Writing and Reporting the News for the 21st Century

Bassim Hamadeh, CEO and Publisher

Kristina Stolte, Senior Acquisitions Editor

Michelle Piehl, Senior Project Editor

Berenice Quirino, Associate Production Editor

Emely Villavicencio, Senior Graphic Designer

Stephanie Kohl, Licensing Associate

Natalie Piccotti, Senior Marketing Manager

Kassie Graves, Vice President of Editorial

Jamie Giganti, Director of Academic Publishing

Cover images: Copyright © 2017 iStockphoto LP/Sensay.
    Copyright © 2013 iStockphoto LP/AlexAndrews.
    Copyright © 2017 iStockphoto LP/apichon_tee.
    Copyright © 2017 iStockphoto LP/alexy_boldin.
    Copyright © 2017 iStockphoto LP/lushik.

Printed in the United States of America.

ISBN: 978-1-5165-2678-9 (pbk) / 978-1-5165-2679-6 (br)

cognella® | ACADEMIC PUBLISHING

Writing and Reporting the News for the 21st Century

The Speed at Which We Travel

First Edition

Yumi Wilson, Gina Baleria, and Grace M. Provenzano

 cognella® | ACADEMIC PUBLISHING

Contents

Introduction   7

1   Definition of journalism in a fast-changing media landscape   11

2   Guiding principles of practicing accurate and fair journalism   19

3   Law for journalists in a digital age   39

4   The basics of writing news for online, print, radio, and TV   51

5   How to create compelling news features   69

6   How to find sources, stories for your beat and more   99

7   The art of interviewing   109

8   Accessing and understanding data, public records, surveys, and studies   123

9   Speeches   145

10   City hall, government, and meetings   155

11   Crime and courts   165

12   Weather and natural disasters   179

13   Budget and financial stories (working with numbers)   191

14   Op-eds and reviews   205

15   Digital media 101: Blogging, micro-blogging, and promotion   219

16   Future of journalism: Is it bright? You bet.   245

Epilogue   255

Glossary   261

Introduction

" I've always said there are four words that every child in the world knows and those are, 'Tell me a story.' Even the people who wrote the Bible knew that. They told stories like the story of Noah."

–Don Hewitt

Welcome to this innovative book on digital journalism. We hope it helps and guides you as you learn the foundations of this venerable field and begin your journey down its ever-evolving path.

The **first section** of this book introduces students to the fast-changing media landscape, going over the importance of embracing technology and social media as a 21st century journalist. This section also goes over the ethical and legal considerations that aspiring journalists must consider when writing, reporting, and disseminating news. In addition, students will learn about the different codes of ethics used by print, online, and broadcast journalists seeking to practice accurate and fair journalism. Ultimately, this section should help students learn how to become ethical journalists.

The **second section** of the book tackles the nuts and bolts of writing well. For students, you'll soon learn that the inverted pyramid formula is an easy and practical way to tell your readers what they need to know. This style of writing is effective when covering breaking news. For example, what would be the No. 1 thing you would tell your friend or sister after Game 7 of the NBA Finals? That's right: You would tell them who won. That's following the inverted pyramid-style of writing—the most newsworthy aspect of a story comes first.

As you hone your writing skills, we also want to emphasize the importance of getting people to open up to you. To do this, you have to step away from your computer and go out into the community. Residents, merchants, city officials, police, and others will tell you what's really going on—if you gain their trust. That goes right back to why ethics matter: When your sources view your story as fair and balanced, they are more likely to speak with you again, introduce you to other movers and shakers, or tell you even more, and that's important because great journalists seek information that no one else has, also known as "a scoop." Great journalists are not just regurgitating the news—they are presenting the news first, as it happens.

The following chapter shifts from hard news leads and inverted-pyramid stories to soft leads and feature writing. By creating a descriptive opening or leading with a powerful anecdote, you are more likely to hook the audience.

In all cases, you can only write well by listening and capturing what others say as accurately as possible, which is why we devote a chapter to the art of interviewing. This chapter will teach you the importance of listening to your sources, asking meaningful questions, and getting and using the right equipment to record the interviews.

While you may get one great interview, we don't want you to forget that journalism requires you to talk to as many different people as possible. This is why our next chapter discusses the importance of seeking multiple sources, mining data, and seeking public records. For example, if your source tells you that he plans to sue the city, ask to see the lawsuit. If another source tells you that he was robbed, ask to see the police report. If these people don't have these records, you will learn that many government records are available to you. While local laws vary on what records are available to the public, remember that you can file a Freedom of Information Act for many documents kept by federal agencies or a Sunshine Act request for government documents in many states.

The **last section** of this book will show students a bright view of their future. A journalism degree can lead to a variety of jobs and opportunities. You can freelance for major media outlets; get hired as a full-time reporter, editor, or producer; or start your own news business. You can also choose to move into public relations, marketing, technical writing, and many other jobs because most companies are looking for clear and concise writers and communicators who are responsible and fair. They are also looking for people who know how to conduct research and interview people. This book is designed to teach you how to write clearly and concisely while also highlighting the need for today's storytellers to be accurate, fair, and compassionate.

Note to instructors: We encourage you to organize the chapters in a way that flows with your class. If you want to save our chapter on freelancing until the end, you'll see it works nicely with our section on backpack journalism and crowdsourcing. Don't worry—if you don't address ethics at the very beginning of your class, you will soon see that ethical guidelines are infused into almost every chapter.

CHAPTER 1

Definition of journalism in a fast-changing media landscape

"When we change the way we communicate, we change society."[1]
–Clay Shirky

What does it mean to practice journalism in the 21st century?

How do you get your news? From your phone? Your iPad? Your watch? The speed with which we consume and share news has changed dramatically in the last decade, allowing almost anyone to become a journalist. The barriers that once existed to producing and publishing the news no longer exist. Smartphones and computers allow us to capture news, and social media and the Internet allow us to transmit and share those stories with a mass audience, yet not every story goes viral, and not every story is told with grace. Important stories are often ignored while sensational stories are given too much weight. How can the public receive a happy balance of news they need with news they want? This book gives aspiring journalists the tools and knowledge they need to write, produce, and publish fair and balanced stories, yet also understand the importance of tone, voice, reach, SEO, and social media in finding and reaching the right audience for their stories.

Better. Faster. Stronger. In the television series *The Six Million Dollar Man* doctors used bionic parts to create a human who would be better than before. Today "bionic parts" in the form of technology, web innovation, and social media have changed the way we consume, produce, promote, and share our news. From the Gutenberg Press to the smartphone, technology has made it infinitely easier to gather, produce, and disseminate information.

Through the Internet and social media, everyone has the potential to become a journalist, as Clay Shirky wrote in *Here Comes Everybody: The Power of Organizing with Organizations.*[2] "Thanks to the Web, the cost of publishing globally has collapsed." Taking pictures, posting a blog, and sharing content with an audience are fairly easy to do, and it's getting easier every year. A November 2017 report by the Pew Research Center found that nearly

---

1   Clay Shirky, *Here Comes Everybody: The Power of Organizing without Organizations*, (New York: Penguin Books, 2009), 17.
2   Shirky, *Here Comes Everybody*, 9.

half of U.S. adult users on Facebook say they get their news from the website.[3] Meanwhile, about 18 percent of U.S. adult users on YouTube say they get their news from there, and 11 percent of U.S. adult users on Twitter say they get their news from there.[4] As we know, platforms such as Facebook and YouTube do not produce news, so what the Pew study illustrates is that people are getting their information from varied and often uncredible sources. Since everybody's version of Facebook or YouTube is slightly or very different, we're often not getting the same news or seeing the same sources.[5]

Traditional news outlets can no longer rely on the audience to pick up a newspaper, tune into the six o'clock news, or subscribe to their favorite magazines. Indeed, many have had to scramble for new profit-making business models, lay off staff, close newsrooms, or shutter printing presses. Some newsroom observers believe that the cutbacks signal the death of journalism, but the truth is that demand for news and information is skyrocketing in the digital age.

What is a journalist?

The traditional definition of a journalist has been "A person who writes for newspapers or magazines or prepares news to be broadcast on radio or television." Things have changed quite a bit, to say the least. The American Press Institute defines journalism on its website as the "activity of gathering, assessing, creating, and presenting news and information."[6] Thus, nearly anyone collecting and sharing news could be considered a journalist. The caveat, however, is this: The public expects journalists to tell the truth. They expect journalists to be fair and transparent. They also expect journalists to listen to them and acknowledge their mistakes. Indeed, the API states that journalism "can be distinguished from other activities and products by certain identifiable characteristics and practices. These elements not only separate journalism from other forms of communication, they are what make it indispensable to democratic societies."[7]

That is why this book integrates ethics into every part of learning how to be the best in the field. When thinking about whom to interview and what questions to ask, adhere to the principles of full disclosure and minimizing harm. When being swayed by all sides, remember to act independently. When deciding what to publish, a journalist should adhere to the

3   Elizabeth Grieco, "More Americans Are Turning to Multiple Social Media Sites for News," Pew Research Center, November 2, 2017. Accessed March 3, 2018, http://www.pewresearch.org/fact-tank/2017/11/02/more-americans-are-turning-to-multiple-social-media-sites-for-news/.

4   Ibid.

5   Ibid.

6   "What Is Journalism?" American Press Institute, Accessed on June 19, 2016, http://www.americanpressinstitute.org/journalism-essentials/what-is-journalism/.

7   "What Is Journalism?" American Press Institute, Accessed on June 19, 2016, http://www.americanpressinstitute.org/journalism-essentials/what-is-journalism/.

basic principles of seeking truth and reporting it. "Members of the Society of Professional Journalists believe that public enlightenment is the forerunner of justice and the foundation of democracy. Ethical journalism strives to ensure the free exchange of information that is accurate, fair, and thorough. An ethical journalist acts with integrity."[8]

In 2013, *TMZ* "posted an audio recording of Los Angeles Clippers owner Donald Sterling making racist remarks." That same year, "it published a video showing Ray Rice knocking out his fiancée in an elevator in Atlantic City. This remarkable string of scoops has highlighted the unexpected power and reach of a gossip website that's not even 10 years old."[9]

Does this make *TMZ* a credible news provider? How about *The Daily Show,* known for taking on serious issues while making people laugh? Add to that Edward Snowden, "a former National Security Agency subcontractor who leaked top-secret information about NSA surveillance activities" to the media in 2013.[10] Some consider Snowden a whistle blower. Some consider him a criminal, saying, "Instead of constructively addressing these issues, Mr. Snowden's dangerous decision to steal and disclose classified information had severe consequences for the security of our country and the people who work day in and day out to protect it."[11]

Yet, others consider him a citizen journalist. Citizen journalism, also known as "participatory journalism," is the act of citizens "playing an active role in the process of collecting, reporting, analyzing, and disseminating news and information."[12] Indeed, a growing number of citizens are actively engaging in journalism, capturing raw video of officer-involved shootings, violent protests, and never-before-seen footage of crimes in progress. As Shirky said, "For the first time in history, the tools for cooperating on a global scale are not solely in the hands of governments or institutions."

What is news?

News is what other people want to know. In today's market, you have to find the people who want your news, especially if you want them to subscribe and/or pay.

From the very serious to the ridiculous, news is what people make it out to be. What are the factors that make people want to know about an issue, a person, a place, or a thing?

---

8   "Preamble of SPJ Code of Ethics," Society of Professional Journalists, Accessed on June 16, 2016, http://www.spj. org/ethicscode.asp.

9   Jonathan Mahler, "Celebrity Gossip Website Extends Its Reach With Scoops on Stars From a Different Field." New York Times, Sept. 9, 2014, http://www.nytimes.com/2014/09/10/sports/football/tmz-broke-ray-rice-donald-sterling-and-jameis-winston-stories-in-10-month-span.html.

10 "Edward Snowden," Biography. http://www.biography.com/people/edward-snowden-21262897.

11 "A Response to Your Petition." White House. https://petitions.whitehouse.gov/response/edward-snowden.

12 Shayne Bowman and Chris Willis, "We Media: How Audiences Are Shaping the Future of News and Information." American Press Institute. http://www.hypergene.net/wemedia/download/we_media.pdf.

Qualities of news

Timeliness:	It's happening now.
Proximity:	It hits close to home.
Impact:	The issue affects many people. A change in law that affects 10,000 people should be given much more importance than something that affects a few.
Relevance:	A lot of people know the person or issue you're talking about.
Odd or unusual:	If we have never heard of it, we want to know more about it.

Though many of these qualities drove news coverage before, the big difference now is the segmentation of the audience. No longer do folks rely on one news source for all their information. An average consumer might get a little information from social media, watch a little TV news, and check out an online edition of a local newspaper. This means that journalists need to understand what their audience wants.

Journalist spotlight

OWEN THOMAS, business editor, *San Francisco Chronicle*

Journalist interview with Owen Thomas

Owen Thomas is the business editor of the *San Francisco Chronicle,* which covers the nine-county-wide Bay Area. He was previously the editor-in-chief of ReadWrite, one of the most widely read and respected tech news sites in the world. Thomas was also West Coast editor of *Business Insider*

and founding executive editor of the *Daily Dot.* He has held editorial leadership roles at VentureBeat, NBC Universal, and Gawker Media, where he transformed Valleywag into Silicon Valley's authority on tech gossip. In addition, he spent several years at Time, Inc. and Business 2.0. Thomas admits that he got into journalism "more or less by accident."

How he got involved in journalism:

"I had experience writing and editing at various publications. I was editor-in-chief of my high school magazine but pointedly not the newspaper. I did become production editor of the newspaper at University of Chicago, but I actually didn't take a journalism course. There was no program at Chicago. Never got a journalism degree. All the skills I learned … learned in the newsroom, as opposed to the classroom."

Figure 1.1

Thoughts on technology and the Internet:

"There have definitely been steady improvements … the devices have improved. Technology has improved. Standards have improved. People are using smartphones to read. We need to think more deeply about that. I was upset to see Circa News fail recently. It broke stories into little chunks and only delivered it to you when there were new chunks. I missed it during the coverage of Greece's financial debacle … because every story (I read) regurgitated everything … Almost makes me want to wait for *The New Yorker* to arrive and tell me what happened. We're still so keen on handing the reader a package with a pretty bow … rather than break it into manageable chunks."

Thoughts on smart devices:

"Again, there is all this video … distributed witnessing capability, but I think that you still have to go to the scene. You can ask smarter questions. You can check people against what they saw on a video. You can ask them about that. It enhances your reporting but doesn't change the value of witnessing things with your own eyes."

"Concept … video editing and manipulation that uses artificial intelligence that creates realistic images such as face swapping. The software can face swap one politician's face for another … and make it look like someone else is speaking."

"All of the technological advances have made me less far less optimistic about citizen-captured video and far more convinced of the journalists committed to objectivity. That is something I didn't really think about a few years ago."

On fake news:

"The way some politicians use fake news is anything you disagree with, anything uncomfortable—fake news, fake videos, fake documents. In the digital world, we have to be suspicious and skeptical all the time."

"The problem is that people are being suspicious of fair reporting of hard-working journalists trying to do their job and gather the facts as best they can."

How technology has changed reporting:

"I think we can think of tweets, blog posts, and other things direct from the source as a building block. Instead of calling up a CEO and asking him about the latest development about Apple, you can find it on Medium or LinkedIn. The practice of journalism … is much more about finding these authentic artifacts … rather than sending a photographer or reporter out to get a photo or quote."

"Is that any better or worse than the canned PR statement? Just be sure to quote them. That does not remove the obligation to follow up and ask questions and make sure you cite them accurately. A lot of stuff is out there, and you certainly don't want to ignore it. You just want to go beyond that."

What should today's journalists have in their tool kit?

"They probably don't need to learn how to code, but I'd like them to figure out ways to use web tools in the cleverest manner possible. They should use IFTTT [https://ifttt.com/] to connect products and apps. You can use Zapier [https://zapier.com/app/dashboard] to connect web services. We need to learn how to build our own algorithm ... don't need massive scale like Facebook ... but you need to learn how to set up a basic filter ... If a tweet gets more than five faves, I want to hear about it ... as opposed to I'm going to follow this person and hope for the best. Journalists need to step ahead of the crude mass algorithms and just be smarter about it. Just as a reporter had to do 50, 100 years ago, you have to see patterns and follow your nose. Rather than knocking on doors, you might be writing a shell script (Unix shell script) or an IFTTT formula."

NOTE to readers of this book: IFTTT, short for If This Then That, is an automation algorithm that enables its users to connect certain web services and smart devices through a series of words. In February 2015, IFTTT made it even easier for users seeking to automate their lives. For example, a user can now type in a command as simple as "Email your parents family-friendly pics," and the program will perform that function on a regular basis.

Thoughts on citizen journalism:

"I think citizen journalism is great in theory. The problem is getting people motivated to do it. In practice, are you actually going to get the story that way? Probably not. You still need the dedicated, persistent persnickety journalist to put it all together in a coherent manner. You need someone with great prose."

"You're not going to be able to aggregate a town hall meeting from afar. You need to go to the meeting. Otherwise, you'll miss things."

Five things journalists must do to stay on top

1. Understand how to use social media and technology
2. Produce stories that include visuals
3. Use data and create infographics
4. Understand how to find and engage audience
5. Learn enough about the back end of web searches and web pages to create smart algorithms to filter news and trends

Credit

CHAPTER 2

Guiding principles of practicing accurate and fair journalism

"Journalism still, in a democracy, is the essential force to get the public educated and mobilized to take action on behalf of our ancient ideals."
–Doris Kearns Goodwin[1]

How does a journalist practice ethically and legally in the digital age?

Digital media allow you to practice journalism—cover a story, share information, and comment on the latest developments—but access does not equal quality. Just because you *can* post something online does not mean you *should*. It does not mean that it is important, relevant, timely, proximal, impactful, unusual, or even accurate. The ethical and legal guides forged in traditional newsrooms have been challenged by digital media, and guidance can now be confusing or nonexistent. Journalists striking out on their own in the digital arena must often find their own way through these quandaries and quagmires. A lack of familiarity with basic legal, ethical, and digital media literacy tenets may lead to incomplete, shoddy, misleading, or false stories. Poor digital media literacy skills may lead someone on deadline or someone who wants to be part of the conversation to post content that is not based in fact but rather was created to push buttons, play on biases, and negatively influence discourse. Failure to be knowledgeable about the law may also open a journalist up to lawsuits, loss of credibility, or ridicule. Worst of all, ignorance of the law and basic ethical principles may lead to a chilling effect—silence on a story that needs to be told.

Journalism's guiding principles

No matter how you choose to practice journalism—independent citizen journalist, reporter at *The Washington Post*, or blogger for *Politico or The Hill*—you must understand how journalists report, interview, write, and publish in a way that's fair to their sources and

---

1 Doris Kearns Goodwin. "Teddy Roosevelt's 'Bully Pulpit' Isn't The Platform It Once Was." NPR. November 04, 2013. Accessed March 20, 2018, https://www.npr.org/2013/11/04/242405056/teddy-roosevelts-bully-pulpit-isnt-the-platform-it-once-was.

truthful to the public, and you must take responsibility for ensuring your work is ethical and accurate.

Though there is no official code of ethics for the journalism industry in the U.S., several organizations have crafted codes of ethics that resonate with journalists across the field. The most commonly cited and foundational code is from the Society of Professional Journalists (SPJ). It begins:

> "Public enlightenment is the forerunner of justice and the foundation of democracy. Ethical journalism strives to ensure the free exchange of information that is accurate, fair and thorough."[2]

The SPJ's Guiding Principles of Journalism are:
Seek Truth and Report It
Minimize Harm
Act Independently
Be Accountable and Transparent

These four principles form the foundation for many codes of ethics across the field, and they resonate well in the digital age, providing all types of journalists from veteran newsperson to solo **blogger** with a structure and principles by which to measure journalistic endeavors.

Seek truth and report it

This principle challenges journalists to always be fair, accurate, honest, and courageous in their reporting. To achieve this, a journalist must always verify information before publishing it, clearly identify sources, ensure sources are credible, give the audience context to help them understand the story, correct information when necessary, and allow people to respond to allegations against them.

This tenet also covers the importance of recognizing that journalists serve as watchdogs of the public interest. That means you must seek to shed light on important information, "hold those in power accountable, give voice to the voiceless," and support public discussion "even views [you] find repugnant" (SPJ).[3]

Kelly McBride, media ethicist and vice president for academic programs at The Poynter Institute, says seeking truth also means defining the story and making sure it is specific and actionable. "If you're a blogger, and you're concerned about crappy public schools and the fact that you have

---

2 "SPJ Code of Ethics." Society of Professional Journalists. Accessed August 25, 2015, http://www.spj.org/ethicscode.asp.

3 "SPJ Code of Ethics." Society of Professional Journalists. Accessed August 25, 2015, http://www.spj.org/ethicscode.asp.

no options for your kids or for the kids in your neighborhood, that's too big of a problem," says McBride. "How do you identify the problem that can be solved? How do you bring data and accountability to that? And then how do you give people a pathway to solving it?"

"How do you identify the problem that can be solved? How do you bring data and accountability to that? And then how do you give people a pathway to solving it?"

A pair of reporters in Cleveland, Ohio have done exactly this. Rachel Dissell and Leila Atassi with the *Cleveland Plain Dealer* got very specific in their work. In the wake of the discovery of eleven bodies around the house of a convicted rapist in 2009, the two began looking into how rape kits were being handled. They filed a public records request to find out how many rape kits remained untested in the system. The answer was about 4,000. With Dissell and Atassi regularly checking in, law enforcement officials tested all the rape kits and discovered that there were several serial rapists, meaning that getting one person off the streets would protect many innocents. You can hear from the two reporters about their work here: https://www.youtube.com/watch?v=_UFGUWy8ZYo.

"One stunning finding that emerged from Cleveland's investigations is that as many as a third of reported rapes were perpetrated by a serial offender, a much higher proportion than officials anticipated," reported *The Columbia Journalism Review*. "The implications are tremendous. It means that every unsolved case is even more likely to be another rape waiting to happen, and that removing even a single rapist from the street eliminates an ongoing threat."

More than 100 people were eventually convicted of rape or serial rape, thanks to Dissell and Atassi's tenacious reporting and news-gathering. Dissell and Atassi's specific and actionable focus on the testing of rape kits led to real results and positive outcomes for the community.

"It's an exemplary instance of local reporting, responsive government officials, and public support coming together to make a community safer," wrote *The Columbia Journalism Review*. "The story has reverberated beyond Cleveland and Cuyahoga

Figure 2.1   Reporters Rachel Dissell and Leila Atassi with the Cleveland Plain Dealer

County. Ohio passed a law in March 2015 requiring every police department in the state to submit untested rape kits to the lab by the following spring. Going forward, all kits must be tested within 30 days. Cleveland's story is also contributing to burgeoning national awareness of how many rape kits remain unexamined, and the potential gold mine they represent; once tested, they can solve old and ongoing cases while providing a wealth of data on sexual assault."[4]

While not every story will have such far-reaching implications, focusing on specific and actionable story angles can help you make a difference, uncover important information that the public needs to know, and help the community and public officials find specific and actionable solutions.

In addition, journalists seeking truth and reporting it must take a closer look at their own biases and how their experiences influence their perspectives and assumptions. This will help you understand how those biases may impact how a story is told. It is important to always label advocacy, commentary, or content taken from someone else. If you are unsure whether you have an implicit bias that is impacting how you are viewing or telling a story, check in with your colleagues or a supervisor. Open discussion always makes newsrooms and the news product stronger and more useful to the public.

"A lie will go round the world while truth is pulling its boots on."

One major challenge to seeking truth and reporting it is the onslaught of what has come to be called **fake news**, which not only involves misinformation, but also the act of delegitimizing quality new outlets. Also called propaganda, misinformation, disinformation, unfounded opinion, or hoaxes, fake news permeates social media feeds. A 2018 study in the journal *Science* found that fake news gets shared and spread far more quickly than actual, fact-based news and information.[5] This gives a grim confirmation to a famous quote, often incorrectly attributed to Mark Twain: "A lie will go round the world while truth is pulling its boots on." It was actually said by C. H. Spurgeon in *Gems from Spurgeon* (1859).[6] While the Twain-Spurgeon misquote is a quaint example of the concept it highlights, in actuality, fake news appears to be causing actual and lingering harm to our public discourse, our ability to respectfully engage with each other, our ability to trust information we receive, and, at its most

---

4   Chava Gourarie, "How an Ohio Reporter Helped Convict More than 100 Rapists." *Columbia Journalism Review.* *September 2, 2015. Accessed June 16, 2016,* http://www.cjr.org/local_news/rape_kit_reporting.php.

5   Soroush Vosoughi, Deb Roy, and Sinan Aral. "The Spread of True and False News Online." *Science* 359, no. 6380 (March 08, 2018): 1146-151, doi:10.1126/science.aap9559.

6   Fred Shapiro, "Quotes Uncovered: How Lies Travel." Freakonomics. April 07, 2011. Accessed March 20, 2018, http://freakonomics.com/2011/04/07/quotes-uncovered-how-lies-travel/.

concerning, the very foundations of our democracy (more on this in the "minimizing harm" section). As a journalist, you must take great care to seek truth and report it when it comes to any information that crosses your feed. This will go a long way toward minimizing harm, the second SPJ guiding principle of practicing ethical journalism.

Minimize harm

This principle focuses on ensuring that you do your best in your reporting to ensure that sources, subjects, followers, and any other person or entity impacted by your story experiences the least harm possible. This is often not as easy as it sounds, because you must sometimes weigh conflicting concepts when deciding how or whether to report on a story, such as the public's right to know versus the privacy rights of the subject in question. However, in many cases, such as when it comes to dealing with fake news, your newsgathering and reporting decisions may actually be quite straightforward.

"Members of the public [are] human beings deserving of respect" (SPJ).[7] That means a journalist needs to weigh and balance the public's right to know with a person's right to privacy. Be sensitive to those who find themselves embroiled in news stories, such as young people, crime victims, those who lost their homes to fire or war, or simply members of the private citizenry. These people are not used to being in the spotlight and likely did not seek it out. They need your compassion. You must still get the story, but you can do so in a respectful, direct way that does not belittle or disrespect them. Poignant examples of this are the mass shootings, mass casualty events, and officer-involved shootings that have become more common or more reported in recent years. From Columbine to Aurora to Sandy Hook to San Bernardino to Las Vegas to Parkland and the many other mass casualty events reporters have navigated, and from Philando Castile to Trayvon Martin to Stephon Clark and the many others who have lost their lives in controversial shootings, this often fraught landscape demands constant attention to the balance between ensuring the public has information and respecting the privacy of victims, victims' family and friends, people connected to the perpetrator, and others who find themselves swept up in the story. While no one is perfect, understanding how to approach these situations journalistically and ethically can take you a long way toward conscientious, respectful, truthful, and impactful reporting.

Remember also that just because you have the legal right to publish something does not mean it is ethical or journalistic. It is easy with digital media to post something sensational, lurid, shocking, or funny because you know you'll get a response, but what about the person who is the subject of that topic? We see this with examples of **public shaming,** including PR executive Justine Sacco who was publicly shamed for publishing an unfortunate tweet that was then retweeted across the world. She ended up losing her job. Dentist Walter J. Palmer was

---

7   "SPJ Code of Ethics." Society of Professional Journalists. Accessed August 25, 2015, http://www.spj.org/ethicscode.asp.

#
Students
for
Parkland

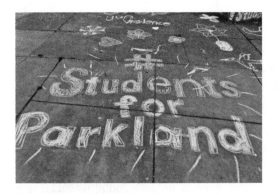

Figure 2.2

Figure 2.3

UNITE
Philando

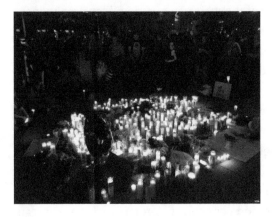

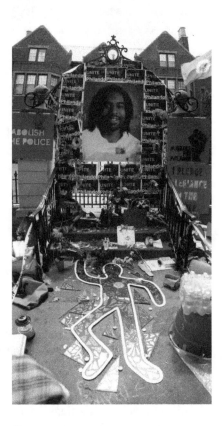

Figure 2.4

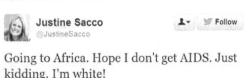

Justine Sacco
@JustineSacco
Follow
Going to Africa. Hope I don't get AIDS. Just kidding. I'm white!
Reply Retweet Favorite More
2,678 RETWEETS
1,206 FAVORITES
10:19 AM - 20 Dec 13 from Hillingdon, London

Figure 2.5

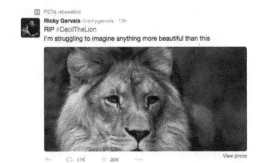

PETA retweeted
Ricky Gervais @rickygervais · 15h
RIP #CecilTheLion
I'm struggling to imagine anything more beautiful than this
17K
20K
View photo

Figure 2.6

forced to temporarily close his dental practice in the face of harsh backlash on social media for killing an endangered lion in Zimbabwe. When Palmer reopened his practice, the media and protesters were waiting at his place of business. Whether or not Palmer faces criminal charges, is it right to punish him over social media? Where does journalism fit?

"The mere act of documenting the public shaming serves to exacerbate the humiliation."

In a Poynter Institute Blog, McBride wrote that journalists play a role in public shaming when they repost or take up a story. "Journalists find themselves in the role of observer and describer, claiming to have no stake in the outcome. Yet the mere act of documenting the public shaming serves to exacerbate the humiliation," says McBride. "A journalistic purpose takes the audience's needs into account and minimizes harm. Public shaming often isn't about the audience's needs at all, unless you factor in the dark emotional rush of validation." In addition, your post does not go away, and you have no control over how others will share or use it.[8]

Figure 2.7

Figure 2.8

McBride tells us that there must be a journalistic reason to cover a story. Otherwise, it's not about journalism. "Most of the news that I'm seeing about Cecil the Lion is by news organizations that have absolutely no journalistic purpose at all. They are simply trying to ride the viral wave of that story. And that's why public shaming has become such an issue. People go crazy, and it drives up your clicks, and you have no journalistic purpose at all," McBride says. "So who has a journalistic stake in that story? If you're a national news organization, you've really got to ask, how can we advance this? Because

---

8   Kelly McBride, "Journalism and Public Shaming: Some Guidelines." Poynter. March 11, 2015. Accessed August 25, 2015, http://www.poynter.org/news/mediawire/326097/journalism-and-public-shaming-some-guidelines/.

it's a national story. If you're a local news organization, and you are not in Minneapolis or Zimbabwe, then you probably don't have a stake in it at all. Or, if you're going to find a local stake, you've got to advance it in a local way."

"Is there is an angle that is relevant to your audience?
If not, then why is your outlet covering the story?"

If you find yourself covering a story that involves public shaming or judgment, ask yourself whether there is an angle that is relevant to your audience—often the local angle. If so, then what are the local or relevant angles? If not, then why is your outlet covering the story? Is there a true journalistic purpose? Or is your outlet just hoping to capitalize on the notoriety of the story and get clicks? If it's the latter, then you may want to speak up and defend the journalistic reputation of your outlet.

As mentioned above, one of the most harmful behaviors to journalism, and to democracy itself, is the spreading of fake news. Often people share fake news because it reinforces their point of view or opinion, but as we now know, much politically oriented fake news was being manufactured and disseminated by so-called troll farms based in Russia. In early 2018, special counsel Robert Mueller indicted more than a dozen Russian nationals for deliberately manipulating social media platforms by creating and posting content designed not to inform but to exacerbate divisions among the American people. Couple this with the fact that many people in the U.S. lack strong digital media literacy skills, as highlighted in a 2016 study out of Stanford that found students from middle school to college had trouble assessing the credibility of information online, and, we get a perfect storm of misinformation, disinformation, and manipulation.[9] Though you as a journalist cannot solve the problem of poor digital media literacy, you can seek to act ethically in your own newsgathering and reporting to ensure that you minimize harm, and that you challenge questionable information in your quest to seek truth and report it.

How to ensure you are not part of the fake news problem

While the spread of false information is not new to our era, social media have made the ability to spread false information far easier than at any other time in history. The primary drivers of fake news, as reported by the Brookings Institution, are talk shows, cable news, citizen journalism, and foreign actors. Says Darryl West, vice president and director of Governance

---

9   Sam Wineburg, *Evaluating Information: The Cornerstone of Civic Online Reasoning.* (Stanford, CA: History Education Group), 2016. 1-29.

Studies at Brookings, "Fake news and sophisticated disinformation campaigns are especially problematic in democratic systems, and there is growing debate on how to address these issues without undermining the benefits of digital media."[10]

As a journalist, you can do your part by verifying information before you release it, being as transparent as possible with your audience, and acting ethically toward your sources and in your newsgathering and reporting process. If you make a mistake, admit it and correct it ASAP. In addition, don't feed the trolls. Respond to and engage with reasonable comments and sincere inquiries on social media but take a pass on posts designed to inflame or divide.

Act independently

This tenet states, "The highest and primary obligation of ethical journalism is to serve the public." You are not serving anyone else—not the president, not a legislator or Congressperson, not the CEO of a private company. *You are serving the people.* [11]

> *"The highest and primary obligation of ethical journalism is to serve the public."*

This means avoiding conflicts of interest. Though receiving gifts is nice, in journalism a gift can be seen as buying influence. Do not accept gifts, even food, if offered by a source or potential source on a story you are covering. No matter how it actually influences you (or not), the perception is what matters. If you do have a conflict of interest, disclose it.

In my own journalism career, I faced a major potential conflict of interest. I was working in a major market newsroom in 2002 when a former priest in the area came under suspicion for child molestation, kidnapping, and murder. I knew the former priest. He had married my step-aunt when I was a child. I immediately went to my news director's office and disclosed this potential conflict of interest. Though I did not feel that my relationship with this individual in any way compromised my ability to do my job, it was still important for me to disclose the information. My news director decided that I should continue to cover and write about the story, but I had colleagues read my pieces to ensure there was no bias. In the end, this person was convicted of child molestation but cleared of any suspicion of murder.

---

10   Darrell M. West, "How to Combat Fake News and Disinformation." Brookings. December 18, 2017. Accessed March 20, 2018, https://www.brookings.edu/research/how-to-combat-fake-news-and-disinformation/.

11   "SPJ Code of Ethics." Society of Professional Journalists. Accessed August 25, 2015, http://www.spj.org/ethicscode.asp.

Thanks to my disclosure and our strong news team, the story was covered fairly and truthfully at every step.[12,13,14]

In addition to your own potential bias, beware of bias or conflict of interest from potential sources, especially in the era of fake news when many would-be sources are simply seeking access, influence, and power. It is generally not a good idea to pay for access to news or content. Known as **checkbook journalism**, the practice could encourage people to fabricate or exaggerate news items for money. Anyone seeking compensation for information that would inform the public should be treated with wariness, and their motives should be questioned.

On the Poynter Ethics Blog, McBride says that "money 'can have a distorting effect' on truth-telling. 'When you offer a monetary incentive to a source, the source may try to give you what you want; they change reality to make what they are offering more valuable.'"

Though some outlets, such as TMZ, have been known to pay for content from time to time, most journalists are wary about the slippery slope and implications on the free flow of information. In 2013, *The Globe and Mail* paid $10,000 for still images of Toronto Mayor Rob Ford doing drugs. The seller wanted $100,000 for the full video, but the outlet negotiated a lower price for the stills. On its website, *Mail* Editor-in-Chief David Walmsley defended the decision. "Toronto is the financial capital of this G8 country and the sixth-biggest government in Canada. Paralysis in Toronto is bad for the country. The mayor is supposed to be the guardian of his city. The photographs we published are a price worth paying."[15]

A good rule of thumb is to avoid this situation entirely. If you find yourself in a situation where the source content must be revealed, and payment is the only option, bring it to your news team and news director or editor-in-chief. Any decision involving payment to a source must be made at the management level.

Be accountable and transparent

This means giving the public as much information as you can about your story, where it came from, how you got your information, and how you interpreted it. This also means taking responsibility for every aspect of your story and making corrections immediately if necessary.

---

12 Janine DeFao, Kevin Fagan, and Jaxon Vanderbeken. "Excavation at Ex-priest's Home / Police Dig in Yard at Truckee Vacation House for Possible Remains of Missing Kids." SFGate. June 6, 2002. Accessed August 25, 2015, http://www.sfgate.com/bayarea/article/Excavation-at-ex-priest-s-home-Police-dig-in-2830691.php.

13 Martha Ross. "Defrocked Priest Stephen Kiesle Named in Suits Alleging Catholic Church Coverup; One Plaintiff Is Stepdaughter." Walnut Creek, CA Patch. August 19, 2010. Accessed August 25, 2015, http://patch.com/california/walnutcreek/defrocked-priest-stephen-kiesle-named-in-suits-allegi46ddb9bfb0.

14 Jesse McKinley and Katie Zezima. "Oakland Priest's Accuser Describes Sexual Abuse." The New York Times. April 11, 2010. Accessed August 25, 2015, http://www.nytimes.com/2010/04/12/us/12abuse.html?_r=0.

15 David Walmsley, "Editor's Note: Why We Published the Rob Ford Photos." The Globe and Mail. May 1, 2014. Accessed June 16, 2016, http://www.theglobeandmail.com/news/toronto/editors-note-rob-ford-photos/article18357133/.

When you make a mistake: "You correct the mistake, and you correct it in every venue and platform that you made it in, so that the audience that saw the mistake is likely to see the correction."

When asked about what to do if you make a mistake, McBride says the answer is easy. "You correct the mistake, and you correct it in every venue and platform that you made it in, so that the audience that saw the mistake is likely to see the correction. On rare occasions, you may actually take down an entire story, but you need to replace it with an explanation that says, 'we took this down because it's not valid.'"

If questions arise about your coverage, answer as quickly and openly as possible. When *The New York Times* came under fire in July 2015 for a story claiming democratic presidential candidate Hillary Clinton was facing a criminal inquiry into the destruction of several emails, it reacted slowly to criticism of the story, taking more than a week to fully backtrack and offer a correction. Many critics felt that the *Times* took too long and did not adequately respond in a timely and transparent manner to questions about the story. This impacted how people viewed the *Times* as a credible news source.

With comment sections and social media, it is easier than ever to open up a dialogue with your public. Encourage this interaction. The public feels heard, and you are building trust. You may even receive important story information from your online sources.

The Poynter Institute: An ethical guidepost

The Poynter Institute, named for newspaper producer Nelson Poynter, offers teaching, ethical analysis, and resources for journalists, whether in a newsroom, school, or at home working on a solo blog. The organization also seeks to innovate and bring people together to discuss the latest trends in journalism and ways to effectively respond. It is an extremely valuable resource for journalists, both rookie and veteran.

Poynter President Karen Dunlap told *Broadway World* that Poynter's core mission over the last four decades has been to improve journalism in the service of democracy. "If we want journalism to stay relevant and influential, then all of us need a framework for understanding our duties and responsibilities in a democratic society."[1]

Kelly McBride, Poynter ethicist and vice president, says the institute focuses on educating journalists. "Our mission as a school is to make journalism the world over better and keep journalism working in service of democracy."

"We consider ourselves a bridge between the academy and the profession, and we work a lot to help the profession stay on top of the latest skills, research, thinking, and leadership that they need to do their jobs, which is a lot, because so much has changed," McBride says. "We also try and communicate back to the academy that here's how you need to train students."

Poynter's blog leads the way in discussing trends in journalism, including new tools, digital developments, ethics, and other issues

---

1   "Poynter Publishes New Journalism Ethics Book." Broadway World. July 31, 2013. Accessed August 25, 2015, http://www.broadwayworld.com/bwwbooks/article/Poynter-Publishes-New-Journalism-Ethics-Book-20130731.

facing the profession. Poynter is a must for journalism students and professionals.

"It's more important now as a journalist that you know what the national conversation about journalism is, because otherwise you're just going to make mistakes that other people have already made," McBride says.

McBride says responding to comments is now part of the journalistic process. "*The New York Times,* when they open something up for comments, they don't leave it open forever," says McBride. "They only leave it open for a certain period of time, and that's because they want to be able to devote the resources to curating it in a way that fosters a healthy conversation. Part of journalism is managing the commentary. It's a test of whether you care about the journalism at all. If you're not willing to curate the conversation, then you probably don't have a journalistic purpose in the first place."

The Guardian was one of the first news outlets to cultivate and curate its comment section, and it has built a rich dialogue between newsroom and public. *Guardian* Editor Graydon Carter told *Vanity Fair* that the paper takes its relationships and its job as a watchdog seriously. "*The Guardian,* with its deep journalistic traditions, is careful about context and explanation. It sees itself as a gatekeeper, and it worries about consequences."[16]

Making choices and the implications of your choice

On August 26, 2015, two journalists conducting a live, on-air interview for their local morning news show were shot and killed while the camera rolled and the public and their newsroom watched. This story was covered heavily across the country, and outlets made different choices about how to cover it. Some choices were based in journalism, some in sensationalism, and some with an eye toward respecting family and friends. We will revisit this example later in this chapter to explore the implications of the choices various news outlets made.

---

16 "The Transparent Trap." Vanity Fair. January 2011. Accessed June 16, 2016, http://www.vanityfair.com/magazine/2011/02/graydon-201102.

When you cover news stories, you, too, have choices to make. Do you choose the photo of the suspect smiling with family or frowning while staring at the camera? Do you choose the image of the public official looking handsome and vibrant or the image of that public official answering tough questions and frowning at the camera (Fig 2.10a–b)?

When O.J. Simpson was arrested in 1994 for the murders of Nicole Brown Simpson and Ron Goldman, *Time* and *Newsweek* each published magazines with his mugshot on the cover. *Time* decided to alter the photo, darkening it for effect (Fig. 2.9). *Time* was then accused of racism because the manipulation made O.J. Simpson look more menacing and threatening than the un-altered photo that appeared on the *Newsweek* cover.

Each image conveys its own messages, and you will need to make the choice that best represents the story you are telling. You must take care not to let your own biases or personal feelings enter into the equation. It is very easy to influence your audience through these choices, and you want to be sure you can defend the choices you make.

Words are also powerful, and your word choice can reveal inherent biases. Some coverage in the wake of Hurricane Katrina revealed clear bias, depending on who was pictured (Fig. 2.11).

In an Associated Press (AP) image depicting a black man chest deep in water, the caption reads, "A young man walks through chest-deep flood water after looting a grocery store in New

Figure 2.9   This is an example of how an image can be manipulated to fit a certain narrative.

Figure 2.10a and b.   An image conveys a story in itself, and the choices we make influence the story that is being told.

Figure 2.11   Image descriptions can reveal our bias.

Figure 2.12   Figure 2.13

Orleans." A similar image from the Agence France-Presse (AFP) but depicting two white people, reads, "Two residents wade through chest-deep water after finding bread and soda from a local grocery store after Hurricane Katrina came through the area." The use of the word "looting" for the black man and "finding" for the white people, when each seems to be engaging in the same behavior, appears to reveal a bias of treating people of different races differently in the same situation.

We also see racial bias in reporting when a mass shooting or mass casualty event takes place. Someone who is of Middle Eastern descent or otherwise darker skinned may immediately be referred to as a terrorist, while someone who is Caucasian is often initially referred to as mentally disturbed or a lone wolf. In a series of bombings that took place in Austin, Texas in March 2018, the bomber, who was white, was called "frustrated," "challenged," a "maniac," and "driven by personal issues, not hate."[17] A graphic that appeared in *The Huffington Post* and a bit on *Family Guy* each visualize how media outlets often initially approach crime, depending on the race of the perpetrator. Though *HuffPo* is a progressive-leaning outlet, the conclusions drawn in this cartoon are supported by several academic studies, which find that non-white perpetrators and victims are either under-represented or reported on in a stereotypical manner.[18,19,20] As a journalist, you can begin to check and minimize this systemic bias by being aware and then looking at your own reporting to see whether you are relying on societal biases or whether you have chosen unbiased language.

Returning to the Roanoke, Virginia, on-air shootings, below are three coverage options. WARNING: The final option contains graphic content. If you were covering this story, what choice would you make? Do you choose images of the victims smiling? (Fig. 2.14)

17 Sean Collins Walsh, Mary Huber, and Claire Osborn. "THE SUSPECT: Mark Conditt Driven by Personal Issues, Not Hate, Cops Say." Mystatesman. March 21, 2018. Accessed March 22, 2018, https://www.mystatesman.com/news/the-suspect-mark-conditt-driven-personal-issues-not-hate-cops-say/gjtbZoq6jaL72FavUu1vHK/.

18 T. Dixon, "Overrepresentation and Underrepresentation of African Americans and Latinos as Lawbreakers on Television News." Journal of Communication 50, no. 2 (June 01, 2000): 131-54. doi:10.1093/joc/50.2.131.

19 Trina T. Creighton, "Coverage of Black Versus White Males in Local Television News Lead Stories." Journal of Mass Communication & Journalism 04, no. 08 (September 17, 2014). doi:10.4172/2165-7912.1000216.

20 Travis L. Dixon and Charlotte L. Williams. "The Changing Misrepresentation of Race and Crime on Network and Cable News." Journal of Communication, 65, no. 1 (2014): 24-39. doi:10.1111/jcom.12133

Do you choose the images depicting the moment before (Fig. 2.15), when the journalist pictured had no idea that she and her photographer were about to lose their lives?

You might choose images from the shooter's POV (Fig. 2.16) or the moment when the reporter knew (Fig. 2.17) she may lose her life.

Or you might show the bodies of the victims after they were shot live on the air. Each choice presents a different tone to your audience and sends potentially different messages. When making choices like these, ask yourself:

- Why would you show the images? What are you trying to convey?
- Is showing the more graphic images adding to the story and giving the audience the information they need? Or are the images simply titillating, designed to get more clicks?
- Do you want to allow the shooter to frame the story?
- Are there larger stories or sidebars that the images will help tell? In the case of the Roanoke shooting, discussion quickly turned to the safety of journalists in the field.

Figure 2.14 We have a choice in how we tell a story. In this image, the victims are in their official capacity, smiling, trustworthy. This image also offers smiling victims, full of life in candid shots.

Figure 2.15 Or, you may choose to tell the story by showing one of the victims the moment before the shooting.

Figure 2.16

Figure 2.17 You may also depict the story by showing the moment of.

There are no definitive answers here. The one constant is that your answers to the questions, and therefore the choices you make, should be based in journalism.

In addition to making choices about how to cover news, you will also need to recognize that doing journalism comes with risks, especially when journalists are telling stories that those in power or those with something to lose don't want told. In June 2018, five journalists at the Capital Gazette in Annapolis, Maryland lost their lives when a shooter entered the building and began shooting. In the early hours of the aftermath, little information had been released, even though a suspect was quickly taken into custody on the scene. In the midst of grieving for fellow journalists lost in a senseless tragedy, journalists in the Gazette newsroom and across the country knew they had to do their duty and cover the story, being as fair and transparent as possible, while taking care not to speculate about the shooter's motive.

In a climate in which the president of the United States had repeatedly called the news media the "enemy of the people"[21] and often used language inciting violence against the media[22] and just days after right-wing provocateur Milo Yiannopoulos texted, "I can't wait for vigilante squads to start gunning journalists down on sight."[23] Many journalists struggled to keep their biases in check.

While navigating the story, journalists were careful to state the facts while also bringing into the public discourse the climate journalists face. It turned out that the shooter was a local resident who held a grudge against the paper for its accurate reporting on the shooter's previous legal issues. As a journalist, you must remember to collect all the facts, report only what you know, and when giving context take great care to avoid making leaps. This does not mean you report in a vacuum. Even though the shooter was not necessarily politically motivated,[24] the incident provided an opportunity to contextualize the dangers journalists face and how certain factors may contribute to an unsafe climate. Journalists who remembered the ethical tenets of journalism were able to effectively contextualize the story."

Plagiarism, patchwriting, and aggregating: Ethical quandaries facing today's journalists

In the age of digital media, it can become difficult to tell what is original reporting and what is aggregated content. Lines can also blur between original content and content that has been aggregated, plagiarized, or patchwritten.

---

21 https://www.nytimes.com/2017/02/17/business/trump-calls-the-news-media-the-enemy-of-the-people.html

22 https://www.nytimes.com/2017/02/17/business/trump-calls-the-news-media-the-enemy-of-the-people.html; https://abcnews.go.com/Politics/back-trump-comments-perceived-encouraging-violence/story?id=48415766

23 https://www.dailydot.com/layer8/anti-press-rhetoric-capital-gazette-shooting/

24 https://www.nytimes.com/2018/06/29/us/jarrod-ramos-annapolis-shooting.html

Let's start with the straightforward baseline that copying work that is not your own and using it without attribution is never OK. It seems simple enough, but in the digital world this simple tenet can get complicated.

We begin with **plagiarism**. This is the flat-out copying of someone else's words, content, or ideas without giving that person credit. Plagiarism can include copying and pasting someone else's exact words, as well as paraphrasing. Even if you rewrite a paragraph or entire article in your own words, you are still plagiarizing someone else's work because it was their reporting, enterprising, and crafting of the story on which you are basing your work. A good rule of thumb is to just make the call to the right source to seek permission or reach out directly on social media to independently confirm information, get your own interviews, and tell your own story. If you must rely on someone else's work, give them credit. Let your audience know where you got your information. However, sometimes even this is not enough, and permission must be sought.

A close relation of plagiarism is **patchwriting**. It is very similar to paraphrasing but a bit more universal throughout a story. It happens when you rely too much on the structure and themes of the original story and write your own story in a way that mimics that original story too closely. It often happens when we take too little time to truly understand a story so that we can write it in our own words. Patchwriting is a very real danger in journalism because we are often relying on other source material, rushing to meet a deadline, and trying to get more content published.

"The litmus test is new value or new ideas," McBride says. "Writing that brings new value to the audience, maybe even writing that merely attempts to bring new value to the audience, is likely to be intellectually honest. And writing that doesn't do that, that merely rehashes the work of others—that's patchwriting."[25]

The moral of the story here is that your own ideas, original reporting, and a fresh take on existing facts and information add value to the journalistic landscape and will set you apart as a quality journalist.

Conclusion

It's easy to post content online. Any of us can do it. I can post to my social media account, start a blog, or comment on an existing story. What sets a true journalist apart from all the noise we encounter online every day are ethics. If you make a commitment to seek truth and report it, minimize harm, act independently, and be accountable and transparent, then you will be guided by strong journalistic principles that should help elevate your work. These principles will also help guide you when the inevitable gray areas arise. With a clear sense of your journalistic ethics, you can do the work that the public needs, be a voice for the voiceless, shed light on important stories, and help inform your audience, so they may improve their communities.

---

25 Kelly McBride, "'Patchwriting' Is More Common than Plagiarism, Just as Dishonest." Poynter. September 18, 2012. http://www.poynter.org/news/mediawire/188789/patchwriting-is-more-common-than-plagiarism-just-as-dishonest/.

EXERCISES AND ACTIVITIES

1. Answer the following questions as a journalist:

    a) Is it right to write a story about the dentist who shot Cecil the Lion over social media? Under what circumstances is this story OK? When is it not OK? How do you balance the public's right to be informed with the potential that you are contributing to public shaming?[1]

    b) How should the New York Times have handled the correction in the Hillary Clinton email story (July 23, 2015)?[2,3]

       Editor's Note:

       http://www.nytimes.com/2015/07/28/us/editors-note-clinton-email coverage.html

       Original Story (corrected):

       http://www.nytimes.com/2015/07/24/us/politics/inquiry-is-sought-in-hillary-clinton-email-account.html

       NOTE AT BOTTOM OF ORIGINAL STORY: "A version of this article appears in print on July 24, 2015, on page A1 of the New York edition with the headline: Inquiry Sought in Clinton's Use of Email."

    c) Should the Associated Press have published its story on Hillary Clinton having the delegates to win the Democratic presidential nomination on June 6, 2016, the eve of the California primary?[4]

---

1 Kerry Howley. "What We Mourned When We Mourned Cecil." The New Yorker. September 29, 2015. Accessed June 16, 2016, http://www.newyorker.com/books/page-turner/what-we-mourned-when-we-mourned-cecil.

2 "Editors' Note: Clinton Email Coverage." The New York Times. July 27, 2015. Accessed August 25, 2015, http://www.nytimes.com/2015/07/28/us/editors-note-clinton-email-coverage.html.

3 Michael S. Schmidt and Matt Apuzzo. "Inquiry Sought in Hillary Clinton's Use of Email." The New York Times. July 23, 2015. Accessed August 25, 2015, http://www.nytimes.com/2015/07/24/us/politics/inquiry-is-sought-in-hillary-clinton-email-account.html.

4 "AP Count: Clinton Has Delegates to Win Democratic Nomination." The Big Story. June 6, 2016. Accessed June 12, 2016, http://bigstory.ap.org/article/779b7012af24446289623a968926ec04/ap-count-clinton-has-delegates-win-democratic-nomination.

Credits

- Fig. 2.1: Source: https://www.youtube.com/watch?v=_UFGUWy8ZYo.
- Fig. 2.2: Source: https://commons.wikimedia.org/wiki/File:Tam_High_Vigil_for_Parkland_School_Shooting_(25427251787).jpg.
- Fig. 2.3: Source: https://commons.wikimedia.org/wiki/File:VOA_Vegas_vigil.jpg.
- Fig. 2.4: Source: https://commons.wikimedia.org/wiki/File:Memorial_to_Philando_Castile_at_the_Minnesota_Governor%27s_Mansion_(28269919222).jpg.
- Fig. 2.5: Source: https://www.theguardian.com/world/2013/dec/22/pr-exec-fired-racist-tweet-aids-africa-apology.
- Fig. 2.6: Copyright © 2015 by Ricky Gervais.
- Fig. 2.7: Source: http://justice4cecil.com.
- Fig. 2.8: Source: https://commons.wikimedia.org/wiki/File:Walter_Palmer%27s_clinic.jpg.
- Fig 2.9: Source: http://images.complex.com/complex/image/upload/t_article_image/knf36sx-d5vvxdi6gyi4r.jpg. Copyright © 1994 by Time Inc. and Newsweek LLC.
- Fig 2.10a: whitehouse.gov, "Official Portrait: President Barack Obama," https://www.whitehouse.gov/sites/whitehouse.gov/files/images/Administration/People/president_official_portrait_hires.jpg. Copyright in the Public Domain.
- Fig. 2.10b: Copyright © (CC BY-SA 3.0) at https://commons.wikimedia.org/wiki/File:Obama_Chesh_2.jpg.
- Fig 2.11: Source: https://advertwatch.files.wordpress.com/2009/12/katrinaracistmediacoverage.jpg
- Fig 2.12: Source: https://www.huffingtonpost.com/omar-alnatour/muslims-are-not-terrorist_b_8718000.html
- Fig 2.13: Copyright © by FOX News Network, LLC.
- Fig 2.14: WDBJ/Associated Press, Copyright © 2015 by Associated Press.
- Fig 2.15: WDBJ/Associated Press, Copyright © 2015 by Associated Press.
- Fig. 2.16: Vester Lee Flanagan, 2015.
- Fig 2.17: WDBJ/Associated Press, Copyright © 2015 by Associated Press.

CHAPTER 3

Law for journalists in a digital age

"Free press can, of course, be good or bad, but, most certainly without freedom, the press will never be anything but bad."

–Albert Camus, French novelist, essayist, and dramatist[1]

While ethics build a foundation for how you should respond to information and sources, law serves as the structural guide for proceeding, protecting both you and others, and clarifying situations when it may otherwise be unclear. The primary laws governing journalists are copyright, defamation, and the First Amendment. It is also important for journalists to consider privacy and shield laws. Some of our legal protections and guidelines come from federal law, while others are state by state.

Copyright: Who owns what, and how can we use it?

Attorney James Wagstaffe handles major media law cases as managing partner of the Kerr & Wagstaffe Law Firm. He says copyright laws in the digital age are old wine in a new bottle. "Copyright laws start with the concept that if someone creates something and it's an original work, they own it—whether it's music or story or a poem. And if someone utilizes that without permission, then it's an infringement. Nothing is different because it's online." A recent court case affirms this. In February 2018, a New York federal court ruled that a retweet of a copyrighted photo of New England Patriots quarterback Tom Brady and Boston Celtics General Manager Danny Ainge was indeed copyright infringement. Outlets sued in this case included Breitbart, Heavy.com, Time Inc., Yahoo, Vox Media, Gannett Company, Herald Media, Boston Globe Media Partners, and New England Sports Network.[2] There is concern that this ruling could lead to a chilling effect on social media, which is partially built on the sharing and re-posting of copyrighted material, and it remains to be seen how this case will impact the social media sharing

---

1   Albert Camus and Justin O'Brien. *Resistance, Rebellion, and Death* (New York: Vintage Books, 1995), 102.

2   Brian Feldman, "How a Photo of Tom Brady Could Change the Way That You See the Internet." New York Magazine. February 16, 2018. Accessed March 20, 2018, http://nymag.com/selectall/2018/02/court-rules-that-embedding-tweets-could-violate-copyright.html.

landscape. The one thing journalists can take away from this ruling is that journalists need to adhere to copyright laws, even if everyone else is sharing at will.

So how do journalists do their work if they need to use copyrighted material to tell their story? Is it OK to use a photo found on Instagram, Facebook, or Twitter? What do you do if another site reposts your work without linking back to you?

Many misconceptions exist about what exactly is allowed when it comes to copyright. Some journalists believe that it is OK to grab a photo from social media in a breaking news situation, but it is not OK unless you've been granted permission by the copyright holder, likely the page owner. Others think using just a few bars of music or less than 30 seconds of video will keep them from running afoul of copyright law, but the actual allowable amount is zero seconds, unless permission has been secured.

The main consideration for journalists when it comes to copyright is **fair use.** Ask yourself:

- How am I using the work? Is it to advance the story (i.e., is it transformative)?
- How much of the work am I using? Is it just enough to tell the story? Or did I use too much?
- What is the nature of the work I am using? Is it factual? Fictional? Does it help me tell the story?
- Does my use take away from the potential market value of the work?

The Society for Professional Journalists and the Center for Media & Social Impact at American University believe the use of "copyrighted material is central to" the work of a journalist and have created a Set of Principles for Fair Use in Journalism,[3] which helps journalists navigate questions of fair use and copyright.

> "Fair use protects journalists' free speech rights from within the structure of copyright. Those rights fuel journalists' mission to inform the public," says the booklet. "Journalists use it, often without thinking about it or even knowing they are doing so, to quote or paraphrase source material, to provide proof or illustration of assertions, and to engage in comment or critique, among other uses."[4]

The booklet outlines seven principles journalists can use to test whether their use is fair use:

1. Copyrighted material captured incidentally in the process of gathering news
2. Proof or substantiation in news reporting or analysis

---

3   "Set of Principles in Fair Use for Journalism." Center for Media & Social Impact. Accessed June 1, 2016, http://www.cmsimpact.org/journalism.

4   "Set of Principles in Fair Use for Journalism." Center for Media & Social Impact. Accessed June 1, 2016, http://www.cmsimpact.org/journalism.

3. Cultural reporting and criticism
4. Illustration in news reporting or analysis
5. Historical reference in news reporting or analysis
6. Starting or expanding a public discussion of news
7. Add value and knowledge to evolving news

If your use falls under one or more of these principles, you are probably covered by fair use, but there are limitations. For example, if you obtained the copyrighted material illegally or by lying, you may not be protected.

"If somebody breaks the law to gather information, that could be crossing the line into some kind of liability," says Roy Gutterman, Director of the Tully Center for Free Speech in the Newhouse School at Syracuse University. "Privacy is a civil issue where there could be monetary damages awarded if it's proven that somebody invaded privacy. It can also be a criminal aspect if it's a really egregious situation, like trespassing or wiretapping or computer hacking or some sort of other data security breach."

However, even though you yourself are not allowed to break the law, if someone else gives you information, you may be allowed to use it. Gutterman explains, "The scenario for that would be an insider, a leaker, a whistleblower, a busybody—somebody with access to information breaches a contract, breaks the law, actually commits some sort of tort obtaining information and then generously gives that off to the reporter. The courts, even the U.S. Supreme Court, have said that is viable journalistic use, as long as the journalist didn't break the law him or herself."

What about drone use? Gutterman says, "The drone issue is up in the air right now—poor metaphor."

"It's not settled law yet," he adds. "In many ways, the traditional elements of reasonable expectation of privacy are out there, but, above and beyond that right now, journalists cannot even use drones for gathering information." A recent FAA ruling "says commercial use of drones is not permitted, and it considered journalistic use a commercial use, which in many ways is a misstatement of commercial use." Journalistic use is not traditionally considered commercial use when it comes to copyright law. However, "somebody else using a drone and then sending that information over to a TV station or website, that would be a perfect use."

Can you take a photo from social media and use it? The answer is no, unless you get permission first (see court case mentioned above). A great tool that helps facilitate permissions is **Creative Commons** (http://creativecommons.org/). Creative Commons helps facilitate permissions by allowing the owners of the copyright to choose a license. Then, when you decide to use the image, video, or other copyrighted work, you know exactly who the owner is and how you are allowed to use the work. You must always attribute, not only to give credit to the source, but to assure your audience of your own credibility. Once you know how to use Creative Commons, you can find images through Wikimedia Commons or Flickr's Creative Commons area.

What about aggregator sites posting your work? This can be a violation of copyright, but enforcement can be challenging. You cannot copyright the news or facts, but you can copyright your depiction of events.

"Aggregators really get close to the line," Gutterman says. However, the issue really is not new. "This has been going on since the wire services at the turn of the last century. There was a big case involving the AP ... a hundred years ago where one wire service was taking the East Coast wire feeds, slapping a new top on them, and selling them to West Coast newspapers, and that was illegal."

What about today's digital aggregators? Time will tell. Many news outlets are forging agreements with aggregator sites in the spirit of embracing the digital paradigm.

Defamation: Fact, opinion, false claims, and consequences

Defamation is publishing a false statement about someone that causes that person to suffer harm to their reputation or mental state. It includes libel (printed) and slander (spoken). To prove defamation, all of the following need to be proven:

- Published
- False
- Injurious
- Unprivileged

Published does not mean printed in a magazine or online article. It only needs to be heard, read, or seen by one other person to qualify as published.

False information must be a purported statement of fact. If someone is expressing an opinion, it cannot be proven objectively true or false and therefore cannot be defamation. In addition, opinion is protected by the First Amendment. Truth is also fair game. For example, in August 2012, two high school football players in Steubenville, Ohio, allegedly raped a 16-year-old girl and posted pictures and comments of the incident on their own social media pages (they were later convicted). A blogger reposted some of those posts with commentary, and one of the accused rapists sued her for defamation, but the suit was quickly dropped because no falsity was contained in the blog. In fact, the blogger used content directly from one of the accused, so a defamation case could not be sustained.[5]

---

5   Alexandria Goddard. "Prinniefied.com." Prinniefiedcom. August 23, 2012. Accessed August 25, 2015, http://prinniefied.com/wp/2012/08/23/steubenville-high-school-gang-rape-case-firs/.

As for injury, "the whole point of defamation law is to take care of injuries to reputation," says Nolo Press. "Those suing for defamation must show how their reputations were hurt by the false statement—for example, the person lost work; was shunned by neighbors, friends, or family members; or was harassed by the press."[6]

Privileged speech includes speech between an attorney and client, some legislative sessions, and speech in court. In these cases, "free speech is so important that the speakers should not be constrained by worries that they will be sued for defamation."[7]

"Happily, most journalists are not engaged in active campaigns of lying," says Wagstaffe. However, journalists do need to proceed thoughtfully and carefully to ensure they do not inadvertently defame someone. First, be sure that the person upon whom you are reporting is actually the person in question. During the early hours of the response to the Sandy Hook Elementary School murders, some reporters mistakenly identified the brother of Adam Lanza as the alleged gunman. They retracted the information as soon as the mistake became apparent.[8,9]

Second, be sure you are reporting only on the known facts and not assuming anything. A headline that reads "Murderer Arrested" can be considered defamatory because the person in question has not been given a trial or perhaps even yet been charged. All you know is that someone was arrested *in connection with* the murder and careful reporting must continue. All you know is that the person is *on trial* for the murder, *convicted* of the murder, or *serving time* for the murder. You were not in the room when the murder occurred, so you do not actually know if the person murdered the victim, and you never will. Keep in mind that people convicted of crimes regularly have their convictions overturned. You can only report on the facts as you know them.

Public figures

There is one more aspect to defamation that needs to be addressed, and that is the public figure. Public figures are celebrities, politicians, and others who have chosen to put themselves in the spotlight, but there can also be involuntary public figures, such as Captain Sully Sullenberger, who landed the plane on the Hudson River (and later became a full public figure by agreeing to become a commentator). In addition, there is the limited public figure, someone

---

6   Emily Doskow, "Defamation Law Made Simple" Nolo.com. Accessed June 16, 2016, http://www.nolo.com/legal-encyclopedia/defamation-law-made-simple-29718.html.

7   Emily Doskow, "Defamation Law Made Simple" Nolo.com. Accessed June 16, 2016, http://www.nolo.com/legal-encyclopedia/defamation-law-made-simple-29718.html.

8   Erik Wemple, "CNN Addresses Ryan-Adam Lanza Mis-ID." Washington Post. December 15, 2012. Accessed January 31, 2016, https://www.washingtonpost.com/blogs/erik-wemple/wp/2012/12/15/cnn-addresses-ryan-adam-lanza-mis-id/.

9   Kashmir Hill. "Blaming the Wrong Lanza: How M edia Got It Wrong in Newtown." Forbes. December 17, 2012. Accessed January 31, 2016, http://www.forbes.com/sites/kashmirhill/2012/12/17/blaming-the-wrong-lanza-how-media-got-it-wrong-in-newtown/.

Richard Jewell: Defining a public figure

Richard Jewell should be considered a hero, but many still consider him a suspect in one of the most prominent terror attacks ever on U.S. soil.

In 1996, Atlanta hosted the Summer Olympic Games, and on July 27, people filled Centennial Olympic Park to enjoy the festivities. Security guard Richard Jewell was on duty that night, and he noticed something suspicious—a backpack left under a bench. Jewell began clearing people away from the area, and then a bomb exploded. More than 100 people were hurt and one killed. However, that toll could have been greater if Jewell had not been there.

At first, Jewell was hailed as a hero, but soon suspicions began to swirl around him and whether he had planted the backpack himself so he could play the hero. Though Jewell was never officially charged or even officially named a suspect, a desire to resolve the case quickly led the news media and investigators to latch onto him.

Jewell's life would never be the same. Even after the FBI officially cleared him as a suspect, public perception persisted. He sued several news media outlets for defamation, and several settled, but *The Atlanta Journal Constitution* fought the suit and won after a court ruled that Jewell was a public figure because he had held a news conference. Some disagreed with the court's ruling, given that Jewell was simply defending himself, but the court ruling stands. Jewell died in 2007.

who is known within a specific community, such as the president of the PTA or mayor of a small town.

The U.S. Supreme Court says that when it comes to public figures, the First Amendment right to free speech must be protected. Therefore, public figures need to prove that there was intent to defame, that the defamer knew the information was false and published it anyway with "reckless disregard for the truth." This gives room for people to comment on fair matters of public interest while balancing defamation protections.

In 2012, a police officer was killed in Cold Spring, Minnesota. Officers arrested Ryan Larson, and the media began reporting on Larson as the prime suspect in the case, with some outlets indicating that he faced charges. No charges were ever filed against him, and another suspect was soon named.

Larson sued for defamation and settled with several stations.

First Amendment and privacy: Speech, access, and information

"*Congress shall make no law respecting an establishment of religion, or prohibiting the free exercise thereof; or abridging the freedom of speech, **or of the press**; or the right of the people peaceably to assemble, and to petition the Government for a redress of grievances.*"

—First Amendment, U.S. Constitution, 1791[10]

---

10 "Amendment I Freedom of Religion, Speech, Press, Assembly, and Petition." National Constitution Center. Accessed June 27, 2016, http://constitutioncenter.org/interactive-constitution/amendments/amendment-i.

The free flow of expression is critical to a functioning democracy, and the news media is a critical part of that free flow of expression.

"If the First Amendment is an umbrella protecting speech, at the spindle of the umbrella, right in the center of it is political expression," says Wagstaffe. "We want to have a democracy where people get to express their ideas on the issues that concern citizens."

However, the First Amendment does not give journalists any extra rights. They must be balanced with the rights of the general public, including their Fifth and Sixth Amendment rights to due process and a speedy trial by an impartial jury, as well as the right to privacy.

Wagstaffe says Americans are fascinated by the criminal justice system, and the numbers support this. "News reports that concentrate on law enforcement activities ... comprise more than 50 percent of news stories, court proceedings ... about 30 percent."[11] This extensive coverage could jeopardize a suspect's rights by tainting the jury pool with information that may not necessarily be presented during the trial. The recent trials of convicted Boston Bomber Dzhokhar Tsarnaev and convicted Colorado theater shooter James Holmes were expected to be appealed on the grounds that pretrial publicity made it impossible to seat an impartial jury.

The Reporters Committee for Freedom of the Press says that, although the Supreme Court has overturned convictions in rare cases, it tends to lean toward free speech. "Juror exposure to news accounts of a crime, the Supreme Court has held, does not by itself deprive a defendant of due process rights. In the case of (former Enron President Jeffrey) Skilling, the Court said, 'Prominence does not necessarily produce

Though the Richard Jewell case reverberated nationally and is still widely used when discussing defamation and the media, cases like this continue to crop up. [1,2,3]

---

11 Ray Surette, *Media, Crime, and Criminal Justice: Images and Realities.* Pacific Grove, CA: Brooks/Cole Pub., 1992.

1 "Olympic Bombing 1996: Richard Jewell, the Wrong Man." New York Times Retro Report on YouTube. October 07, 2013. Accessed June 16, 2016, https://www.youtube.com/watch?v=euxX2TPw8Oo.

2 Ronald Ostrow, "Richard Jewell Case Study." Columbia University. June 13, 2000. Accessed June 16, 2016, http://www.columbia.edu/itc/journalism/j6075/edit/readings/jewell.html.

3 Erin Fuchs, "How the Media Ruined an Innocent Man's Life After the 1996 Olympics Bombing." Business Insider. April 17, 2013. Accessed June 16, 2016, http://www.businessinsider.com/lessons-from-richard-jewell-2013-4.

NY Times v. Sullivan and the dawn of actual malice

NY Times v. Sullivan (1964)[1,2] still stands as an historic Supreme Court case, pivotal to protecting the First Amendment rights of journalists, reducing the danger of a chilling effect on journalists, and holding public figures to a higher standard when it comes to defamation. It settled many of the press questions and is still widely utilized today when disputes arise.

In 1960, *The New York Times* ran an ad in support of Martin Luther King called "Heed Their Rising Voices." It detailed actions taken by law enforcement against civil rights protesters, and it did contain minor mistakes. No law enforcement official was mentioned by name, but Montgomery Public Safety Commissioner LB Sullivan sued for libel and won in an Alabama court.

However, the U.S. Supreme Court overturned that ruling using a concept that the justices developed while deliberating the case—actual malice. In a unanimous decision, Justice William Brennan wrote: "[D]ebate on public issues should be uninhibited, robust, and wide-open, and … it may well include vehement, caustic, and sometimes unpleasantly sharp attacks on government and public officials."

To ensure that Freedom of Speech is not curtailed, public figures are now required to prove that the publisher of any false information must have done so knowing that the statement was false and with reckless disregard for the truth. Subsequent cases have continued to refine the balance between defamation and the First Amendment to ensure that the rights of individuals are protected and fairly considered.

prejudice, and juror impartiality, we have reiterated, does not require ignorance.'"[12]

Reporters must also understand their rights and limitations when it comes to access. "The First Amendment is not a hunting license. It is not a vehicle by which you can commit the tort of trespass," says Wagstaffe.

"A journalist has no right to enter a purely private space (such as a home) without consent, and that consent must be freely given," Wagstaffe says. "Investigative journalists make an ethical choice that they're going to take the legal risk in order to cover the story, but in fact they have no right."

Public spaces are a different story. People in public are basically agreeing to be seen. However, anti-paparazzi laws passed in several states have curtailed this right. Those laws say, "even in a public space, if the person is engaged in what the law calls familial activity, and if you're using extraordinary means such as a zoom camera, directional mic, or a drone, it may be that although you are in a public space, you are entitled to your private space," Wagstaffe says.

Places considered quasi-public, such as a shopping mall, are allowed to have rights of exclusion, but those exclusions must be applied equally. Businesses are not allowed to exclude specific groups of people such as women, minorities, protesters, or journalists, but if the exclusion is reasonable, such as late at night or in an emergency, then it is allowed. Businesses may also exclude people with cameras, which could impact journalists trying to gather visuals for a story.

1   "New York Times v. Sullivan Podcast." United States Courts. Accessed January 31, 2016, http://www.uscourts.gov/about-federal-courts/educational-resources/supreme-court-landmarks/new-york-times-v-sullivan-podcast.

2   Andrew Cohen. "Today Is the 50th Anniversary of the (Re-)Birth of the First Amendment." The Atlantic. March 9, 2014. Accessed January 31, 2016, http://www.theatlantic.com/national/archive/2014/03/today-is-the-50th-anniversary-of-the-re-birth-of-the-first-amendment/284311/.

12 Rob Tricchinelli, "Pretrial Publicity's Limited Effect on the Right to a Fair Trial." Reporters Committee for Freedom of the Press. March/April 2013. Accessed June 16, 2016, http://www.rcfp.org/browse-media-law-resources/news-media-law/news-media-and-law-spring-2013/pretrial-publicitys-limited.

There is also the question of what a journalist chooses to reveal and not reveal. Shield laws can project a journalist who refuses to reveal a confidential source, but this is not a federal protection, and whether or not you are protected by a shield law depends on the state in which you are reporting. Luckily, 49 states currently have shield laws (Wyoming is the lone exception).[13] The U.S. Supreme Court, however, has not made shield law a blanket federal protection. "The key U.S. Supreme Court case *Branzburg v. Hayes* in 1972 found that a journalist does not have an absolute constitutional right to refuse to reveal sources in court," writes the SPJ. "However, the court did acknowledge that government must 'convincingly show a substantial relation between the information sought and a subject of overriding and compelling state interest.' In other words, it's a balance, and the government needs to have a good reason to force journalists to cough up their notes or sources."[14]

Whether you are protected by shield law also depends on whether or not the courts consider you a journalist. In 2006, blogger Josh Wolf initially refused to hand over video he shot of a protest in which an officer was injured. The court ruled that he was not a journalist and held him in contempt. Wolf spent 226 days in jail before the matter was resolved—the longest contempt term ever served by a media professional.[15,16] The Wolf case set in motion discussions about who is considered a journalist. Now many organizations, including the SPJ, focus on doing acts of journalism, rather than defining a person as a journalist.

Conclusion

To be effective as a journalist, be familiar with the laws governing the field and know your rights and limitations. Always pursue important stories with the vigor necessary to bring the story to the public, and don't allow fear or ignorance of the details of the law to have a chilling effect on your work.

Gutterman says proper preparation, research, diligence, and copy editing can protect you from most legal issues. "One of the things I tell all my students—and I teach undergrads and Masters students—is your legal defense begins at your reporting stage. Good reporting and thoughtful reporting, reliance on public records, and really good sourcing and double checking will do more than hiring the best lawyer in the world. Your defense begins when

---

13 Christine Tatum, "Federal Shield Would Protect Public's Right to Know." Society of Professional Journalists. Accessed June 16, 2016, http://www.spj.org/rrr.asp?ref=58.

14 "Federal Shield Law," Society of Professional Journalists. Accessed June 16, 2016, http://www.spj.org/shield-law-faq.asp.

15 Howard Kurtz, "Jailed Man Is a Videographer and a Blogger But Is He a Journalist?" Washington Post. March 08, 2007. Accessed June 16, 2016, http://www.washingtonpost.com/wp-dyn/content/article/2007/03/07/AR2007030702454.html.

16 Bob Egelko and Jim Herron Zamora, "The Josh Wolf Case: Blogger Freed After Giving Video to Feds." SFGate. April 4, 2007. Accessed June 16, 2016, http://www.sfgate.com/bayarea/article/THE-JOSH-WOLF-CASE-Blogger-freed-after-giving-2576757.php.

you're checking your facts," Gutterman says. "Copy editors save more people than lawyers in defamation cases."

Wagstaffe tells journalists, be not afraid. "The First Amendment is a halo of protection, if you are acting in good faith," he says. "Mistakes get made. Happily, the law will forgive an honest error. … It will not tolerate deliberate fabrication. … That lets you sleep at night. Then, hire a good lawyer."

EXERCISES AND ACTIVITIES

1. Is it OK to use a photo found on Instagram, Facebook, or Twitter? Why or why not?
2. What do you do if another site aggregates and reposts your work without linking back to you?
3. How might you handle the following scenarios? Explain your reasoning.

   - If someone robs a bank and then discusses it on social media, can you report on this and name the people involved in the discussion? Why or why not?

   - If someone is convicted of murder, can you begin identifying the person as "the murderer" in your news stories? Why or why not?

   - You arrive on a crime scene and see that the door to the house where the crime was committed is open, and no one is guarding it. Are you allowed to enter? Can you use the news gathered inside the house? Why or why not?

CHAPTER 4

The basics of writing news for online, print, radio, and TV

"We are the first eyes, the first ears, the first to tell a certain story because without us who? Without us who?"

—Christiane Amanpour[1]

When two journalists at WDBJ-TV were shot and killed during their live shot on the morning of August 26, 2015,[2] reporters from their station and other news outlets hustled to find out what happened and why. They also wanted to know who did the shooting, who was shot, where it happened, and when it happened. Also, how did it happen? These are the questions journalists are trained to ask any time they learn someone has been shot, a famous person has been arrested, a politician has announced a tax hike, or about any other event that the community should know about. An easy way for budding journalists to remember what to ask is to think of the list of questions you need to ask as **the Five Ws and the H:**

Who—Who shot whom?
What—What exactly happened?
When—What is the exact time the crime was reported? When did police or other authorities respond? If it was a fire, when did firefighters respond, and when was the fire extinguished?
Where—Where exactly did the shooting or other event happen?
Why—What motivated the assailant to take action?
How—How did things unfold?

Great journalists seek specific details to answer each of these questions, and they are dogged in their pursuit of truth. Remember the first principle of the SPJ Code of Ethics: "Seek truth and report it." To that end, great journalists will seek to answer the Five Ws and the H by talking to authorities, officials, witnesses, neighbors, and anyone else they can talk to before deadline.

---

1   Wolf Blitzer, "War Correspondents Record History, Report Reality," CNN.com. Accessed March 30, 2018, http://www.cnn.com/2003/US/11/05/wbr.war.correspondents/.

2   German Lopez and Alex Abad-Santos, "Virginia shooting: 2 journalists were killed on live television. Here's what we know," Vox.com, August 28, 2015. Accessed August 30, 2015, http://www.vox.com/2015/8/26/9211229/virginia-shooting-video-vester-flanagan.

The challenge for journalists covering the WDBJ shootings, however, was that so few details were known in the first few minutes of the shooting. It was still unclear who did the shooting, and no one knew why a gunman would shoot a young reporter and her cameraman on live TV. Reporters didn't even know exactly how it happened. All anyone knew was what the American public saw on TV. Do you report a story without knowing all Five Ws and the H?

The answer is yes. Because the public has witnessed this horrific shooting, journalists must act quickly to report the facts and help put the shooting into some sort of context.

When journalists don't know all the facts, they report only what they know, let their audience know what they don't know and that they are pursuing more information, and update readers and viewers as they get new information. At the end of the day, journalists can compile all the facts into a basic news story, which is what we are going to learn how to do in this chapter.

The basic news story

The basic news story consists of five important elements:

- The lead
- Elaboration of the lead
- Strong quote from someone involved or knowledgeable about the event
- Different perspective
- Reaction from those who witnessed the event

The news lead

When a movie comes out, the people going to see it for the first time don't know what's going to happen. For the audience, this is part of the excitement of watching a new movie. For a journalist, however, not knowing what's going to happen at the end can be tough. When a shooting, earthquake, or protest first happens, journalists are expected to tell readers and viewers everything they need to know in the first paragraph of the story. This is called the **news lead.**

A good lead should be short and to the point, and answer as many of the Five Ws and the H as possible. A good lead should also be 35 words or less.

If you can't answer all Five Ws and the H, you should still write the news story. Don't hold back. Readers and viewers still want to know what's happening as a story unfolds, as in the case of the WDBJ shootings. When viewers witnessed live footage of an unidentified assailant shooting cameraman Adam Ward and then TV reporter Alison Parker during WDBJ's morning news,[3] they began asking questions via the web and social networks. The story went viral within minutes. To stay on top of the story, journalists were not only expected to find out what was happening, but to share what they knew via their news programs, websites, and social media. It's the job of a good journalist to "seek truth and report it," as stated in the SPJ Code of Ethics. In this case, journalists must act quickly to find out what's happening by reporting what they observe and then verifying their observations through interviews with witnesses at the scene, first responders, elected officials, and anyone else who can provide more details and give context to a breaking news story. It will be days, weeks, or even months before all the facts are known, but great reporters share their knowledge with their audience as soon as they can. It was later reported that the shooter was an angry former colleague. New details become part of a revision or update of the story, informing the audience of what it needs to know as journalists learn and verify the facts.

Elaboration of lead

Because the lead should be short and to the point, you'll need to give your readers and viewers the details in the second paragraph. For example, if you're covering a fire, you'll tell your audience a fire has raced through an apartment building, but you won't mention details in the lead. You'll save that for the second paragraph. Here's an example:

LEAD: A fire raced through a historic apartment building at 1500 Western St. yesterday, injuring 12 residents and forcing the evacuation of 30 others.

ELABORATION OF LEAD: About a dozen firefighters responded to a call from a frantic resident at 6:45 a.m., and it took about 12 minutes for firefighters to put out the blaze, which damaged a total of six units and caused nearly $3 million in damage, according to fire department spokeswoman Lana Miller.

The rest of the story: Inverted pyramid

Once a journalist tells readers and viewers what they need to know in the lead, what about the rest of the story? A basic news story needs to be clear and concise throughout, and the **inverted pyramid** allows journalists to write a story that makes sense to their audience.

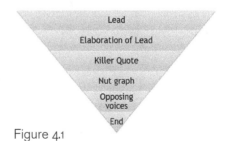

Figure 4.1

---

3   German Lopez and Alex Abad-Santos, "Virginia shooting: 2 journalists were killed on live television. Here's what we know," Vox.com, August 28, 2015. Accessed August 30, 2015, http://www.vox.com/2015/8/26/9211229/virginia-shooting-video-vester-flanagan.

Why an upside-down triangle? You want to put your most important information at the top. Each paragraph becomes less important as we move down the inverted pyramid structure.

After the killer quote, which essentially means finding and using the strongest quote you obtain through reporting, you'll want to follow with the nut graph.

The nut graph

The **nut graph** or "nut graf" tells readers why they should care about the story. For example, if a fire breaks out at a building where 20 people are forced to evacuate, your readers who don't live there might wonder why they should care. This is where a strong nut graph can explain why the entire community should care about something seemingly far away or irrelevant. A nut graph can tell readers that the fire was started by an arsonist who has not been caught. Readers can start looking for the arsonist and report any suspicious activity in their buildings or neighborhoods to police. Perhaps the nut graph reveals that there have been other fires at the same building, and the owner hasn't added any additional sprinklers or firearms. Learning details about a crime, a case, or an event can get people to care about your story, which is one huge reason we write nut graphs.

After the nut graph, the journalist should bring in opposing views on the same subject. For example, if a reporter writes that authorities are investigating the owner for not doing enough to prevent fires, an ethical journalist will reach out to the owner and give him or her a chance to respond. Journalists could also interview people who are not directly involved in a case. For example, why not interview city planners to talk about fire safety codes or interview a tenants' rights group to find out what can be done for renters who are now homeless after the fire? The list of people journalists can interview is long, and it's up to the reporter to use imagination, curiosity, and tenaciousness to seek all sides of the story.

As various voices are brought into the story, the reporter should think about how to end the basic news story. Often writers will end their news stories with a final quote from someone quoted earlier in the story.

Features

Not all stories have to be told with such brevity and force. Indeed, a great number of stories are told as great tales, with the ending not given away off the top. This allows the audience to savor the journey. We will dive into the structure of a news feature in the next chapter of this book.

Difference between hard and soft leads

For basic news stories, journalists usually write hard news leads. As described in this chapter, hard news leads answer as many of the Five Ws and the H as possible. Hard leads should be written in active voice, meaning starting with the subject followed by a strong, powerful verb.

Is this lead passive or active?

Ex: Three puppies were rescued in San Francisco this morning by a quick-thinking firefighter who used his jacket to catch them as they fell out of a woman's bike basket.

The answer: It's passive.

To make a sentence active, you want to answer this question: Who did what to whom? In the case of the rescued puppies, an active sentence would look like this:

> A quick-thinking firefighter saved three puppies this morning by scooping them up with his jacket as they fell out of a woman's bike basket.

> The firefighter, who was off duty, was biking near the woman when he saw that the puppies were trying to climb out. The woman, who had on headphones, did not hear the dogs, and she could not see them because they were in the back.

Multiple sources and data

When seeking sources for a story, there are two primary considerations: covering all sides and verification.

Covering all sides: It is important to seek out multiple, diverse perspectives to ensure you are fully covering all relevant sides of a story. For example, if you are covering a story about gentrification and the explosion of condo construction in a local neighborhood, you must seek out as many sides as are relevant to fully covering the story. In this case, that would include developers, city leaders, community and neighborhood activists, longtime residents, new residents—the list goes on. If you plan to continue covering the story, you will come up with new angles that lead to additional sources, such as how the construction is impacting traffic, crime, local businesses, etc.

Verification: When trying to verify information, you should not rely on just one source. You must seek out two or more sources to ensure the information is actually accurate. To complicate matters, you must also ensure that your second source is not simply someone who also received the information from your first source.

This situation played out during the early hours of the Boston Marathon bombing story. CNN and a handful of other news outlets, including the Associated Press, Fox News, and Boston Globe, reported early on that a suspect had been arrested. CNN Anchor John King, who called in the information, based it on one internal source that he said had been "briefed on the investigation."[4]

---

4   David Carr, "The Pressure to Be the TV News Leader Tarnishes a Big Brand," New York Times. Accessed June 20, 2016, http://www.nytimes.com/2013/04/22/business/media/in-boston-cnn-stumbles-in-rush-to-break-news.html?_r=0.

It quickly became apparent that no arrest had been made, and indeed no arrest was yet imminent. This became a high-profile embarrassment for CNN, and it prompted the FBI to speak out about the incident, urging all news media "to exercise caution and attempt to verify information through appropriate official channels before reporting." The moral of the story: Get two or more independent sources to verify information before going with it.

Full quotes

Quotes are your proof, your evidence, and often your detail and color. When quoting someone, you must quote accurately, verbatim, and in context. Failure to do this can be misleading, can cast your source in a false light, and can call into question your credibility.

The best way to ensure that your quotes are accurate is to record all interviews with sources. You may take notes during the interview to help you remember moments and quotations that you want to revisit, as well as ideas for follow-up questions and story angles, but relying on written notes is dangerous. Recorded interviews faithfully capture the interview, inflection, and context of all quotations, helping you write an accurate and fair story.

It is also OK to do some basic cleanup, so that you do not embarrass your source. If your source stumbled or said "um" or "uh" a lot, there is no need to include that. However, don't go too far, or you run the risk of changing the meaning or tenor of the interviewees thought.

When using quotes in your writing, be sure the punctuation—commas and periods—at the end of the quote are *inside* the quotation mark. If you want to use two sections of a quote, you may separate them with an ellipsis (...) or by separating the quotes with the interviewee name and title.

Here is an example of what a reporter can do with the quote:

City activist Josie Smith tells you, the reporter:

"We want the city to stop relaxing regulations on housing construction. It's ridiculous, and we won't stand it! These new condos are causing traffic problems, parking issues, and impacting businesses."

Here's how you can write it in a news story:

"We want the city to stop relaxing regulations on housing construction," said city activist Josie Smith. "These new condos are causing traffic problems, parking issues, and impacting businesses."

OR

City activist Josie Smith wants the construction to stop. "We want the city to stop relaxing regulations on housing construction. ... These new condos are causing traffic problems, parking issues, and impacting businesses."

Journalist spotlight

KALE WILLIAMS, reporter for the *Portland Oregonian*

Kale Williams (Fig. 4.2) is a former staff reporter for the *San Francisco Chronicle* who began his professional career right after graduating with a B.A. in journalism from San Francisco State University in 2013.

On how he got hooked on journalism:

"Originally, I wanted to do creative writing, but I found I was not creative enough. I was having trouble coming up with stories that people would be interested in. Journalists, as a whole, tend to want to put the focus on other people, not themselves ... and I felt more comfortable with that writing. Distance from my own self was what I was looking for."

On what he likes to write about:

"I'll cover pretty much anything. A lot of my coverage focuses on crime and criminal justice. What I love about my job: It's different every day."

One of his most exciting days early in his career:

"In mid-July 2015, I was dispatched from the San Francisco office to a murder-suicide of a young woman and her ex-boyfriend in Walnut Creek. I found out about the story through Nixle (a privately held U.S. corporation that offers free and

Figure 4.2

paid notification services for local police departments, county emergency management offices, municipal governments and their agencies). The news on Nixle had no names, no location. All I knew was the police were investigating a murder-suicide. It was in a community that didn't get this kind of violence, and the people were young. Multiple reporters were assigned to it."

The process of reporting a breaking story:

"The first version of my story was based solely on a press release. I called the medical examiner's office, and they released name and city of residence but nothing more on the cause of death."

How to find information:

"I looked her up using DMV records on LexisNexis. I wrote a preliminary story for online ... the SFGate and SF Chronicle sites."

Importance of ditching your computer and driving to the scene:

"I got to the house where it happened. I knocked on the door. No one answered. I then went to the house of neighbors. They talked to me. They gave me a little context for the neighborhood and the quote about it being rattling. I tried to get into the gated community where the young man's family lived—unsuccessful."

On how technology has changed journalism:

"For better and for worse, it has made dissemination of information a lot faster. You can find out about something and tweet out what you know without waiting for the reporting and research to be done. If all lanes are closed because of a fire, yes, tell your readers. But at the same time, you might not really have the right information at first. ... With RTs and shares, you can spread the wrong information fast."

On preparing for a career in journalism:

"I would advise them to study journalism: The skills you learn in journalism can be applied to many careers. You'll learn skills applicable across a wide variety of jobs, especially with journalism. Being media literate, skeptical, and effective in communication is important in any job setting."

Writing for social media

Social media is a place to share your stories more widely, directly engage with your audience, and develop sources. Your goal on social media is to inform the public and encourage participation, conversation, and community. It is also to build awareness and credibility so that your audience trusts you and your outlet to be honest, transparent in delivering the news, and responsive to them.

The most important thing to keep in mind when it comes to social media writing in journalism is that the rules and foundations of good journalistic writing still apply. Social media is not a place to soften those foundations or let those rules slide. That being said, the style of writing for social media in general, as well as for specific social media sites, is quite different from the more traditional forms of journalistic writing, such as print, broadcast, and blogging.

In this section, we will explore the general tenets of social media writing and then delve into more specific approaches for specific social media platforms, including Facebook, Twitter, and Instagram.

The most important aspects of social media writing apply to all forms of journalistic writing but particularly when writing for social media platforms: know your audience, understand your outlet's voice, and use ethics as your guide.

The primary difference between social media writing and other forms of journalistic writing is that your audience can immediately engage and interact with you. They can also easily pass on or share the information you provide. You need to keep this in mind as you write. Your goal on social media is to convey information to your audience and give context and meaning to the information you convey. Remember that context does not mean opinion. It means the circumstances and information that enable people to more fully understand a situation. You are also helping the audience engage with the information and their world, and you are cultivating sources.

Social media content should be:

- ☑ Relevant, useful, and interesting
- ☑ Easy to understand and share
- ☑ Friendly, conversational, and engaging
- ☑ Action-oriented

Know Your AUDIENCE

Understand Your Outlet's VOICE

Use ETHICS as your guide

Your target audience gets multiple messages from many sources every day, so you must ensure that your posts are **relevant, useful,** and **interesting** to keep your audience engaged. This does not mean posting clickbait or sensational headlines. Keep it journalistic. The challenge is to speak to your audience without resorting to the lazy and unseemly practice of using clickbait.

Ensuring that your content is easy to understand makes it easier for your audience to share. If they understand and relate to it right away, then chances are they may want to share it with their own audience. In addition, if the content is simple and the file size is small, that also makes it easy to share.

Given that engagement is the primary purpose of social media platforms, it is important that your content is friendly, conversational, and engaging. Of course, you still want to keep it journalistic and professional, but social media is a place where the voice of the news outlet may be more casual or conversational than on the website or other content distribution channels.

Your writing should also be active and action-oriented. Active verbs and straightforward content is easier to read and more interesting than passive or convoluted content.

To ensure that your content is compelling, ask yourself:

- What are you writing about?
- Why are you writing about this?
- Who is your audience? To whom are you speaking?
- Why do you want to speak to that audience?

In addition, your news outlet should decide how it wants to speak to the audience and what interactive elements will most resonate with that audience. For example, an interactive element that allows the user to click on different elements to learn about the pros and cons of a ballot initiative may resonate with an audience of millennials but not with an audience of baby boomers. The baby boomer audience may prefer a less interactive tool but one that has larger graphic elements.

Beyond simply writing for social media, you have another layer of journalistic responsibility. Social media is not just a place to share information; it is also a forum for discussion and criticism. As a journalist, you must avoid the extremes of public opinion in your own posts, and you must curate the comment sections to keep conversations on track. As we know, the internet will not self-correct. As social media manager for your newsroom, it is up to you to keep it on track or get it back on track when the comments begin to go off the rails.

Many outlets, including *The Guardian,* post guidelines for how to engage in comment threads. This provides parameters for the public and helps keep discussions on track, but it is not always foolproof. You may need to delete offensive comments, respond to and clarify for people, and add your own comments to guide the discussion in a more journalistic direction.

One example of the power of curation is how TED's social media team handled the comment thread when they posted Monica Lewinsky's talk, "The Price of Shame." In a blog post about the experience, Nadia Petschek Rawls, director of social media and audience development at TED, wrote:

> "As soon as her talk went up on Facebook, in too little time for anyone to have actually watched the 20-minute video, the comment thread was deluged with vitriol and hatred. People called her a slut and a whore, made jokes about sucking dick, and said she deserves the shaming because 'shaming is an important part of how we shape our culture.' They attacked her character, her appearance, her choices, even her right to live."[5]

Though Rawls said she was unprepared for the onslaught of what she described as "hideous" and "hateful" comments, and she was moved to tears over what Lewinsky had gone through, she was not deterred. Three people monitored and aggressively curated the comments section of Lewinsky's talk, deleting comments that "attacked, disrespected, or shamed" and responding to comments that were positive or thoughtful. Eventually, their work paid off, and they began to see productive, rich conversation emerge.

The moral of the TED Lewinsky story is that it is important to demonstrate for your audience what is acceptable and not acceptable in the comments. The can be done by posting comment guidelines and best practices, deleting offensive content, and actively responding to content that demonstrates what you hope to see on the comment thread. In this way, you can make your social media feed a rich space for discussion. You may even find that your audience trusts you enough to offer story ideas, serve as sources for a story, or otherwise respond to your newsgathering needs.

Social media platforms are such an important aspect of news content delivery and engagement because that is where your audience is spending their time. Therefore, you are reaching them when, where, and how it is convenient for them. This helps the audience feel that your content is available to them, which may help your audience feel more satisfied with you and your news outlet. In short, it is *not about you.* Your audience thinks it's about them, and they will not welcome you into their feed unless you understand and embrace that. In general, the following tips should help hone your social media writing:

When it comes to specific platforms, the landscape is constantly evolving. At the time of this writing, the most popular platforms for news content are Facebook, Twitter, and Instagram, so this book addresses writing specifics for these platforms, but social media platforms fall in and out of favor, and so you will need to hone your skills for whichever social media platform(s)

---

5   Nadia Petschek Rawls, "This Is What Happened When We Posted Monica Lewinsky's TED Talk," Ideas.ted. com, November 01, 2017. Accessed March 24, 2018, https://ideas.ted.com/want-to-help-prevent-online-bullying-comment-on-facebook/.

are popular at the time you are writing, as well as the platforms that are most appropriate to your specific audiences.

Facebook

Facebook writing has no length limits, so limit yourself. In general, the most effective posts are one-to-three sentences long. However, a handful of pages have success posting longer-format content, including KTVU's Frank Sommerville, Humans of New York, and former Secretary of Labor under President Bill Clinton, Robert Reich. However, these are special cases, and they have carefully built their audiences. You should stick to the short rule, at least to start, but feel free to experiment to see what works best for you, your outlet, and your audience.

As mentioned above, incorporating visuals is important to encourage engagement. Visuals can include images, graphics, slideshows, memes, GIFs, and even video. Keep in mind that nobody wants to engage with video after video. It is important to vary your visual content.

Of the current social media platforms, Facebook is the place where the most engagement and conversation happens. One of your major goals is to build relationships with your audience before the story breaks. That way, they trust you when something does happen. Building relationships involves posting content of interest to your audience (that is also newsworthy), responding to comments, and keeping your audience updated and informed. It also means letting them know when you don't know something, telling them you're making efforts to find out, and posting corrections when necessary. Stick to the facts, of course, but learn and know how to talk to your community.

Twitter

Twitter posts are limited to 280 characters, including links, mentions (@), and hashtags (#). Even though you are limited, your posts still need to make sense. On Twitter, your focus will be to craft compelling headlines or comments and encourage people to click your links for more in-depth information. Twitter is also a great place to update stories regularly. In general, use few to no hashtags (0–3) and mention only to help advance the story or make important connections.

Instagram

Given that Instagram is all about the visuals, your written content will likely be limited to a short headline or caption, so make it good. Many Instagrammers throw away the opportunity to utilize the caption because they expect their images to speak for themselves, but this is a waste of an opportunity to frame the story, provide additional information and context, or otherwise communicate. Though multiple hashtags are common on Instagram, in a journalistic setting you should be judicious and only use the hashtags that will advance your story and help you connect with your audience. Finally, as with Twitter, give the audience a link, so they can follow up and find more information.

Social media summary

Above all, remember that on social media, engagement is the goal. Frame your posts to encourage engagement, sharing, and clicks (but no clickbait!). When people do engage, respond and also weed out the trolls. Most importantly, continue your journalistic mission to inform, update, and communicate with your audience as you pursue news to help inform.

Writing news for radio and television

You tune into National Public Radio or your local all-news or news-talk radio station. You know the call letters. You take a seat on the sofa and grab the remote. You want to know what's happening in the community, so you punch up your local TV station for news, sports, and weather.

This is traditional news dissemination, and, unlike turning to online reporting or social media for headlines, this news is consumed in a linear fashion. The reader and viewer are taking in information as it is distributed from start to finish. There's no jumping ahead or clicking on a hyperlink to find out more on a specific aspect of the story.

A listener or viewer of linear traditional news needs to "stay tuned." It may seem quaint and old-fashioned, but many American still consume their daily news this way.

A study by The Pew Research Center found that as of August 2017, 43 percent of Americans claimed to receive their news online. That's seven percentage points lower than the 50 percent who often get news on television. That same survey shows that 37 percent of Americans claim they often watch local TV news as compared with 46 percent in early 2016.

Online reporting often requires the audio and visual element of storytelling. It's a reason why the skills accrued as a radio or television reporter will live on in a news media landscape with an emphasis on 24/7 news gathering and dissemination.

The methods in which news is gathered and disseminated in traditional media rely on the gathering of accurate facts, just like print and digital reporting mentioned earlier in this chapter.

Differences lie in sentence structure, visualization elements, and storytelling. Broadcast reporting lays out key information throughout the body of the story, not just in the nut graph or lead. Broadcast stories do require a "hook and point" at the top to entice the listener and viewer to want to stay tuned. Then, it's up to the writer to unfold the facts as the story is told. This is true for the 1:30 packages on the local news and for the long-form documentary style of reporting seen via outlets such as Reveal.

Differences between print and broadcast writing

Broadcast	Print
One chance to be understood	Audience can read and refer back to the story
Weave information throughout story	Inverted-pyramid format
Conversational tone with contractions	More formal tone and no contractions
Short, declarative sentences	Sentences may include subordinate clauses
Dates, titles, and numbers written to be said	Dates, titles, and numbers written in AP style
Numbers rounded up or down to simplify	Specific figures used
Attribution at start of sentence or early	Attribution may come after quote
Identify and use pronouns sparingly	Pronouns may work better
Use of sound and visuals to help tell story	Story relies on words (with some images)

Similarities between print and broadcast writing (in a side box)
- Storytelling
- Fact-gathering
- Interviewing skills
- Journalistic tone

Keep it conversational

Broadcast writing is conversational. This doesn't mean simple. Sentences should be relatively short and concise so that the viewer or listener can follow without working too hard to dissect complex sentence structure. It's helpful to keep length to no more than 10 words. Shorter sentences are likely to be to the point with one subject, one verb. Avoid beginning your sentences with a dependent clause. This makes sentences unnecessarily complex and difficult for the ear to follow, causing your audience to tune out and change the station.

Part of maintaining a conversational tone is placing a title in front of names as you would speak it. For example, "Iowa Governor Jane Wilson is signing the measure today." Attribution is also placed at the beginning of a sentence, which better reflects how people talk to each other.

In broadcasting, a reporter needs to highlight key facts, just like print reporters do when writing in inverted-pyramid style. The difference is that a well-produced broadcast piece will sprinkle key details throughout the storytelling process with the goal of maintaining the audience to the very end of the piece. You do this through proper use of sound bites, natural sound, and visualization.

Sound bites

A sound bite is an excerpt from a recorded interview. Most sound bites in reporter packages are relatively short. You could interview someone for five minutes, but the sound bite may only be 12 seconds. Sound bites in broadcast are like quotes in print. They are statements directly from the source. Sound bites, like quotes, add credibility to the story and allow the audience to hear first-hand what the witness, police chief, star athlete, etc., has to say.

In broadcast, edits may be made that are not apparent to the viewer or listener. For video, you can use a wipe or other transition to indicate that a cut has been made in the middle of the quote. In radio, that cut will be less apparent. No matter what, it is important to keep the context and spirit of the quote intact. As with print and digital, removing "ums," "uhs," and other non-sequiturs is OK to slightly clean up the quote, but don't go too far or you run the risk of changing the tenor or meaning of the quote.

Natural sound

Natural sound is environmental sound captured by a microphone that is hand-held or built inside a camera or smartphone. When used in a broadcast report, it helps the audience to feel part of a story. Natural sound could be the sound of a bird chirping, the implosion of a building, the murmur of a crowd, the sound of a train whistle, the sound of a protest going by, or the whoosh of a golf ball being hit by a nine iron. This transports the audience to the story environment.

Visualization

Television reporters look for any relevant footage that will help relay the story. Stories need to be constructed based on the kind of visuals obtained in the field. This "writing to visuals" is also called visualization. Often with stories containing numbers, such as those involving budgets, these reports will also include graphics or illustrations to help the viewer understand the layers of statistics.

Sometimes beginning TV reporters will use generic footage to tell their story, and this is called "wallpaper video," which you want to avoid. Use specific shots to report specific facts and events in the story.

News stories appearing on television and online provide audiences with a unique opportunity to see

Broadcast tip sheet

Remember to:

- Keep sentences short. Try to use one subject per sentence to help the viewer or listener understand key facts of the story.
- Do not use symbols in broadcast writing such as $, #, @, &. Instead write "12 dollars," or "number 15" or use the words "at" or "and" even if you are quoting a source. This makes it easier for the broadcaster to read copy.
- Write out numbers zero to eleven and use digits for numbers 12 and up. The reason is, if "0" appears in a script it can be mistaken for the letter "O." Also, if you write the number 11 instead of spelling it out, it could be mistaken for the lower case letter "L."
- Attribution should be at the beginning of the sentence, such as "Police say …" or "According to witnesses … ." It is more conversational than placing an attribution at the end of the sentence.
- Complete addresses are often found in print stories. In broadcast writing, an address is usually not given because it is detailed information that is difficult to grasp for a listener or TV news audience member. Detailed info like addresses, phone numbers, or emails is best left to a full-screen graphic or the print medium.
- Round your numbers. While a print or digital story may include the exact figure, that level of detail is difficult for a listener or viewer to follow, so "712,326" becomes "more than 700 thousand."
- Write unfamiliar or difficult names phonetically. For example, of the authors of this book, Yumi Wilson would be written, "YUU-mee Wilson," and Gina Baleria becomes "Gina buh-LAIR-ee-uh," and Grace Provenzano would be: Grace proven-ZAH-no." Note that the emphasized syllable is capitalized.

what is happening and to witness the sources give their statements. When visuals and copy are used well together, broadcast becomes a powerful storytelling medium.

EXERCISES AND ACTIVITIES

- Dissect a story online or in the newspaper and label each of the Five Ws and the H.

- Take that same story and identify the lead and the nut graph. What are the differences in those two paragraphs?

- Go to a busy park, a packed venue, or weekend festival and write an inverted-pyramid story about the most interesting thing that happens that day. Some basic rules: You have to witness the event, and you have to talk to at least three people (not friends or family) to quote them in your story. Be sure to get their full names, ages, and occupations. The story should run between 300 to 400 words. Be sure to follow the formula defined earlier in the section.

- Go to Google News and read the top news for the day. Choose five stories that are written in inverted-pyramid style and note whether the story was about a crime, disaster, or breaking news story.

Credit

CHAPTER 5

How to create compelling news features

"Writing well means never having to say, 'I guess you had to be there.'"

–Jef Mallet, creator of "Frazz"[1]

Introduction

The goal of a feature is simple: Tell a good story. You want to have a strong beginning, something that sets readers on the edge of their seats. You want to have a well-formed middle, jam-packed with rich details, credible sources, and diverse perspectives that offer balance and accuracy. Finally, you want to have a strong ending, something that ties the whole story together. While some features focus on the lifestyles of the rich and famous, other features examine the complexities of war or the challenges faced by climate change. Regardless of the topic, every great feature usually contains these five major elements:

1. Powerful opening
2. Strong nut graph (unique angle or hook)
3. In-depth interviews and research
4. Compelling characters
5. Tension or conflict

1. Powerful opening

Every great feature must start with a soft lead that intrigues readers and compels them to keep reading. When a big rig smashes into three parked cars and injures a dozen people or a 6.0 earthquake strikes a busy neighborhood causing hundreds of injuries, we want our readers to know what happened right away. That's why we write those stories in inverted pyramid style (Fig. 5.1), which means that we give readers the most important information first (as learned

---

1   Jef Mallett, Frazz, July 29, 2007, http://www.quotationspage.com/quote/40151.html.

Inverted Pyramid

Figure 5.1

in an earlier chapter). As we learned earlier, the first paragraph of an inverted news story is called the hard news lead.

In a feature, the most important information doesn't have to come right at the beginning. Indeed, a good feature creates intrigue by starting with a soft lead, which gives readers a hint of what's to come next. Let's look at how Eli Sanders of *The Stranger*, the 2012 Pulitzer Prize winner for feature writing, begins "The Bravest Woman in Seattle":

> The prosecutor wanted to know about window coverings. He asked: "Which windows in the house on South Rose Street, the house where you woke up to him standing over you with a knife that night—which windows had curtains that blocked out the rest of the world and which did not?"
>
> She answered the prosecutor's questions, pointing to a map of the small South Park home she used to share with her partner, Teresa Butz, a downtown Seattle property manager. When the two of them lived in this house, it was red, a bit run-down, much loved, filled with their lives together, typical of the neighborhood. Now it was a two-dimensional schematic, State's Exhibit 2, set on an easel next to the witness stand. She narrated with a red laser pointer for the prosecutor and the jury: "These windows had curtains that couldn't be seen through. These windows had just a sheer fabric."
>
> "Would your silhouettes have been visible through that sheer fabric at night?"

After three paragraphs of the story,[2] readers can guess that a woman is being questioned in a courtroom, but they still don't know who the woman is or whether the man who held a knife to her is dead or alive, and if alive, the kind of charges he is facing. One thing, however, is certain: The story is intriguing. The opening compels readers to care and want to know more, and that's the goal of a well-written news feature. This kind of opening is called a **soft lead.**

A **soft lead** in a print or online news feature usually runs anywhere from one to five paragraphs. It generally provides rich details of an event that has already happened, which is one reason why the

---

2   Eli Sanders, "The Bravest Woman in Seattle," http://www.thestranger.com/seattle/the-bravest-woman-in-seattle/Content?oid=8640991. Copyright © 2011 by Index Newspapers, LLC.

story is not considered breaking news. Readers might have heard about a murder case, for example, but they may not know much more than that. That's where a good feature writer comes in, just as Truman Capote did when he wrote In Cold Blood, a book giving us a deeper understanding of why two young drifters decided to kill a family as they lay sleeping in their Kansas farmhouse in 1959.

There are many kinds of soft leads, including:

Anecdotal lead—Focuses on a person, place, or thing that exemplifies what the story is about.

> 1999-05-12 04:00:00 PDT San Francisco: Eleven-year-old John O'Connor thought he had the perfect solution for busy parents and overworked staffers at the Presidio branch of the San Francisco Public Library: donate a half-hour of his free time every week helping kids learn how to read.
>
> John, an avid reader since age 6, planned to wear a jester's hat, fake spectacles, and a black cape as the Reading Wizard. He had already selected his first book, *The King's Giraffe.* He even drafted flyers to invite neighborhood kids, ages 3 to 6, to the library on Wednesday afternoons.
>
> "Instead of sitting in front of the TV all day, they could do something fun with reading," John said.
>
> But instead of getting a big thank-you for his proposal, John, a sixth-grader at St. Vincent de Paul School, got the big kiss-off.
>
> Library officials say they already have reading programs for preschoolers, which are run by librarians who have training on how to "present stories to various age groups."
>
> Yumi Wilson, San Francisco Chronicle, 1999
>
> http://www.sfgate.com/education/article/S-F-Library-Closes-Book-On-Boy-s-Idea-2931204.php[3]

Narrative lead—An opening that creates vivid details and dramatic action that make readers feel as if they are there. *The New York Times* won a Pulitzer, the highest award in journalism, for its riveting 2012 "Snow Fall" series,[4] which examined how a group of well-trained skiers ended up in a deadly avalanche. Many of those stories had powerful narrative leads.

---

3   Yumi Wilson, "S.F. Library Closes Book On Boy's Idea / 11-year-old wanted to volunteer to read to younger children," http://www.sfgate.com/education/article/S-F-Library-Closes-Book-On-Boy-s-Idea-2931204.php. Copyright © 1999 by Hearst Communications Inc.

4   John Branch, "Snow Fall" New York Times, December 2012. Accessed Jan. 8, 2016, http://www.nytimes.com/projects/2012/snow-fall/#/?part=tunnel-creek.

T he snow burst through the trees with no warning but a last-second whoosh of sound, a two-story wall of white and Chris Rudolph's piercing cry: "Avalanche! Elyse!"

The very thing the 16 skiers and snowboarders had sought — fresh, soft snow — instantly became the enemy. Somewhere above, a pristine meadow cracked in the shape of a lightning bolt, slicing a slab nearly 200 feet across and 3 feet deep. Gravity did the rest.

Snow shattered and spilled down the slope. Within seconds, the avalanche was the size of more than a thousand cars barreling down the mountain and weighed millions of pounds. Moving about 70 miles per hour, it crashed through the sturdy old-growth trees, snapping their limbs and shredding bark from their trunks.

The avalanche, in Washington's Cascades in February, slid past some trees and rocks, like ocean swells around a ship's prow. Others it captured and added to its violent load.

Somewhere inside, it also carried people. How many, no one knew.

Figure 5.2

In the example above (Fig. 5.2), writer John Branch offers bits of action, drama, and vivid details that help readers visualize the event.

Descriptive lead—An opening that uses vivid details to set the stage or scene. *The Milwaukee Journal Sentinel's* Mark Johnson became a finalist for the 2014 Pulitzer in Feature Writing by creating a powerful series on medical students working with cadavers.[5] One of Mark's stories offers a great descriptive lead:

One afternoon before the end of the fall semester, students from each of the 36 dissection teams troop over to the Medical College of Wisconsin Alumni Center, a large auditorium with a balcony. Andrew Kleist is the lone emissary from Table 1.

A projector glows in the darkened room.

Gary L. Kolesari, one of the professors helping teach gross anatomy, beams a single image onto the screen, a bland government-issue sheet of paper with little boxes, similar to a tax form.

The death certificate for the old woman they've been dissecting at Table 1. Her name is blacked out, but not the rest.

Figure. 5.3

---

5   Mark Johnson, "The Course of Their Lives," Milwaukee Journal Sentinel, Oct. 12, 2013. Accessed Jan. 9, 2016, http://archive.jsonline.com/news/health/The-Course-of-Their-Lives-Medical-College-of-Wisconsin-students-gross-anatomy-class-225058322.html#!/the-weight-of-her-brain/.

Question lead—Ask a question of your readers so they'll stick around to see what the answer is in your story. Use the question lead sparingly and be sure to answer the question high up in your story. This tends to work best in online news stories.

Summary lead—Different from a hard news lead, a summary lead in features can offer readers a quick burst of information, a snappy quote, or a preview of what's to come in a feature.

Most important, avoid clichés in your leads. Here are some examples of what NOT to do:

1. The good news, bad news lead.

The good news: It's going to be sunny in the Bay Area for the weekend. The bad news is this means there will be no rain for this drought-stricken region.

2. "Thanks to" lead.

Thanks to the fast-thinking efforts of firefighters, a family of five was rescued from a burning boat yesterday.

3. The "get no respect" lead.

Lawyers get no respect, but they can help you fight a lawsuit.

2. A nut graph (unique angle or hook)

As defined in an earlier chapter, the **nut graph** or "nut graf" tells readers why they should care about the story. A nut graph typically follows the soft opening in a news feature, helping the audience understand why the story is important and relevant to the public. Often, the nut graph will explain the significance of an event and/or the impact it has on a group of people.

Learning activity #2

Write an **anecdotal lead and nut graph** based on the following facts and details.

The Martins come home from a weekend trip to discover that their house has been burglarized. They call police. Police say it's the fourth house in the neighborhood that's been burglarized in the past 90 days. In the police report, Officer Tom Green says they got the call at 8:45 p.m. and arrived to the house at 9:15. The police report shows that the family says that their 48-inch TV is gone, along with two laptops, a ruby ring, and an old printer. Also missing is their golden retriever, who answers by the name of Brownie. Brownie is eight years old. Brownie is a special dog, the family told police, because she helped their youngest child to sleep through nightmares. Now their daughter, who just turned five, can't sleep, they told police. They release a statement to the media: "We are heartbroken without Brownie. Our daughter needs her. Please bring her back. No questions asked."[1]

There are plenty of great stories, such as an in-depth look at homeless youth, the gentrification of a neighborhood, or a new law passed by the local city council, but without a clear and focused nut graph, the story will sound and feel like every other story that's been done.

To avoid sounding like everyone else, be sure to conduct enough interviews and research to answer this basic question: So what? Why should readers care about homeless youth, for example? Has there been an increase in the number of youths living on the streets in your neighborhood? Is there a rise in the number of arrests of homeless youths? If you can answer the question, you have yourself the start of a very promising nut graph. This paragraph, which usually comes at the third to fifth paragraph of a feature, answers why we must know about an issue right now, as opposed to next month or next year.

3. In-depth interviews and research

Great writing in journalism can only happen after great reporting. Unlike novels or short stories, where you can use your imagination, features must be based on truth and facts. One way that writers seek truth and report it, a key principle under the SPJ Code of Ethics, is to get all sides of the story: the good, the bad, and the ugly. Indeed, the success of *In Cold Blood,* which examines why two young drifters killed a family inside their Kansas farmhouse in 1959, can be attributed to the fact that the writer, Truman Capote, interviewed the killers. Without those interviews, it would have been very tough for any journalist to craft a riveting feature about the murders.

Spend as much time with the subject(s) of the story as you can. This will allow you to observe and record

---

1 Diana Marcum, "Scenes from California's Dust Bowl," Los Angeles Times, April 14, 2015. Accessed June 20, 2016, http://www.latimes.com/local/great-reads/la-me-c1-drought-toledo-20150414-story.html#page=1.

details and dialogue necessary to recreate scenes for the story. Powerful features feel, read, and sound like a good movie or novel. When reporting details, be as specific as possible. If you're describing someone in a baseball cap, tell the audience about the logo on the cap and whether the person was wearing it to the side or backwards.

Above all, be sure to verify the information you observe and receive from the subject(s) of your story. Verify information by cross-checking information with other sources, documents, and data. For example, a reporter writing about a political candidate should visit the Department of Elections to review that candidate's voting record, not just take their word for it.

4. Compelling characters

Each story comes to life through the eyes of the people involved in it. For example, if you're writing about skateboarders who have created a secret ramp late at night at their local church, you'll need to interview lots of skateboarders, enough to provide a diversity of views. Remember, not everyone thinks alike, nor should they.

Most important, a news feature can't be written without interviewing the people affected most by the issue you are covering. As soon as you have an idea for a story, try to get in contact with as many people as possible and line up time to spend following them around for hours, if not days or even longer.

In addition, use details to describe each person so that he or she comes alive on the page. What's his favorite color? What high school did she attend? What does she like to wear the most? Do he have a Mohawk, and if so why? What issues does the person care about most? Spend time getting to

Learning activity #3

Go to a busy café on campus or in your neighborhood. Observe the scene for at least 30 minutes and write as much as you can about the interactions and conversations you hear during that time. Write at least 1,200 words. Try to capture exact dialogue by using a recorder. If you plan to use names of people in conversation, be sure to identify yourself, ask for their names, and ask to record them. Be sure to describe as many details about each person as possible.

know each person so well that you could answer a long list of questions. Even though most of this information might not make it into the story, it will help you develop a sense of authority about the characters that help bring your story to life. Remember: People care about people.

5. Tension or conflict

What makes a story so darn interesting? Conflict, tension, the bump in the road that forces the character(s) to take a different route or to overcome that hurdle. That is why it's important for you to learn as much about your subject(s) as possible. Often, you'll discover the road to success wasn't easy, and it's that struggle that helps to create drama in a story.

Another way to capture conflict or drama is to interview people who have views that differ from the main subject(s) of your story. Notice how *Los Angeles Times* writer Diana Marcum creates tension in this short passage below. Marcum went on to win the 2015 Pulitzer Prize for her series on California's drought.

 By Diana Marcum · Contact Reporter

APRIL 14, 2015, 3:00 AM | REPORTING FROM POPLAR-COTTON CENTER, CALIF.

It was done. Over. No more waiting for rain, hoping for snow.

The 32-year-old farmer in the barber's chair said his well wouldn't make it to summer.

"I held on a little longer than some," Adam Toledo said. "But only the richest will survive now."

"Bro!" protested Sammy-the-barber. "You're scaring me."

Sam Agcoili liked to keep his small shop cheery. Pictures of his lush native Philippines and Hawaii, where he went for his anniversary, hung on the walls. Christian pop music played on the stereo.

Figure. 5.4

Story organization

Another difference between breaking news stories and feature stories is the way each is organized. In feature stories, you typically have a beginning, middle, and end, but you can vary organization depending on the way you want readers to consume the information. Here are some forms below:

Chapter structure

A **chapter structure** allows the writer to create blocks of a story that can be broken up into chapters or packages, which works well for web stories.

Below, you will see an example of how the *Journal Sentinel organized a big series*[6] titled, "The Course of Their Lives" into chapters or sections. Above the headline, you can see small pictures that serve as tabs with a short headline: The First Cut, the Living & the Dead, A Heart in Your Hand, and The Weight of Her Brain. Once the user clicks on any of these icons, he or she will be taken to the story, which also offers great visuals—key to presenting a strong package online. Indeed, this series was a 2014 Pulitzer Prize finalist in the Feature Writing category. As you think about the organization of your story, long or short, be sure that each section or chapter offers the audience a new angle or look at the issue. Mark Johnson, the author of this series, offers different perspectives as he tells the story of how first-year medical students in Wisconsin get an up-close and sometimes uncomfortable look at the human body through cadavers.

Figure 5.5   Go to the link provided in the footnote below to see how the newspaper used animation and music to help tell the story.

---

6   Mark Johnson, "The Course of Their Lives," Journal Sentinel, Oct. 12, 2013. Accessed on June 20, 2016, http://www.jsonline.com/news/health/The-Course-of-Their-Lives-Medical-College-of-Wisconsin-students-gross-anatomy-class-225058322.html#!/the-first-cut/.

List approach

A list approach offers information in a bulleted list. Lists work well online and on mobile because you can create a visual chart of pictures and words, making it easier for consumers to understand the news. Indeed, visuals only take one-tenth of a second for the brain to process, which is one reason why more media outlets are using the list approach in stories. For example, BuzzFeed used a list approach in "26 Beauty Products Our Readers Loved in 2015."[7] In this article, BuzzFeed creates a visual list of makeup that readers bought during the year (Fig. 5.6). Each item features comments from readers, an image of the product, and a snappy headline. The reader must continue scrolling down the page to look at each product, which means readers end up spending more time on BuzzFeed's pages.

Figure. 5.6

Q&A

We often see Q&A formats in magazines, such as *Rolling Stone* or *Vogue,* and they work well when a journalist conducts an in-depth interview with a rock star or other celebrity.

Wall Street Journal method

The *Wall Street Journal* method typically starts with a **soft lead** (see below) and then moves to the main point of the story. It often contains an anecdotal opening followed by an informative nut graph.

SOFT LEAD: The first one-to-four paragraphs should set up the scene with a powerful lead. Remember to tease your readers; don't give it all away.

NUT GRAPH: Once you've enticed your readers, be sure to explain why this story matters to them. How does the story relate to your audience? Why is it news today and not yesterday or last year?

BODY: This next section should include backup for the lead and nut graph. It should also include quotes from a variety of sources to make sure that the story is balanced and fair.

KICKER ENDING: End with something that gives readers food for thought. Perhaps it's a quote from one of your sources or thoughts about the future.

---

7   "26 Beauty Products Our Readers Loved in 2015," BuzzFeed. Accessed Jan. 8, 2016, http://www.buzzfeed.com/maitlandquitmeyer/beauty-products-you-loved-in-2015#.qkv9yvXLrM.

Let's take a closer look at the WSJ method in action. In this practice feature written for a class assignment, San Francisco State journalism student Karina Bueno focuses on one person and then describes the scene. (Note: Names have been changed.)

> After spending most of his week teaching college math, Tom Smyth goes from teaching parabolas and the quadratic equation to a large, brick building along the east end of Golden Gate Park.
>
> Although it doesn't look like much on the outside, inside there are men and women flying through the air, weightless and others hanging precariously from the ceiling by brightly colored silk curtains.
>
> There are women sitting on trapeze swings several feet from the ground, twisting the bar and the rope they hang from to create shapes with their bodies and hang upside down.[8]

Because this opening focuses on Tom Smyth, we can call this an anecdotal lead. In addition, the great details and active verb choices create a very riveting scene. This compels many readers to want to know more about the story, and it's a great way to start a feature.

NEXT SECTION OF STORY:

> "What seemed to only be doable by circus folk is now turning into a full-fledged workout for some of San Francisco's longtime residents."

Learning activity #4: How to create a riveting opening

Q: Why do you think the opening works well?
A: Notice the rich details used by the writer. Do you feel like you can see things unfold as they happen? Rich details are key to telling a good story, so be sure you take copious notes, not just on what people tell you, but what they are wearing and doing. If possible, go to the scene and watch the action and take photos and video to use in a multimedia project. Describe the setting. Be sure to get people's names, hometowns, ages and contact information.

"I tried it once in New York, a few days before I graduated college, thinking I'd never have the chance again. I loved it so much, I decided to start teaching it," said Smyth, a math teacher by day and trapeze instructor by night.

The people that attend Smyth's beginning trapeze classes range from seven to 60. Men and women learn how to balance on one another, using each other's arms and legs to support each other. Some sit on hoops that hang from the ceiling, dancing and spinning faster and faster only to stop on a dime with their toes.

The section above comprises the nut graph and backup for the nut graph and lead. The nut graph explains that the number of people "flying through the air" is growing, and this represents a trend. A trend or pattern that a reporter discovers is a great reason to write or produce a feature story. Notice how the writer brings in Smyth's voice. Be sure to quote someone high up in your story, preferably the person "starring" in your opening.

The center not only offers trapeze instruction for beginners and advanced flyers but also offers trampoline instruction, aerial technique, Chinese pole, silks, an entire class devoted to stretching, acrobatics, handstands and much more.

Classes may seem slightly intimidating to someone who has only stuck to a running and weightlifting regimen but on the contrary, classes aim to teach beginners and also help seasoned professionals stay on their game.

"I really like exercising, but got tired of running on the treadmill," said Lisa Palmish, 32, an avid cyclist and runner. "These classes help me to mix up my workout and have fun in the city."

There are other centers that offer alternative workouts. One offers trampoline jumping.

"The great thing about trampoline workout classes is the trampoline makes the workout low impact on joints, bones, muscles etc.," said trampoline instructor Lon Brue. "If you try to do a plank jack on the floor, you do not have as much absorption as you do on a trampoline."

A well-known study published in the *Journal of Applied Physiology* found that "the magnitude of the biomechanical stimuli is greater with jumping on a trampoline than with running." The study, published in 1980, has been cited in numerous blogs and articles on the benefits of bouncing on a trampoline.

Notice how the reporter introduces a new idea and new person, so the feature becomes more than just a profile on one person or one place. Also, notice how the journalist cites data from a study published in the *Journal of Applied Physiology.* This goes right back to the basic SPJ principles of seeking truth by using credible sources of information.

The rest of your feature should bring in more scenes and voices. Also, try to end with a kicker. A good way to end is to do a circular ending, which means to end with a thought from the person who was introduced first.

"I never thought my hobby or the thing I love to do most could be my work," Smyth said. "Thanks to a whole new generation of people willing to try something new, I'm living the dream."

Journalist spotlight

Interview with **MEREDITH A. MAY,** writer

Meredith May is an award-winning journalist, author, and a fifth-generation beekeeper (Fig. 5.7). She taught digital journalism and podcasting at Mills College in Oakland for 10 years.

Her forthcoming memoir, *The Honey Bus: A Girl Saved By Bees,* reveals the life lessons she learned in her grandfather's Big Sur bee yard that rescued her from a difficult childhood. To be published April 2019 by Park Row/HarperCollins, the book will be translated into eleven languages.

In 2017, Meredith wrote *I, Who Did Not Die,* the true story of a 13-year-old Iranian child soldier who risked his life to save an enemy fighter during the brutal Iran-Iraq War, only to reunite with that enemy fighter by chance twenty years later at a Canadian help center for torture survivors.

Learning activity #5: Create an infographic

When you have a lot of numbers or data in your story, or if you want to give your audience a list of places to go for an acrobatic workout or trampoline jumping, you might want to consider creating an **infographic.** An infographic gives readers a visual display of information, making it easier for them to understand the most important points about that data. Be sure, however, to use credible sources of information for your chart.

Figure 5.7

A former *San Francisco Chronicle* reporter, her *Operation Lion Heart* series about a war-wounded Iraqi boy, won the PEN USA Literary Award for Journalism and the Pulitzer Prize for photography; and her investigation into sex trafficking at San Francisco massage parlors earned first-place feature writing awards from the Society of Professional Journalists and the Associated Press, and was turned into a graphic novel by Stanford University. Her writing is included in the book, *Best Newspaper Writing 2005*, published by the American Society of Newspaper Editors.

She maintains several beehives at a community garden in San Francisco and gives talks on urban beekeeping, most recently at the Monterey Bay Aquarium.

On how long it takes to teach feature writing:

"I set aside two or three weeks of the semester to do feature writing."

On some writers to read:

"Gary Smith, a well-known sports writer, Susan Orlean, who wrote the book, *The Orchid Thief*, Katherine Boo, who wrote the book, *Behind the Beautiful Forevers*, and Sonia Nazario, who wrote 'Enrique's Journey' for *The Los Angeles Times*."

On how she teaches feature writing:

"I storyboard the whole story with them and talk about how to break it down into scenes. I tell them it's like putting a movie together. I ask them questions: How would you report those scenes? Which scenes would you pick?"

On choosing the most dramatic or comical scenes:

"There is a feeling ... an emotion you want to convey ... like courage. So, you pick your scenes that reflect that emotion. Scenes convey the emotional truth of the story. Readers figure this out and that's when reading becomes enjoyable."

On how it was to write Operation Lion Heart:

"It was such an adventure to report. The photographer (Deanne Fitzmaurice) and I had to chase that story for a year because it just kept changing. Will the boy survive? Will he ever see his mother again? It morphed into a story about him meeting his mother into a story of how a kid from a war-torn country survives in Oakland."

"The challenge was to unlearn my journalism brain. I had to recreate everything that happened up to the point when I first saw him. I had to go back in time. I tracked down the surgeon … wasn't hard finding the people to tell me the story. The first version was very flat. My editor, David Lewis, sat down with me. Editing took five months. Any success I had with the story was due in a large part due to David Lewis."

Meredith's six tips for aspiring feature writers:

"1. The story has to interest you or don't do it.
2. Put together a wish list of scenes that you want.
3. Find your guide (a navigator into the story … don't just wander into a place … figure out someone who would love to tell you all about X … sort of like Yoda)
4. Be flexible. Be willing for the story to turn … or jump off your scene list. Don't stick so tight to what you have in mind that you can't see what's happening in front of you.
5. Make sure your story has emotional truth, and you choose scenes that reveal that emotional truth.
6. Make sure your story moves the ball forward. Make sure it tells the reader something new, or it offers a lesson learned. There has to be a reason for reading. Your story has to be a gift."

To read *Operation Lionheart*, May has provided this link:

http://www.sfgate.com/news/article/OPERATION-LION-HEART-Part-One-An-Iraqi-boy-s-2726186.php

Different types of features

Features come in many different shapes and sizes. Some features are very long, such as the ones you find in the *New Yorker* magazine, and other features are really short, such as some articles you might find on BuzzFeed. Here is a list of some feature types:

Follow-up

When a disaster strikes a community, journalists will initially report and write the story as breaking news. This alerts residents that something has happened. After a story breaks, journalists will often continue reporting on the issue to find out what happens next. If the story is newsworthy, the reporter will write a **follow-up.** While the follow-up is usually not as urgent as a breaking news story, journalists will often try to get this story out quickly, and they tend to produce the story in a day or less, so you might also hear the term **daily**. This term is used less frequently nowadays, given the fact that most news outlets are producing news 24/7, meaning that reporters will often publish or air follow-ups in less than a day.

Trend feature

Another kind of feature involves trends. A trend feature goes beyond the profile because it examines a trend or a pattern. For example, a reporter who interviews a variety of police officers and then discovers through interviews and statistical data that an increasing number of police officers in California have died in the line of duty could write a news feature on that issue. The story would not just focus on one police officer's story; it would focus on the stories of many police officers. The story would also have a strong nut graph (the paragraph that comes just after the opening to explain why this story is important to understand).

Obit

Obituaries are very similar to profiles in terms of focusing on one person, but they are written to announce the death of someone prominent. Many news outlets feature paid obituaries, where family members can pay the news outlet to publish the announcement of their loved one's death, but journalists will publish an obit on a prominent person free of charge. In fact, the obit of a well-known person will often be featured on the front page or home page of a major news outlet, as in the cases of Princess Diana, Michael Jackson, or David Bowie.

An obit tells readers the name and often the age of the person who died in the first paragraph or lead of the story. The lead or the second paragraph will then contain how the person died. The obit will also include the person's highlights, quoting people who knew the person very well. An obit will also include any surviving relatives and information on any memorial or funeral services, depending on when the story is published.

Commentary

A news outlet often will offer opinion pieces or commentary in which a journalist or guest commentator can offer his or her opinion about an ongoing issue. For example, KQED offers listeners a chance to offer viewpoints in a series called "Perspectives." Commentary is often written in first-person style, different from most news stories that appear in news outlets.

Op-eds

Opinion editorials or op-eds are different from news stories because they offer the writer's opinion (but different from talk in that the opinion is based on an educated analysis of news and information). Op-eds can be written either by a staff writer or a guest. Most major news outlets enlist staffers to write opinion pieces opposite the editorial page, which usually features perspectives offered by the entire editorial board.

Editorials

An editorial is an opinion piece written by the editorial staff of a newspaper, magazine, or any publication. Editorials are often unsigned, which means no one person's name appears on that editorial.

Analysis

After a story breaks, journalists can interview a wide variety of experts on a topic such as terrorism and write a story that offers readers deep insight into the complexities behind the issue.

Profiles

The **feature profile** focuses on one person, place, or thing. However, this kind of story, done correctly, is not a Wikipedia entry, a chronological biography, or corporate press release. A well-done profile goes far beyond a simple biography entry by one person or glowing highlights offered up by one company. A feature profile offers multiple viewpoints and interesting, unusual, or even unknown facts about the subject and balance.

Feature focus: Writing profiles

Journalists write profiles on celebrities, politicians, unusual characters in the neighborhood, and people who emerge as heroes from disaster. The list of possible "stars" in a profile is endless. The key to writing an interesting profile is to choose someone who is willing to be honest and open with the reporter. The subject must share the good, the bad, and the ugly. Of course, the reporter shouldn't expect all of this information to freely flow into their lap. Indeed, the key is to use your best interviewing techniques to get your subject to trust you and open up. That's why it's important to follow the basic principles of the SPJ Code of Ethics,[9] including:

- Avoid stereotyping. Journalists should examine the ways their values and experiences may shape their reporting.
- Balance the public's need for information against potential harm or discomfort. Pursuit of the news is not a license for arrogance or undue intrusiveness.
- Show compassion for those who may be affected by news coverage. Use heightened sensitivity when dealing with juveniles, victims of sex crimes, and sources or subjects who are inexperienced or unable to give consent. Consider cultural differences in approach and treatment.

---

9 "SPJ Code of Ethics." Society of Professional Journalists. Accessed August 25, 2015, http://www.spj.org/ethicscode.asp.

- Realize that private people have a greater right to control information about themselves than public figures and others who seek power, influence, or attention. Weigh the consequences of publishing or broadcasting personal information against privacy concerns.

Different forms of the feature profile

You can write many kinds of profiles, but here are examples based on form.

Snapshot profiles

This is a mini-profile focusing on one element of a person's life. For example, a snapshot of a musician might just focus on one night at a bar, and the journalist would follow the musician from start to finish at the show.

Broadcast profiles

These profiles show the subject in action and concentrate on helping viewers understand the person as they do things.

Web profiles

Think about a multi-pronged approach to storytelling. Perhaps a timeline is necessary to highlight the subject's accomplishments. Perhaps a video should be added to the package so viewers can see and hear the person in action.

Personality profile

This type of profile focuses on how the person behaves in relation to their craft. We learn about the person through words, actions, dress, and mannerisms. We also learn about this person by what others say and do around them. Below is an example of a soft lead for a personality profile, written by a journalism student at San Francisco State:

> Guitars clatter and buzz as the band sets up shop. The dimly lit bar stands silent, waiting for the rock star to begin. The lead singer ruffles the wavy mop-top on his head and fixes his over-sized sweater, muttering, "check, check" into the mike. This is a regular weekend for Brad Hagmann.
>
> "I tried doing other stuff. I mean I sell sofas for God's sake. But playing music is the only thing that makes me feel fulfilled," Brad says as he's bundling up a cord after a band practice.

Preparing for the profile

Before you interview your subject, be sure to research your subject by running searches not just on Google or Yahoo but also on Google Scholar and library databases such as LexisNexis. Look for all articles that have been written about your subject previously, not to copy what others wrote but to look for potential sources and to make sure you don't sound like everyone else. Also, look for any public documents about your subject, either through electronic records or by going to city hall or other places where records on taxes, marriages, divorces, property, court files, and other documents are kept. You will also want to look for sources that don't necessarily agree with or like your subject, so you can eventually seek balance and fairness in reporting the story. Be sure to prepare a list of questions or topics that you want to talk about. This is particularly helpful if you know your subject is busy and has allotted a certain time for the interview.

Setting up

When you arrive to the location where you'll be interviewing your subject, you'll need to find a place to sit and assess the technical options, depending on whether you are planning to do a print, online, or multimedia package. Profiles are a great opportunity to do multimedia packages, so it's a smart idea to bring an audio recorder, video camera, and notepad. Even if you don't have fancy equipment, you can use a smartphone, which often has adequate video and audio recording options. Be sure to use icebreakers (How are you? What have you been up to?) before jumping into your questions.

On the technical side, be sure to find a quiet spot if you plan to use audio in your video or podcast. No listener wants to hear the bustling sound of wind or noisy chatter of passers-by during an interview with a notable author or celebrity, right? If you plan to capture video, be sure to bring a tripod so you can keep the camera steady. Affordable tripods are available for smartphones. Most important, be sure to ask your subject if they want to be recorded. If the subject says no, then bring lots of notepads and don't be afraid to ask the subject to slow down or repeat words that you miss. Remember, you need full quotes in a profile, and that means capturing what the subject says word for word. Of course, don't forget to ask to take photos. Important to remember: Move around to get the best shots. Get close-ups, wide shots, and action shots. Even if you don't use all of these photos, they will help you write the story by helping you to recall what your subject did during the interview.

Before the interview

In addition to interviewing your subject, you will also want to talk with some of the people who know your subject well. This can include co-workers, fellow students, peers, bosses, parents, friends, partners, customers, clients, etc. If possible, try to schedule time with your subject while they are at work or in action. For example, if you are interviewing an artist, ask to visit his or her studio while he or she is painting a portrait, or ask to attend an exhibit where there will be visitors, the curator, and others who can speak about the artist and his or her work.

To ensure quality audio, you may also want to use a lavaliere or dynamic microphone.

If you're doing a one-on-one interview with the subject, be sure to follow up with others who know your subject, so you can have a well-balanced story. Be sure to ask your subject for names of other people you should reach out to for the profile.

If you are doing a video story, you may also want to capture b-roll (supplemental or secondary footage) of other sources, as well as b-roll of the subject and any interesting visuals and cutaways you see at the scene. In addition, you may want b-roll of the subject in action, even if these action shots don't happen during the interview. This means you'll need to set up several appointments with your subject, which is always suggested for an in-depth profile. Also, be sure to gather details about your subject's mannerisms, fashion style, and interactions with others.

In addition, you should prepare a list of questions, even if you don't plan to ask all of them. Here are some basic questions you should always ask, in addition to some that might encourage your subject to go beyond the surface:

1. Full name and nicknames; former names
2. Age
3. Education (be sure to find out if they got a degree or just studied there and cross-check with multiple sources)
4. Jobs
5. Life ambitions, dreams, and goals
6. Failures
7. Things they'd still like to do
8. What they enjoy doing most
9. Places they have visited; places they'd like to visit
10. Hobbies, past and present
11. How has life changed since childhood
12. Childhood
13. Honors and awards (ask to see a resume and LinkedIn profile)
14. Details about current work and family life
15. What bothers you the most and why?
16. What makes you the happiest and why?
17. Take on politics
18. Take on money
19. Who are some of your role models?

20. Who are some of the people you dislike or don't trust?
21. What are the major lessons you've learned in life?
22. Best advice for people who want to be like you?
23. What were some of your greatest mistakes?
24. Things that you could change if you had a do-over?

Here is a good example of a profile from a 2015 online ABC News story[10]:

Heroic Firefighter's Story

By ABC NEWS
Oct. 4

f Share with Facebook Share with Twitter

326
SHARES

After 21 years of fighting some of New York's toughest fires, including a 1998 blaze that almost killed him, firefighter Timothy Stackpole proudly served his first day as captain on Sept. 10.

The next day, he was one of the hundreds of firemen who answered the call after the World Trade Center was struck by two airliners — and one of the 343 who was killed when the twin towers collapsed.

Stackpole, who was a legend in the Fire Department after surviving the 1998 fire, was dedicated to his job to the end.

"The greatest high you can get in life is by helping somebody," he said in a public service announcement that was taped before his death. He taped the message for the hospital that helped him recover from the terrible burns he suffered in the 1998 fire.

Figure. 5.8

Journalist spotlight

MYKI ANGELINE, red carpet host, radio personality, podcaster, video journalist

Myki Angeline had only one minute to interview Queen of Funk Chaka Khan before Chaka Khan accepted an award at the 2016 "She Rocks" Awards event[11] in Anaheim. How did Angeline prepare for that minute?

Figure 5.9

10 "Heroic Firefighter's Story," ABC News, September 2015. Accessed June 20, 2016, http://abcnews.go.com/Primetime/story?id=132189.
11 She Rocks http://www.thewimn.com/events/she-rocks-awards/

Q: How did you come up with your questions?

A: Knowing that I only had one minute with her, I did a lot of research. I wanted to ask something that was important to Chaka Khan and something that had not been asked a million times before. I learned that she had founded the Chaka Khan foundation in 1999, which had been originally started to help autistic children and later expanded to at-risk women and children. So I decided to focus my big question on the foundation and her philanthropic work. I first congratulated her and went over her history. It was my icebreaker. I then asked her about her foundation. My last question was: Did she feel a responsibility as a woman in that role to inspire and motive other women in music? She said, "I feel we are all responsible." That was very powerful.

Q: Should you interview people you admire or people who do things you like?

A: Whether you interview people you admire, or you're assigned a profile about someone you don't know, or even someone you may dislike, do the best you can and learn everything about that person. If you're not into the subject matter or you don't really know what they do, research, learn, and care about them and ask questions that haven't been asked. Be ethical, of course. Don't just ask questions that embarrass or anger people just to get a reaction. Remember, your career as a journalist goes far beyond one interview or one story. People need to trust you to really open up.

Writing a radio news feature

When it comes to producing a feature for radio, all of the information in this chapter applies. The primarily difference is that you are telling your story through sound. Because of that you must give some thought to how you might use sound to tell a compelling story and most effectively communicate with your listeners.

There are three primary types of sound you can use: sound bites, natural sound or nat sound, and sound beds.

Sound bites are cuts from those you have interviewed. The sound bite should advance the story, add to it, and enhance it. Try to avoid using sound bites that you can say yourself. Also, do not use a sound bite to repeat what you have just said. It should be something that only the interviewee can say.

Natural sound or nat sound is sound from the environment. It helps the listener be present and feel as if he or she is there. For example, if you are covering a rainstorm and flood, then appropriate natural sound would be a river rushing, water pouring down a drain, or footsteps through mud. Natural sound should be sound you gather on the story, rather than sound you have on file.

A sound bed is a piece of music or ambient sound that is placed "under" your voice track. Some rules of thumb are:

1. Your sound bed should not contain lyrics. Lyrics will often compete with your voice track for attention, distracting the listener.
2. Your sound bed should be at a level or volume soft enough so that your voice track is heard clearly but loud enough that it can also be heard.
3. Your sound bed should relate to the story and set a tone for your listeners.

Here are some examples of radio features that effectively utilize sound to tell a story, inform listeners, and capture a moment and feeling.

1. "As Ebola Pingpongs in Liberia, Cases Disappear into the Jungle" (NPR)

   a. (Winner: 2015 Columbia-DuPont Award for Use of Sound)

   b. Note the use of nat sound to help transport the listener to the location of the story. In addition, the reporter and producer began with a scene-setting sentence, rather than a fact or piece of important information. The reporter and producer then take the listener on a journey by letting us hear as they make the journey. The reporter also talks to locals and keeps the listener in the loop by describing what she sees and explaining what she seeks to find. NOTE: Also included on the website are images and other visual information that helps enhance the story.

2. "Delinquent Mines" (All Things Considered)

   a. (Winner: 2015 National Edward R. Murrow Investigative Reporting Award; 2014 Investigative Reporters and Editors Award)

   b. This story weaves facts and interviews with those who live near and work at the mines, as well as nat sound, news archival audio, and data analysis to tell an important, compelling, and groundbreaking story.

3. "Youth in Ferguson: 'I Want More for My City Than What It Is Now'" (KBIA)

   a. (Winner: 2015 National Edward R. Murrow Feature Award)

   b. In this story, the voices of the community dominate. The reporter and producer successfully weave those voices and sound bites together to tell a compelling story and give voice to people who do not usually have a voice in mainstream media.

4. "Star Spangled Banner" (CBS Radio News)

   a. (Winner: 2015 Edward R. Murrow Feature Award)

   a. This story is on the lighter side, but it still compels the listener with gorgeous sound, strong production, and clean storytelling.

5. "Trans Families" (State of Re: Union)

   a. (Winner, Edward R. Murrow Documentary Award)

   b. The reporter for this documentary feature spends a moment at the beginning setting the stage and then personalizing the issue to help the listener relate to those discussing trans issues. The reporter then explains why it was important to produce this story. Again, you will hear strong production, natural sound, and sound bites that advance the story and help the listener connect. For this long-format documentary, you will also hear sound beds to help set the tone at various points in the story.

As you can hear, each of these stories, whether less than two minutes long or more than an hour long, utilize natural sound, strong storytelling, and voices from the community. In addition, each story focuses on an issue impacting or of interest to many people. Many of the stories also focus on issues that don't often get attention.

Keep in mind that strong feature stories involve more than just the person whose voice you hear. Often many people in the newsroom help produce these pieces, including producers, writers, editors, and the news director. This helps ensure that the story is told well.

Creating a feature for television

Television news stories are all about the visualization of the story, and writing an investigative or feature piece is no different. The steps you'll take to develop an investigative report require patience and determination to dig for information until you have confirmation or data.

More information about obtaining public records for your research through the Freedom of Information Act and sunshine laws will be provided in Chapter 8. Before you use these references and approach the fine details of reporting, it's necessary to know how to begin producing a feature or investigative piece for television and selecting appropriate visuals.

When planning your story, in addition to considering whom to interview and other potential sources, you will also begin to figure out what visuals you need. Creating a video shot list will help you begin to think of the **b-roll** you will want to shoot. B-roll is supplemental video footage to help visualize your story. It contains content that is descriptive, such as landscapes, crime scenes, event wide shots, or your subject in action.

Tip on feature or investigative series work

A **series** consists of at least two or more reports that build off the other yet the stories must stand alone. For example, if you were investigating unhealthy or unclean conditions at a local hospital, your first report would establish the issue at hand and educate viewers to the problem or alleged problem. The second report, or episode, might focus on a person whose life is, or has been, affected by hospital conditions. The third episode might include strategies underway to remedy the problem(s). Once you begin accumulating data you'll begin sketching out the number of episodes needed to tell your story fully and in an organized fashion using appropriate visualization.

Overall, it's important to remember that you have a wide variety of options when writing or producing a strong feature package. Though we give you some examples, be sure to try new ways of telling a story and share them with your peers, instructors, and editors.

Here are steps to achieving a visual investigative or feature report and/or series:

1. Be curious about the world around you to discover a story that would interest and affect people in your community. Return to the basics of reporting when searching for a feature or investigative idea: What are the Five Ws and How? Also ask yourself, "If I had to tell the story through visuals, no words, how would I do it?"

2. Do an Internet search of local TV newsrooms, online publications, and community newspapers to see if anything has yet been done on the subject. What kinds of photos are available? Is there any archival footage to help tell the story? Is there a person whose life can best illustrate the issue or problem?

3. Write down all the visualization potential (archival, photos, graphics, charts and new b-roll). Do you have enough? At this stage you'll discover some reports are best told on radio or in print if they lack opportunity for shooting b-roll and sound bites. Court stories often fall into this category because cameras at times are not allowed in the courthouse, so you're dependent on sketches and general shots of courthouse exteriors. This visual limitation makes it very difficult to complete a television story or take it beyond one episode.

4. Remember it's always best to humanize a story, especially in an investigative piece, because you want to relate the story to others. Mentioning early on how this issue affects a life can create immediate empathy among the audience for the story and its subject.

Journalist spotlight

ROBERT CARTAGENA, boxing correspondent at SFBay.CA

Robert Cartagena, a writer for SFBay.CA [https://sfbay.ca/], an online news site that covers the Bay Area, has profiled top boxers in the Bay Area, including Karim Mayfield, Jonathan Chicas, Amir Khan, and world champion Andre Ward. He has also profiled boxing promoter Blanca Gutierrez and wrestler extraordinaire Thunder Rosa.

Figure 5.10

In this interview, Robert, who graduated in journalism from San Francisco State in 2011, talks about how he got the interview with Thunder Rosa and how he got her to open up.

Q: How did you get the interview with Thunder Rosa?

A: I met her at a wrestling show in summer of 2014 ... just went up to her to take a picture. She had been wrestling locally, and I would see her at the events and talk to her briefly. We became friends on Facebook in March 2015. To get the interview, I tweeted her and told her I wrote for a local online newspaper (SFBay.CA) and wondered if I could write about her.

Q: What tip would you give to aspiring journalists about contacting potential subjects for a profile?

A: I would encourage aspiring journalists to research them, learn about them, attend their events, and connect or follow them on social media. Make a good first impression. Don't ask for the interview the first time you talk to them. I would hand them my business card, tell them what I do, and say something like, if you are ever interested, I could interview you and share your story with our audience.

Q: Where did you interview Thunder Rosa?

A: We met at Yerba Buena Gardens (San Francisco). I didn't have a car ... so we met up somewhere close to BART (Bay Area Rapid Transit system). We found this little area next to a playroom for kids ... we sat outside. After the interview, we walked across the street and got something to eat.

Q: What was your first question?

A: How would she sum up her experience in Japan?
She said it was amazing. She couldn't believe after spending all that time, she was back in the Bay Area. She had to get back to work. She was really, really busy.

Q: How did you take notes?

A: I recorded it. I asked for permission first. I used my Zoom recorder. It's easier to focus on that person and not look down all the time.

Q: How much time did you spend with her?

A: The interview was about 63 minutes ... and then we shared a meal for nearly three hours. Based on everything, I did get to know her. She actually took acting classes before boxing. She was born in Mexico, and English wasn't her first language. She ended up trusting me and wasn't afraid of sharing personal things with me. I feel like I earned her trust.

Q: What was the theme of your story?

A: If you work hard and set your goals, you can achieve anything you set your mind to. She was a great example of that. Also, I wanted to talk about the ups and downs. ... She started off a ring card girl, holding up the signs in the ring. ... She was telling me that people only saw her as that. She didn't have too many downs but just that doubt ... she had to prove people wrong ... and she wanted to be a role model for young people in Oakland.

Q: The question that really opened her up?

A: When I asked her about her thoughts on the current divas division in wrestling, I also asked her if she thought the term "diva" was negative. She didn't think it was a negative term, but she didn't think it was the most positive term. She also said she didn't want to be recognized as a diva. That really stuck out to me ... and she really opened up after that.

Q: How do you stay objective?

A: I make sure I don't favor the people I write about. If someone loses a match, for example, I don't say they were robbed. Objectivity is very important. I'm not here to favor one side or the other.

Here is a link to Robert's story on Thunder Rosa. He has given permission for us to use the article in the book: https://sfbay.ca/2015/07/27/thunder-rosa-takes-to-the-mat-in-japan/

Overall tips on creating a great feature

No matter the type or format of your feature, the aim is to reveal something we don't know about the subject or topic, so remember: Surprise us, shock us, tell us something new. Don't tell us what we can read elsewhere or look up on Wikipedia. We want to learn, laugh, cry, and grow by reading a strong feature. Remember that the strength of your feature will depend on the information you obtain. Here's a quick list that will help you write a compelling feature:

1. Choose subjects who are willing to allow you access into their lives.
2. Come up with questions before you interview your subject.
3. Create a storyboard or outline of the story before you create your final project.
4. Research your subjects and sources before your interviews.
5. Choose a focus or theme for your story. Though you'll learn a lot of interesting facts, a feature must start with an intriguing opening that hooks the audience.
6. Develop a strong nut graph that helps the audience understand the significance of the person, place, or issue(s) that your story tackles.
7. Look for documents and data to help explain what your story is about and its impact on the public.

After publication

For all stories, not just features, be sure to use social media to promote your content. Remember, if you don't call attention to your story, very few people will see it. Be sure to tweet a link about your story offering an enticing hook so that readers will want to click on the link. Also, promote your story on Facebook, Twitter, LinkedIn, Snapchat, and Instagram, if it's appropriate. Each social network has a slightly different audience, so be sure to craft the message to fit the medium. Use visuals in every post because studies show that followers and friends are more likely to engage with posts that have visual content.

EXERCISES AND ACTIVITIES

1. Interview your classmate and ask him or her the questions listed above. Ask if you can record him or her and also take notes by hand. Write a profile about your classmate that reveals something we wouldn't expect about them.
2. Choose a breaking story and discuss with classmates what types of features could be produced to follow up on this story.
3. Choose a local journalist and set up an interview with that journalist. Produce a package that includes 400 words of text, three still images, and either a short video or podcast.

Credits

CHAPTER 6

How to find sources, stories for your beat and more

"This instrument can teach, it can illuminate, yes, and even it can inspire. But it can do so only to the extent that humans are determined to use it to those ends. Otherwise, it's nothing but wires and lights in a box."[1]

–Edward R. Murrow

Check out any news website. They are in abundance. Newscasts are filled with them. Where do these story ideas come from? The breaking news stories are easy to identify. Most others are the result of reporter ingenuity and awareness.

Journalists starting out in newsrooms cover general assignment stories, which can range from a homicide to a feature story about a fundraising event in town. Eventually, many journalists zero in on a particular area of specialization, often based on their personal interests, such as politics or consumer news. This area of expertise is known as a "beat."

In film noir, detectives scour the crime scene and police stations for any sign of clues that will lead them to answers. That is a "beat" the detective cultivates, and they make contacts well inside the police force and legal system to uncover facts no one else has discovered. That makes for an excellent detective. Those are the same skills that make for an excellent investigative reporter. It all starts with a beat.

Basics of news reporting for all platforms

One thing to remember is that good, basic storytelling doesn't change regardless of platform or reporting specialization. The experts quoted in this chapter confirm this. A successful news story contains as many of the Five Ws and How as possible. It will be written in an inverted pyramid to make it most easily understood by the audience. The reader/viewer/listener needs to relate to the story, so involving a human element, making it a "people story," will better

---

1   "Edward R. Murrow's 1958 'Wires & Lights in a Box' Speech." RTDNA. Accessed March 31, 2018, https://rtdna.org/content/edward_r_murrow_s_1958_wires_lights_in_a_box_speech.

communicate the core elements of your report. Once this is accomplished, the story can be printed, broadcast and/or posted online. The technical means by which the story is disseminated is a secondary concern. Getting the facts right, double-checking sources and lining up information so it is clear and concise are your primary responsibilities as a news reporter. It's a multitasking, multimedia convergent world of news gathering and dissemination.

Developing a beat using social media

Be aware of trends. Be aware of your surroundings. Attend community meetings. These are just a few ways to find stories. Potential news stories are all around you. To be enterprising, reporters need to go out and look around. Don't stay hooked up to your iPod or glued to your phone. Look at the world and begin wondering why things are the way they are, and if something appears amiss, you may have the makings of an original, enterprising report.

Explore everything from neighborhood reporting to courts to sports to entertainment and offer the basic steps every journalist should take when covering a beat.

Wayne Freedman, KGO-TV reporter in San Francisco and author of *It Takes More Than Good Looks to Succeed at Television News Reporting,* says there always needs to be a beginning, middle and end. When it comes to news gathering, Freedman recommends being curious and patient. He also adds, "If you have a hobby or passion outside of the newsroom, use information gleaned from that part of your life and find ways to use it in your professional reporting life."

Freedman recalls the day a plane crashed off the California coast and how his interest in aviation put him ahead of the game. "No one in the newsroom understood the technical language from the initial crash report." The report referenced a jackscrew and horizontal stabilizer as possible reasons for the airplane flipping over and crashing. He explained to others in the newsroom the vital role these items play in flight. It also placed Freedman in a small group of reporters who could give true insight into the downed aircraft story. "Every reporter needs an area of expertise that makes them more knowledgeable in a particular area than anyone else." Freedman also covered the NASA beat for five years, so his interest in all things science paid off.

If you want to focus on a political beat, find out all you can about the legislature and government system. Start with the basics. Know how many legislators there are and how state government works; know the role of state constitutional officers and how their roles differ from the federal or local government officials. Pay attention to high school civics lessons; know about political parties. Having that basic understanding is an integral part of being a good reporter.

Finding stories, whether you're on a beat or not, requires research and knowing where to go for original information.

Finding stories and locating sources using traditional methods

Keeping up with the latest news by reading a variety of websites is a good way to stay informed, but if you are trying to find a story to pursue, you need to dig a lot deeper. In short, meet people and talk to them about what's going on in their world.

Stop by the police department, visit the courthouse and check out public records, attend community functions, get to know public relations staff at companies. The concept of neighbors talking about life over the backyard fence has been updated with social media and digital communication advancements, but it's still a way to keep in contact with family, friends, and acquaintances, all of whom can offer story tips and leads. Seek primary and secondary sources for information. Primary sources would be a witness or the person experiencing an event. Secondary sources will analyze or interpret primary-source data.

The people on the scene who can update you on the who, what, where, when, why, and how are public information officers. Every agency has at least one that is dispatched to the scene of a fire, crime, or even feature event. Witnesses, neighbors, and others affected directly by the story are key factors in relaying your report to an audience. It's the human element. The best reporters are constantly searching for people to tell the story. Freedman says stories need universal appeal. "Find commonalities in a story. If you can make the story relevant to your audience, then you've succeeded as a journalist."

PBS journalist Thuy Vu agrees. "The best stories are always about people. When stories are heavy on policy, ask yourself whom it affects. If it affects Mrs. Jones, single mother of five, well, go out and find Mrs. Jones and see how she lives the daily effects of a policy. That's a good way to get into your story. It's a good way to get people to watch your story and have an emotional investment because in some way they feel a connection to a real-life human being who is affected by a policy and that it's not just some nebulous law somewhere."

Scott Shafer, Vu's colleague at KQED, adds that it's very important to introduce yourself to people around the newsmakers. He recommends making friends in high and low places. "These are contacts you can call on a regular basis. For example, develop sources who work in the bowels of government who aren't used to being quoted, and you don't need to quote them, but they can give you a heads-up if something is going on."

Also, Shafer advises, don't follow the pack. "There's a lot of pack journalism out there. It's important to cover news conferences but also important to go in the other direction, too. For example, government audits a lot of reports. Download them, read them over because there are always interesting things to be found in them. It isn't necessarily a headline; it might be a sentence that might make you think, 'I want to know more about that.' This kind of research can lead to other stories buried deep inside, so dig around and don't just follow the pack."

Finding stories and locating sources using social media

Twitter, Facebook, Instagram, and Snapchat are just a few social media sites. Reporters in recent years gravitated to Twitter and Facebook to help in the gathering of breaking news information and story dissemination.

Doug Sovern has more than 30 years of experience as a news reporter. He works at KCBS Radio in San Francisco. He has updated his reporting skills and says it's important to stay up to date with the latest technology. According to Sovern, "Social media has changed everything about how we gather and report news in general." He views Twitter as an unfiltered wire service that people can access themselves.

"The material you're going to see on the Associated Press wires in 10, 15, or 20 minutes is on Twitter first. You have to be careful who it's coming from and that it's vetted and accurate, but you're getting the raw information that in the old days, people would phone into a newsroom and now people are tweeting it out."

Every day, Sovern searches for original story ideas and about half of those ideas are rooted in social media. "I will often find out about breaking news on Twitter. Rarely will I find a story I didn't know anything about unless it's a breaking news story." Checking the most used social media sites is just the beginning of this daily routine. "You need to check national stories for local angles. When I go on the road covering a national nominating convention debate, I look for the California angle." Always ask what's important. Look for local angles to a national story or issues that people can relate to.

Sovern is a self-proclaimed "Twitter junkie." "I follow other reporters, people involved in politics, political operatives, and strategists. We all follow each other." He adds that on social media, "you're going to receive data and information as people want to give it to the world, but it won't always prove useful. You have to separate the wheat from the chaff and figure out what's legitimately valuable and what's self-serving. You can click to other links and information to confirm and verify."

This news veteran of 30 years is a big advocate of double-checking the facts, even if they come from a reliable source on social media. Says Sovern, "Once I find something on Twitter, I'm not just going to go on the air and say, 'Hey look what happened.' You're still going to go through the regular journalistic standards and principles, which are to confirm it, attribute it, (and) source it. If somebody tweets out something that I can't confirm, I'm not going to report it."

Shafer says his job cannot be accomplished without reaching out on social media. "As a journalist I'm tweeting out all the time what I'm doing, and if I do an interview with someone, I'll tweet out details of it ahead of time to gin up some interest in it. I'll also send out pictures. We all use LinkedIn, Facebook, and Twitter as tools for finding people, tracking down sources and for getting out our message and getting the quick responses politicians use on Twitter.

It has become an unfiltered way to alert journalists to a press conference or the State of the Union or whatever it might be. We do use Storify and Tumblr and different websites like Mashable—sites that have interesting stuff and ways for us to get out and tell stories using audio, video and pictures."

Vetting and validating information gleaned from social media

Cherry-picking information from social media to use in a news report can be dangerous. No matter the data, big or small, you must double check the information and source. Is the source reliable? How do you know? Is the source relaying wrong information on purpose? Sometimes in the best cases, honest mistakes are made due to the hurried nature of gathering facts in the effort to be first. In any case, this could spell bad news for your credibility as a reporter.

There are ways to double and triple check the bits of info retrieved from social media platforms.

1. Eavesdrop on social media chatter. Tap into and follow circles of journalists who are known for breaking news stories; find out who these news breakers follow and follow them, too; find tweeters in common.
2. Cross check and organize your social media information by using resources such as Tweetdeck and/or Hootsuite. These sources help to organize columns for tracking data and timelines. Create columns that will summarize recent tweets from an individual reporter known for breaking news and obtaining exclusives. View their information on a particular beat or story. Also, follow a variety of respected newspapers and broadcast networks.
3. Twxplorer (twxplorer.knightlab.com) will provide you with a snapshot of related activity in the last 500 tweets on the subject. Double-check your information through recent history.

In addition to vetting and validating your social media information, continue to ask yourself these questions: "Where is this information coming from? Who is this tip coming from? What might be his or her motivation?"

There are consequences for not following through with your research and confirming key information, especially any tidbits picked up on social media. You, the reporter, will be held responsible for any incorrect or harmful information placed in your story. If there is news on social media about your community, pick up the phone or drive over to talk to a local official about your findings. Get that source on the record first-hand.

Understanding the power of social media in news dissemination

"Sometimes, the folks back at the station don't understand the fluidity of the situation in the field and will want to send you to cover another story, so you, as a reporter, need to make your 'find' as compelling as possible and come up with the best story of the day from the Capitol," says political reporter Mike Luery of Sacramento station KCRA-TV.

"We follow Twitter a lot, although you need to double and triple check information that comes across in a tweet. It can be a good starting point, however. Social media is a crucial tool in reporting today since we receive many tips and reach many sources to confirm information even before the story ever makes mainstream media. This is more often the case especially when breaking news happens. If you sit and wait for a news release, you're going to miss the story. You need to be dialed into LinkedIn, Twitter, and Facebook. In fact, a lot of stations are using Facebook as a means for viewers to weigh in on stories. We ask viewers, 'What do you think about this bill or that trend?' Based on how many people follow the story, the station knows which story to lead with that day."

The life of an online reporter also requires a mix of traditional and non-traditional sources. Rob Nikolewski of New Mexico Watchdog.org and energy reporter at the *San Diego Union-Tribune*, says that online reporting is "... great because I can use an interview about a very controversial subject and run the entire 45-second sound bite. This way, the viewer and reader are getting information in context. Also, the policymaker I'm talking to cannot say, 'Well, you took that out of context.'"

"I use what I call 'journalism jujitsu,' where I try to get as many aspects of a story as I can and make myself a little bit different from the many voices out there. What I mean by that is my background before I started covering politics was as a sports anchor for about 20 years. I had this television background and used a flip cam very often. It's not just a good use for making sure I have someone on the record and get their quote accurately but also a way for me to get sound bites. It's similar to how I worked in television, but sound bites in TV could only be ten to twelve seconds." Once Nikolewski writes a story, he posts it on Facebook and Twitter and other sites. He finds with each passing day more people follow him on social media. "As a journalist, you work hard on your stories," he says. "You want people to read your stories. The social media are great, maybe the best way to expand your voice, to have your story read and be heard."

News aggregators

News aggregators are technological platforms or social storytelling tools that let you take media from various social networks and combine them to tell a story on a different site or app. News aggregators can help journalists look across different social networks and be able to find important information and add it to their stories.

Burt Herman is the director of Innovation Projects at the Lenfest Institute for Journalism, founder of Hack/Hackers for journalists and co-founder of Storify, an early news aggregator that was acquired by Livefyre in 2013 and announced its shut down in May 2018[1]. "When we started Storify, we knew we wanted to bring together social media and journalism. Storify required that we pick and choose very carefully what we put in a story. It was more like a blogging tool to write a story. We saw people take to it quite quickly. It seemed to be the right time for something like this. The main purpose behind Storify was to bring together the curation, filtering, editing, and instincts of journalism and skills reporters used for decades to shift through budgets and press releases, selecting the best quotes," Herman says.

In 2018, News360 was considered a top news aggregator app, allowing users to choose the topic(s) they wanted to hear about.[2] Google News and Reddit were also considered other top news aggregators in 2018.[3]

Discussion questions

1. Check out two different news sites and compare content. Do they have similar information and digital elements such as embedded video, photos and graphics (maps, charts, etc.)?

2. If you had to turn a passion of yours into a news beat, what would that be? What kinds of stories would you generate from that interest?

3. A news aggregator will post several reports relating to breaking news or a top story. Review a news aggregator, such as Storify.

Key pointers for solid basic reporting

- Research your topic for the day thoroughly
- Read as much as you can and be familiar with every side of the issue
- Constantly ask yourself, "Who does this story affect most?"
- Know the key players of a story and keep in touch with them using social media accounts
- Interface social media tools (use Facebook, Twitter, and Instagram to promote stories)
- Use Photoshop when communicating via social media; use photos to tease story
- Post photo essays a few times a week to get a lot of followers that watch for the story

How different is each story that is reporting on a single event? Does each story contribute different information? Here is a link to the top news aggregators of 2018: https://www.doublemesh.com/best-news-aggregator-websites/.

4. Watch or listen to a news story. Does it include the Five Ws and the H? How high up in the report? Would you shuffle the information differently if you were to rewrite the information?

EXERCISES AND ACTIVITIES

Finding stories anywhere

Find a place near the classroom where there is some activity or action, like the campus quad. Close your eyes for one minute and write down everything you hear. This exercise is designed regenerate the senses and unplug from the "noise" mentioned in this chapter. Expect to hear and notice things that you likely see every day, but now they take on a whole new light and possibly provide a story idea.

Types of beats

Exercise: Study a few websites to locate one of the following "beats." Figure out two sources you should track down for a sound bite or quote. Think of someone who might be in a position to offer "off-the-record" tips for you to pursue a more innovative approach to covering a story. Eventually, make connections on a regular basis with officials, staff members, and even those who work in a mailroom. They all have the potential to give you story ideas about your "beat" to which no other reporter is privy. In addition, think of visuals that you would use to highlight the story in a television report or video that you would embed online.

- Courts
- Crime
- City hall
- Politics
- Education
- Consumers
- Health
- Investigative
- Regional
- Tech
- Science

For your reference

These links and websites will help you investigate stories and find out more about newsgathering and dissemination practices.

- Poynter.org
- Pewresearch.org
- Mashable.com
- Muckrack.com
- Opensecrets.org
- Buzzfeed.com
- To spot and understand trends: Trendsmap.com

- There are also the traditional and more commonly used sites:
    - Twitter.com
    - LinkedIn.com
    - Tumblr.com
    - Instagram.com

- National and International Broadcast News Organizations (i.e. ABC, CBS, CNN, NBC, BBC World, Deutsche Welle International)

- Additional places to crosscheck information:
    - Twxplorer (search hashtags)
    - Factcheck.org
    - Politifact.com

CHAPTER 7

The art of interviewing

> *"The first thing I tell anybody who's going to be doing interviews is homework. I do so much homework, I know more about the person than (they) do about (them)selves. ... But, here's the important thing—you've got to know your questions, so you can throw them all away, if you have to."*
>
> **–Barbara Walters[1]**

One of the primary tasks of a journalist is to gather information, and one of the primary ways to gather information is through the interview. If you want to be a journalist, you will need to know how to interview someone. Luckily, if you know how to have a conversation, then you may just be able to master this interview thing, because in the end, what you're really doing in an interview is having a conversation on a news topic. You might be interviewing a politician, grieving parent, person on the street, witness to a crime, or celebrity. While there are certainly specific strategies for each different type of interview, the one major commonality is that you must *listen*. If you don't engage in the simple act of listening, then you will certainly miss a lot, and you may miss out on the scoop of the century.

Los Angeles Times Sacramento bureau chief John Myers interviews all types of people every day, including politicians, lobbyists, political staffers, bereaved family members, and other sources. For him, knowing how to conduct an interview is paramount. "Interviewing strategy is important because you're there to get information out of people, and people don't generally sit down and offer information easily," Myers says. "So if you don't really understand how to conduct an interview and how to get information out of people, you're going to miss a lot of what you need."

Beyond the actual act of interviewing, the steps you take leading up to the interview will set you up for success or failure. You must be able to identify and connect with diverse sources that are relevant to your story. You must thoroughly research your topic, so that you understand the story and its potential angles. You must also be comfortable reaching out to sources,

---

1   http://www.citationmachine.net/items/678184068/copy

tracking them down, and getting them to agree to be interviewed, and then you need to get them to trust you so that you can develop a relationship, and they will tell you what you need to know.

Before: Getting the interview

When getting an interview, you first need to understand why you are interviewing a specific source and what you hope to get from that source. As a journalist, your primary goal is to get information that informs and enlightens your audience. You sometimes must work to uncover information, even if the interviewee may not want to share it. Through it all, you want to be fair.

Veteran KTVU-TV news reporter Rita Williams was a trusted journalist in the San Francisco Bay Area for almost 40 years, earning Emmy, Peabody, and Murrow awards. She had many exclusives and earned the respect of sources far and wide, even from those on the wrong side of the story. Williams says that was because she used fairness as a barometer.

"I always told my sources I would be fair ... tough but fair. And when folks on both sides of an issue called to complain or push back on a story I had reported, I knew I had achieved that balance and fairness and told the story well," Williams says.

When Williams retired in 2013, politicians from the left and right and middle, folks from law enforcement and defense, all sides honored her for her consistency and fairness. One called her "a pit bull dog with a heart."

To achieve the praise and respect Williams earned, you must prepare. Do your homework. Before you walk in the room and sit down with a source, you must know:

- What the story is
    - Subject and topic
    - The history of the story

- Whom you're talking to
    - Back story to their life

- Whom or what you're talking about

To do this, you must:

- Research the topic and the person
- Listen to previous interviews with the person
- Listen to previous interviews on the topic
- Get familiar with the latest developments

"I try to approach it at the outset of figuring out what the story is," says Myers. "I figure out what the subject of the story is. What is the point I'm trying to make to the consumer, to the audience? Then I figure out who can offer the best insight into this issue, this dilemma, this problem, this thing. ... I try very hard to figure out which voices will inform the consumer of the news best about what point I'm trying to make."

Research will not only help you prepare for the interview, it will also show the interviewee that you took an interest, that you care about and understand the topic, and above all that you cannot be fooled.

As Myers points out, when you "do your homework before you sit down to do the interview, you do know, in fact, what you're there to ask, and this person is not going to run roughshod over you and tell you that you don't know what you're talking about because you did the research. You trust yourself."

As you research, you will begin devising a theme for your story. You may go in a different direction during the research process or during the interview itself. In fact, you must be prepared to let go of every pre-conceived notion that you developed before and during your research. However, during the research process, you do begin to get a sense of what you need from each interview, what type of story you're telling, and potential angles.

You also want to think about the potential response a source may have to your questions. Often, journalists are asking tough questions to hostile or unfriendly sources who would rather not be asked about these things. How are you going to get this person to talk to you, to trust you? Part of the answer is in thinking about potential responses and how you might respond in those situations. Above all, says Myers, be polite.

"A lot of young journalists seem to equate politeness with being a pushover. I don't think that is a very good strategy to have in this business," Myers says. "The worst thing you can do with people is be rude and too pushy, because it feeds into their perception of the press."

Myers equates this behavior with insecurity. "Too many young journalists adopt that strategy when they feel uncomfortable about their own skill set, and they mask it with this abrupt, rude manner, and it just turns people off. You don't lose power by being polite. You can be assertive and in control of the conversation and still be polite to the person. It's just a matter of being confident about who you are."

Once you've done your research, write your questions or, as an alternative, a series of bulleted topic areas you'd like to cover. However, these should serve only as a guideline to the areas you want to cover. Remember the first rule of interviewing: Listen. Be prepared to go off script if the interviewee leads you down an interesting path or a path worth fleshing out. If you try to insist on following your list of questions, you run the risk of losing or failing to make a connection with your interviewee, missing out on a major scoop or story angle, and getting only a bland, mundane story. Approach every interview as the opportunity to develop a new relationship. You can't do that if your nose is buried in a list of questions.

When you do write your questions, it is OK to explain a bit leading up to the ask but not too much. Avoid yes-or-no questions. These are generally dead ends, allowing the interviewee

Tips for writing questions

- Consider a list of topics, rather than specific questions.

- Avoid YES or NO questions.

- It is sometimes OK to ask yes-or-no questions when you need a direct, definitive answer, but be sure to follow up with something that allows for a meatier response.

- Ask just one question at a time (or you run the risk that the interviewee will choose to only answer part of what you asked).

- Think about potential follow ups.

- Don't be afraid to re-ask a question, if you don't get the answer you want.

- You can always phrase it as that you're trying to be sure you heard it right or get clarity.

- Be prepared to go off script—LISTEN.

to get out of doing any explaining at all. Think about potential follow ups to your questions, and be prepared to go off script.

Former *New York Times* reporter Mirta Ojito told the Poynter Institute that she does her research on both the story and the person. "I try to know almost as much as they do about their subject, so it seems we are 'chatting.'" By taking an interest in the person and not just the information they have to provide, you help forge a connection that may get them to open up to you. [2]

During: Conducting the interview

You've identified your sources, booked the interview, done your research, identified potential story paths, and now you are sitting down with your source.

Step 1: Turn on your recorder.

Step 2: Check your demeanor. Your body language should be direct, welcoming, and strong.

Step 3: Establish ground rules.

Before a single on-the-record question is asked, establish the ground rules and set the tone. Is this interview on or off the record? On-the-record means that anything the source says can be used in the story. Off-the-record remarks must be clearly defined before they are said. By taking the time to be sure everyone is on the same page (and hopefully you've recorded this part in addition to your interview), you help head off potential misunderstandings later. It's also OK to let the interviewee know

---

2   Chip Scanlan, "How Journalists Can Become Better Interviewers." Poynter. March 04, 2013. Accessed April 5, 2016, http://www.poynter.org/news/media-innovation/205518/how-journalists-can-become-better-interviewers/.

that they can re-start or re-phrase an answer if they stumble or want to say it more clearly. However, this does not mean you are giving the person license to take back what they said.

You may also use this time to connect personally with your source. It is perfectly OK to be gracious, welcoming, and put someone at ease. If you know that this person has a child playing soccer, it is perfectly acceptable to inquire about it. You may also ask about the weekend or another non-interview-related question. This will make your source feel as if you took the time to get to know something about their life. Your demeanor throughout the interview should be calm, confident, and in control.

Be sure to ask logistical questions off the top, so you get the right identifying information and begin the interview on neutral ground. These include name, spelling of name, and title. Be sure to get this on tape.

During this time, especially if your interview is on a tough or touchy subject, you want to acknowledge that you are doing a job and so are they. This means that you must ask the tough questions to help inform your audience, and that they have every right to say "no comment" or answer however they like. By taking the time to make this simple acknowledgment, you build trust, demonstrate that you will act fairly, and lay the groundwork for a potential lasting relationship. It also establishes that it is OK to ask tough questions, which are integral to a journalistic interview. Remember, your job is not to be nice. It is to be fair and to get information that your audience needs to know. Politeness is part of this, but that does not mean you are a pushover.

Step 4: Begin

Now it's time to begin the interview. Be sure your questions are relevant to the story you are pursuing and listen to see if there is anything in the answers that you should explore further.

"The more you can make the conversation feel informal, the better off you are. People will shed some of their anxiety if you talk to them like they're a person, and not like you are interrogating them," says Myers. "When they give you something you didn't expect, stop and say, 'that's really interesting. So what do you mean by that?' versus going back to your list of questions and just being too programmed and staying on topic too much. Engaging people with the information they give you is a valuable skill."

> *"When they give you something you didn't expect, stop and say, 'that's really interesting. So, what do you mean by that?' versus going back to your list of question. Engaging people with the information they give you is a valuable skill."*

The intangibles

Be patient—shut your mouth—wait
Listen
Empathize
Look around

While you're listening, be sure to respond to the points being made by asking follow-up questions, asking for clarification, or making connections to the information you already know.

Through it all, remain calm and collected, and always remember that you are driving the interview. You are in control, and you do not want to allow the interviewee to gain the upper hand.

Patience is really your friend in an interview. Instead of jumping to the next question when an interviewee pauses, remain silent and see what happens. Allow the interviewee to collect their thoughts. Your interviewee may reveal something after that pause that becomes the crown jewel of your story.

We've already talked about listening, but I'll say it again. LISTEN.

Empathy can get you far. When you listen, allow yourself to respond on an emotional level. If an interviewee feels that you're giving a truthful response, more trust is built.

Looking around may seem to be the opposite of listening, but when you get the opportunity, check out the space to see what you can learn about the interviewee. You never know what you'll be able to use to help you connect.

After: Choosing sound bites and crafting the story

Now that you've got your interview, it's time to craft your story. It can be difficult to choose from a lengthy conversation with a source. One way to approach choosing sound bites or quotes is to handle the facts, figures, and information yourself, and use quotes from your interviewee that only the interviewee could say.

Myers says journalists have the expertise to construct facts and information into a coherent narrative. Interviewees provide color and perspective, "that thing that you the journalist just can't say."

"Anything that you know you can say in your own voice as the reporter is probably not the strongest thing you should use as the comment from your interview," Myers says. Journalists should handle the meat of the story. "You want your quotes or sound bites to be ways to understand the facts or someone's opinions on the facts or someone's frustrations with the facts or the meat of your story."

Above all, remember that you are imparting information, and your story should be fair to all involved, free from bias, and focused.

Types of interviews

Depending on the type of interview, you may need to calibrate your tone and approach. Of course, you still want to listen, ask relevant questions and pursue tangents, but you need to pay attention to the body language and other signals given by your source and respond accordingly.

There are two main types of interviews, and then several sub-types within those: the news interview and the profile. The news interview is when you gather information to help explain an idea, event, or situation in the news. The profile focuses on an individual. Usually, a **news peg** is used to justify the profile. For example, during the Olympic Games, many profiles are done on athletes.

The most common type of news interview is the informational interview. Here, you want to cover the basics: who, what, when, why, where, and how. Of course, you are always listening to be sure you don't miss something beneath the surface of these often-straightforward exchanges.

Political interviews are another type of news interview, but they are not just with politicians. In addition, they include interviews with PR reps, law enforcement, fire, and other officials. These are often the most difficult interviews a journalist has to do, but they are the most important. Through political interviews we get substantive information to share with our audience.

When conducting a political interview, understand that your goal is to get information, but your interviewee's goal is to sometimes conceal information, advocate for one side of a story, spin perception, or otherwise set themselves or their clients in a positive light.

Knowing this, you can expect that some interviewees may not directly answer your questions, and that is OK at first. It is perfectly fine to give the person a chance to make their case. In fact, that can often set you up to ask very pointed and important follow-up questions. Your follow ups will hopefully help reveal flaws in the version put forth by the interviewee. Remember to listen, so you can ask relevant follow ups and hear when something needs to be explored further.

If you are interviewing someone who is armed with talking points, do allow them to answer and then follow up and prompt him or her to answer the question you actually asked. Remember, you can do this politely but firmly. In these types of interviews, you will need to be prepared to interrupt, rephrase, and repeat, but there is no need to be rude. Again, everyone in the room knows that we are all doing our jobs, so be persistent. Your job is to get information for your audience.

Keep in mind that if you are interviewing a public official, that person is beholden to the citizens. That person cannot plead ignorance. If the head of finances for a city government says they do not know what happened to five million dollars, that is an unacceptable response given their position and the knowledge that comes with that position. It is OK for you to push back (politely but firmly) to hold the public official accountable for information they are expected to know.

Sometimes an interview can turn hostile, with the interviewee giving monosyllabic answers and clearly indicating that they do not want to be there. Again, you have a job to do. Build trust as best you can, take some non-sequitur paths, and work to get the interviewee to trust that you'll be fair. A direct approach may also work here, a reminder that you are both doing your jobs and that the people need to know the answer. If the person insists on continuing to be hostile, then that is what you go with in your story. "No comment," or "the interviewee declined to answer our questions," is perfectly fine.

Myers says it is important to let the interviewee know that the story will run. "I make it clear to people that we make our decisions to run a story independent of whether or not you talk to us. You don't get to control the ultimate outcome, but I want you to be part of it. It's always better that you talk to me. The story is always easier for everyone if you'll sit down and talk to me. If there are things you don't want to talk about, you have every right to tell me that, but you shouldn't just not talk to me."

> *"I make it clear to people that we make our decisions to run a story independent of whether or not you talk to us. You don't get to control the ultimate outcome, but I want you to be part of it. It's always better that you talk to me."*

Another kind of interview a journalist may conduct is with a bereaved person. In this case, the person has lost a loved one, and it is your job to talk with the grieving source, get information relevant and important to your audience, and treat this person fairly.

It is OK to put yourself in that person's shoes, but don't go overboard. Some detachment is necessary to do your job well. Show respect and empathize, but do not tiptoe. Be direct. This should turn into a conversation that allows the bereaved source to open up and discuss.

Do understand what you're trying to get from the interview and what you're *not* trying to get. Journalism is *not* sensationalism, and it is not our job to exploit people who are grieving.

The technical stuff

Asking the right questions is one important part of an interview. Using the right equipment is another. This section will outline some technological options and composition tips for interviews.

Technology

To the digital or mobile journalist, your smartphone is your best friend. It can shoot quality video, capture audio, and snap images. It even allows you to share your work with your news-room or editor—or publish it.

If you rely on your smartphone, you must choose apps that allow you to effectively capture interviews. New apps are being developed all the time, and it is important to stay on top of the latest developments.

At the time of this writing, some of the primary apps for journalists include:

- For audio interviews
    - iPhone: The Voice Recorder App
    - Android: The ACR App

- Editing audio
    - Ferrite
    - KineMaster
    - AudioDroid
    - RecForge II

- Shooting & Editing Video
    - Your phone's built -in video app (be sure to shoot horizontally)
    - On the iPhone, the Videolicious app helps make shooting and editing video easy
    - iPhone: Videolicious, Mavis, and Filmic Pro
    - Android: KineMaster, Filmic Pro

You may also consider purchasing audio equipment, which may be easily connected to your smartphone or used separately. The Zoom H4N boasts two XLR inputs, as well as the ability to mix audio. The Zoom H1 is the less expensive version. While there are no options for using XLR mics, the built-in audio recorder is solid.

To hook up the Zoom H4N to your smartphone to record phone interviews, simply use one of the following cables:

- 1/8-inch / 3.5mm / mini to ¼-inch cable
- 1/8-inch / 3.5mm / mini to XLR
- 1/8-inch / 3.5mm / mini to Dual XLR

1/8-inch, 3.5mm, and mini are three names for the headphone input on your smartphone. The H4N is equipped to take an XLR, dual XLR or ¼-inch input. You then plug your headphones into the Zoom, hit record, and you will be able to hear your interviewee on the phone and record the interview to the Zoom.

For in-person interviews, you may use the built-in microphone on the Zoom or hook up a handheld or lavaliere mic using the appropriate cables.

When it comes to video, your smartphone's video camera will do the job quite nicely. Just be sure you're all charged up and have enough memory to accommodate your interview file. Also, when shooting video, your audio may not come out as strong unless you've hooked up some sort of handheld or lavaliere mic to the smartphone and placed that mic close to the interviewee. You may also record audio separately onto your Zoom and then pair the audio and video later using a nonlinear video editing system such as iMovie, Adobe Premiere, or Final Cut Pro.

Here are some interview package options for the budding journalist:

- PACKAGE 1
    - Smartphone
    - Apps

- PACKAGE 2
    - Smartphone
    - H4N Zoom
    - Cables

- PACKAGE 3
    - H4N Zoom
    - Cables
    - Handheld or Lavaliere mic

If the interview will be written, then you may manually transcribe your interview, which I prefer, so that I can hear everything that was said and begin to make choices about what I want to use, or you may use transcription software, such as Dragon, and then add the punctuation to the transcribed document. In addition, YouTube also provides a closed caption transcript for all uploaded videos. You can simply download this file, remove the time codes, and then clean up the transcription by listening to your interview.

If you plan to craft an audio or video piece, then you will use an audio or video editing app or piece of software to complete your work. As mentioned above, video editing apps on your smartphone include Videolicious (iPhone) and KineMaster (Android and iPhone). Strong audio editing apps are Ferrite (iPhone) and RecForge (Android). On your laptop or desktop, popular video editing software includes iMovie or Final Cut Pro (Mac) or Adobe Premiere Pro (Mac or PC). When it comes to audio editing on your laptop or desktop, Audacity is free software that works great. You may also use GarageBand (Mac) or Adobe Audition (Mac or PC).

Many local and national news outlets now use Videolicious (iPhone) to capture and present stories, including *The Washington Post*, *The New York Times*, *Chicago Sun Times*, and *KTVU*.

Composition

Composition refers to the look of your interview. Just because you can turn a camera on someone and ask some questions does not mean you are engaging in quality journalism. To ensure that people will actually want to watch it and will respond to it positively, you should become familiar with the basics of framing and lighting.

For more on composition and lighting, be sure to check out these videos from photographer Mike Browne.[3] Though they are specific to photography, they apply perfectly to videography for journalism.

Window light

Pt. 1   https://www.youtube.com/watch?v=mlsb7rnzdVo
Pt. 2   https://www.youtube.com/watch?v=_uAat-6OqTk

Rule of thirds

https://www.youtube.com/watch?v=fSSOZxLnNyc

Leading lines

https://www.youtube.com/watch?v=Ea27KqihGtk

Composition

Pt. 1   https://www.youtube.com/watch?v=VW8L8zxDtTo
Pt. 2   https://www.youtube.com/watch?v=dfMFL_g5E2w

---

3   Mike Browne, "Mike Browne Photography." Mike Browne Photography on YouTube. Accessed June 16, 2016, https://www.youtube.com/user/photoexposed.

How to use a tripod

https://www.youtube.com/watch?v=ggUJpKqOZVY

Before you begin the interview, be sure the atmosphere is relatively quiet, so you get a clean recording.

Also, if you're shooting video, be sure that there is light on the interviewee's face and not behind them. If there is a window, be sure the interviewee is positioned to look out the window so that the natural light will be on the interviewee. If outside, be sure you are entirely in the sun or shade to avoid shadows.

If the sun is at high noon, position the interviewee so that the sun is slightly behind them. That way, no shadows will fall across the interviewee's face.

Interview pitfalls

We've all seen those interviewers who just rub us the wrong way, make us feel uncomfortable, or alienate us. Don't be that interviewer.

You want to avoid:

- *Being overly aggressive*. You need to allow the interviewee to make their point. You can always ask a follow-up question, but only interrupt if it is absolutely necessary.
- *Sticking just to questions on the list*. This pitfall is where interviews go to die. Listen and respond accordingly.
- *Acting superior*. This interview and this story are not about you. You are not a diva or celebrity. Journalists are stewards of the public trust, and you must keep that in the forefront.
- *Allowing the interviewee to drive*. This can happen because you failed to prepare, lack confidence, or are intimidated. However, it should never happen. Do everything you need to do to ensure you remain in control and get the information you need to advance the story.

Above all, remember why you are there: to inform the audience, shine light on a topic, share important perspectives, and increase public discussion. With these tenets as your guide, you should be able to conduct a strong interview in service of your audience.

EXERCISES AND ACTIVITIES

1. Personal interview
   a. Choose a parent or friend.
   b. Research that person and develop a series of 5–10 questions. Consider each question for its newsworthiness.
   c. Conduct the interview and be sure to audio record it.
   d. Listen back to the interview.
      i. Identify important story points that you want to use.
      ii. Pull quotes to help tell your story.
      iii. Note places where you could have asked follow-up questions.
         1. What questions could you have asked?
         2. Could the follow-up questions have led to a more interesting story path?
         3. How might you ensure you hear these opportunities while conducting the interview?
   e. Craft your story, either written or podcast (or both).
2. Interview with professor or mentor
   a. Choose a professor or mentor who has a story you want to tell.
   b. Do your research. Be able to say why this person is newsworthy.
   c. Follow steps c–e in option #1.
3. Interview with newsmaker
   a. Choose a person whom you do NOT know and who has a newsworthy story.
   b. Do your research.
      i. Be able to say why this person is newsworthy.
      ii. What story can you tell that may not have been told before?
   c. Follow steps c–e in option #1.

Sources

"BBC Journalism Skills: Interviewing Techniques." YouTube. October 26, 2015. Accessed March 20, 2018, https://www.youtube.com/watch?v=dHUn6zSGEJ8.

Browne, Mike. "Mike Browne." YouTube. Accessed March 20, 2018, https://www.youtube.com/channel/UCs4So7E5NCoR7pVuzBJoe8Q.

Couric, Katie. "Katie Couric on How to Conduct a Good Interview." YouTube. June 26, 2009. Accessed March 20, 2018, https://www.youtube.com/watch?v=4eoynri2etm.

"Interviewing Principles." Columbia University. Accessed March 20, 2018, http://www.columbia.edu/itc/journalism/isaacs/edit/Mencher-Intv1.html.

"Riz Khan—Overview on Interviewing Technique." YouTube. June 26, 2009. Accessed March 20, 2018, https://www.youtube.com/watch?v=y0KzvT3ckDE&.

Scanlan, Chip. "How Journalists Can Become Better Interviewers." Poynter. March 02, 2017. Accessed March 20, 2018, https://www.poynter.org/news/how-journalists-can-become-better-interviewers.

CHAPTER 8

Accessing and understanding data, public records, surveys, and studies

" Distinguishing the signal from the noise requires both scientific knowledge and self-knowledge: the serenity to accept the things we cannot predict, the courage to predict the things we can, and the wisdom to know the difference."

–Nate Silver[1]

Introduction

To report thoroughly, you need to check facts, know how to gain access to information, and understand how to decipher data, surveys, and studies. Then present it to your audience in a way that makes sense and tells a story. Whether or not you call yourself a "data journalist," your work will involve data, public documents, news releases, and reporting on various research studies.

Often, data are publicly available, but sometimes they're not. If they're public, you must know where to find the data and how to access that data. If government agencies have not made the data publicly available, then you'll need to know how to file a **FOIA** or **Sunshine Act** request to gain access to the data. This can be a daunting task. There is so much to discover online and usually even more in person digging through paperwork at the local city hall.

If dataset is given to you through research studies, polls and surveys, or other means, you must then be able to decode whether the agency, organization, or company that originated the data has a vested interest in telling a biased story—or perhaps veiling part of the story. Understanding how to read and analyze research will help you tell the story that needs to be told, the one that informs your audience.

This chapter will dissect this investigative method of confirming data. It will also provide case studies that show the importance of researching facts and information as you search for attribution and acknowledgement. This is especially key when reporting on sensitive material involving a person's life and privacy. Ethical decision making plays a role in deciding how much

---

1   Nate Silver, *The Signal and the Noise: Why So Many Predictions Fail.* (New York: Penguin Books, 2012). Accessed March 30, 2018, https://goo.gl/eX7Q53.

information to use. Just about anyone with years in the business of investigative reporting will tell young journalists that one of the best qualities you can bring to the job of digging through documents and datasets is curiosity about your subject and about the world around you.

Finding and confirming information can lead you to important story details. Being able to translate that data into news people can use is a skill that begins with identifying data, knowing where to find the data, and understanding how to "read" data. Today's news stories flow from multiple sources such as eyewitnesses, blogs, and websites. It's crucial for reporters to know how to dissect information from these vehicles. Data can give insights into what is happening and how it might affect us. Becoming knowledgeable in searching for and visualizing data is transformative for the profession of information gathering.

Data journalism

Nearly everyone in a newsroom uses data journalism, as does anyone in the business of communicating. Reporters, editors, graphic artists, web designers, and app developers all translate data into information that makes their work more understandable and accessible to their audience.

What is data journalism?
- A specialty focused on using data to tell stories and present information
- Interaction between content producers, designers, computer scientists, developers, and statisticians

Data journalism has become such a phenomenon because of the tremendous amount of data currently available and the increasing power of computers to crunch that data. By using data well, whether it's the source of the story or a tool to tell a larger story, data journalism can help the public understand important concepts and trends that may impact their lives.

Any journalist can feel daunted when faced with pages and pages of rows and columns with seemingly indecipherable facts and figures. However, there are stories in the data—often important stories that your audience needs to know. It is up to you to curate the data, make sense of it all, and then help present that data to your audience. Digital tools such as Tableau Public, Google Fusion Tables, Excel, SPSS, and others make it easy and quick to crunch large amounts of data and create visuals to help you see patterns, trends, and important stories in the data. This allows you to explore new and in-depth story angles and tell compelling stories.

For example, in the wake of several recent mass shootings, Vox plotted the data for each mass shooting since Sandy Hook in December 2012 onto a Google Map.[2] It is one thing to discuss or write about data, but seeing the many red dots all over a map of the contiguous U.S. drives the

---

2   http://www.vox.com/a/mass-shootings-sandy-hook

point home that there seem to be a large number of mass shootings and that they seem to be concentrated in certain parts of the country. In its write-up, Vox pointed out that the regions with more gun ownership happen to also have more gun violence. Vox also discussed the varying definitions of a "mass shooting." This is an excellent example of using and visualizing data to make the story more accessible to the audience.

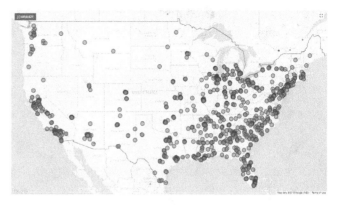

Figure 8.1   Gun Violence

Background

Data journalism is nothing new. It has been part of the industry since the late 19th and early 20th centuries, but it has come to prominence in recent years because of increased computing capacity and access to information over digital channels. In the 1970s, as computers became part of the process, it was termed "precision journalism" or computer-assisted reporting (CAR). Computers allowed for large-scale crunching of data and became a game-changer for investigative journalists, providing them the opportunity to gather and analyze data to enhance their reporting. In the late 1990s and 2000s, the power of the Internet led to a resurgence in the use of data journalism.

When to use and not use data

Not every story will involve data, nor should it. Data should be used to enhance a story, help the reader understand trends, and reveal patterns. See the table below for more information on when to use or not to use data.

When to use data	When NOT to use data
- To show hierarchy - To browse large databases - To envision alternate outcomes - To show change over time - To compare values - To show connections - To trace flows	- When the story is better told through text or multimedia - When you have very few data points - When the data has little variability

WikiLeaks and Edward Snowden: Two different ways of handling data

WikiLeaks and Edward Snowden[1] are two notable recent stories grounded in the use, curation, deciphering, and communication of data to inform the public about potentially egregious activities by the U.S. government.[2]

Figure. 8.2
Edward Snowden

In 2013, Snowden, a contractor for the National Security Agency (NSA) acted as a whistleblower by leaking details of classified U.S. government surveillance programs to The Guardian news outlet.[3] He chose to work through the news media rather than releasing all of the data and documents himself to ensure that the information was curated, culled through, and digested. His hope was to prevent putting anyone in danger that might be serving undercover, as well as ensure that the data were reported correctly. This did not prevent repercussions. The U.S. government charged Snowden with theft of government property, unauthorized communication of national defense information, and willful communication of classified intelligence to an unauthorized person. Snowden is now in Russia, where he cannot be extradited to the U.S.[4]

1   http://www.theguardian.com/us-news/2015/jun/01/charges-against-edward-snowden-stand-despite-telephone-surveillance-ban

2   https://www.theguardian.com/world/2013/jun/09/edward-snowden-nsa-whistleblower-surveillance

3   https://commons.wikimedia.org/wiki/File:Edward_Snowden-2.jpg

4   https://upload.wikimedia.org/wikipedia/commons/6/60/Edward_Snowden-2.jpg

What to do with data once you've got it

Often, the data you get ahold of will not be ready to post. The data will need to be cleaned. Cleaning data is the process of filtering the data to ensure you're isolating only the data elements that you need. For example, if you are looking into job trends and receive a dataset from the U.S. Department of Labor, that dataset may contain hundreds of columns and thousands of rows, including breakdowns by state, county, city, ethnicity and race, age, income level, and many other data points. If you want to look only at job trends in your region, then you will "clean" your data by isolating just the columns and rows that deal with counties or cities in your region. If you want to further look just at data involving millennials, then you will clean out data involving other age ranges.

In other cases, you may have data with holes, meaning that data points may not be available for various elements or fields. In the jobs example mentioned above, perhaps salary information is not available for various jobs that millennials may have. If the data are not available, then the cell in that column and row will be blank. This does not mean that the dataset is useless. It simply means that you need to make clear to your audience which information was not available.

The term "cleaning" may sound suspicious, but it is a perfectly normal process of handling data. Those with agendas and biases, however, can misuse this technique to spin the data toward a specific outcome. For example, if someone wanted to cover up the fact that job growth among older Americans declined by twice as much as from 20 years ago, that data may be scrubbed or minimized in some way. This is a clear violation of ethics. Data should never be manipulated to fit the story.

Accessing data

The process of accessing data can be fairly simple or fairly complex, depending on the situation. In this section, we will cover scraping, FOIA, and research, including surveys, polls, and studies.

Scraping data

"Scraping" is basically using code to "read" a website or app and pull, harvest, or extract data from that website or app. Scraping can also involve organizing unstructured data into some sort of spreadsheet, often an Excel or .CSV file. If an outlet wants to prevent you from accessing its raw data, it may present its data only in .PDF form, making extraction more difficult. The exact mechanisms of scraping are beyond the scope of this book, but there are many resources to learn how to do this, some of which you can find in the reading list in the appendices of this text.

In addition to PDFs, other challenges to obtaining usable scraped data include the fact that not all data are well written. That means that scraped data may be indecipherable. In addition, data behind paywalls, authentication-based websites, and websites with session-based interfaces are difficult to access.

Scraping has become a common practice; however, the ethics surrounding scraping can be somewhat gray. In general, accessing government-based data is considered OK. However, it is not always seen as acceptable to scrape data from private companies or NGOs. Your scraping effort may be seen as a hack or an attempt to sabotage the site. Scraping can slow down a website and be read as a Denial of Service (DOS) attack. There are also concerns that people who scrape data will then violate copyright by claiming the data as their own. In addition, even though public data are generally available, sites that scrape public data and then aggregate it in one place (such

In the case of WikiLeaks,[5] U.S. Army intelligence analyst Chelsea Manning leaked government files to WikiLeaks, an international non-profit organization that publishes secret information, news leaks, and classified material from anonymous sources.[6] Its founder Julian Assange released the information in bulk, leading to concern that the data should have been analyzed first to ensure that no one was harmed by the release. Manning was tried and convicted in 2013, and served part of a 35-year prison sentence before being pardoned by President Obama.

Figure 8.3
Chelsea Manning

The main difference in these two cases is how the data were handled. In the Snowden case, *The Guardian* and *New York Times* curated the data to help the public understand what it meant. Conversely, WikiLeaks engaged in a data dump, making all files available for the public to see.

5   http://www.nytimes.com/2010/11/29/world/29cables.html?pagewanted=all
    https://www.washingtonpost.com/world/national-security/judge-to-sentence-bradley-manning-today/2013/08/20/85bee184-09d0-11e3-b87c-476db8ac34cd_story.html

6   https://upload.wikimedia.org/wikipedia/commons/4/44/Chelsea_Manning%2C_18_May_2017_%28cropped%29.jpeg

1. Who conducted the study?
2. Who funded the study?
3. What interest does this group have in the study?
4. How was the study conducted?
5. Do the results diverge greatly from the body of research in this area?
6. What did the research actually measure?
7. Can the conclusions drawn be supported by the research?
8. Are you able to see the raw data?
9. Are you able to see a list of questions that were asked?
10. How was the sample chosen for the research?
11. What is the margin of error?

as Spokeo, FamilyTreeNow, and others) can be seen as violating privacy because even publicly available data can be too revealing if compiled all together.

Most importantly, there may be privacy issues in accessing certain data. In a cautionary tale, in April 2015, Twitter lost $8 billion (25% of its value) when a tech startup called Selerity ran a program to scrape data from Nasdaq and then revealed earnings results prior to Twitter's planned announcement. The early announcement reverberated throughout the day on Wall Street and severely impacted Twitter's stock value. Selerity's actions amounted to the breaking of an **embargo**—a big no-no in journalism.

So how do you determine whether you are scraping or hacking?

1. Is the data public or private? If it's public, you are probably scraping, but if it's private, your actions can be seen as hacking.
2. Are you obeying the law?
3. Did you ask for the data before scraping it? Often a simple request to the entity whose data you would like to access is all you need to gain access.
4. In your scraping query, are you identifying yourself in the code? Many journalists who use scraping to access data always include information about who they are. This gives anyone from the organization being scraped information to determine whether or not they are OK with the scrape.

Surveys, polls, and studies

Often data—or more specifically, a completed analysis of some dataset—will be given to you for reporting purposes. This may involve the results of polling data on the latest campaign, information on a new research study showing that wine/chocolate is good/bad for your health, or a survey on how Americans feel about regulating gun sales. In each of these cases, it matters a great deal who compiled the data, who asked the questions, how the questions were worded, and how the data were analyzed. Many groups have a vested interest in disseminating their agenda, rather than reporting objective and unbiased facts. This is most often seen in the political realm, but private commercial organizations may want to sell products and show people that their product is somehow superior.

The questions of who conducted and who funded a given research study can give you an indication as to whether or not there could be bias. For example, if a company that makes cereal conducts a study on people's favorite choice for breakfast, and 72 percent say cereal while 18 percent say eggs and another 10 percent say oatmeal, then you should wonder whether the cereal company's funding impacted the way the questions were asked and therefore the outcome of the study.

Another red flag is whether the results of a current study diverge greatly from all other studies conducted in a given area. This is not to say that breakthroughs are impossible, just that you must be aware of the potential for bias.

In addition, when conclusions about a study are drawn in a news release, you must ask yourself whether they are supported by the actual research that was conducted. For example, a recent study purported to find that "bacon gives kids cancer." In actuality, though, the researchers found a correlation between eating cured meats and leukemia risk among children; they did not establish causation, meaning they could not rule out environmental, hereditary, or other factors.

In another example, *CNN* reported "Lack of Sleep May Shrink Your Brain." However, in the article, it makes clear that this is not necessarily the case. "It is not yet known whether poor sleep quality is a cause or consequence of changes in brain structure," says author Claire Sexton of the University of Oxford in the United Kingdom.

In yet another example, *Live Science* reported: "Facebook Users Get Worse Grades in College." However, a quote in the article reads, "This does not necessarily mean that Facebook leads to less studying and worse grades—the grades association could be caused by something else."[3]

The manner in which questions are asked plays a big role in how they are answered. For example, when Congress was voting on the Affordable Care Act, also called "Obamacare," people were asked whether they supported "The Affordable Care Act." They were also asked whether they supported "Obamacare." Depending on their political leanings, people were more or less likely to support one or the other, even though in actuality they were the same thing.[4,5]

---

3 "Facebook Users Get Worse Grades in College." LiveScience. Accessed June 27, 2016, http://www.livescience.com/3495-facebook-users-worse-grades-college.html

4 http://www.popsci.com/scitech/article/2009-07/overhyped-and-misleading-health-headlines-revealed?image=5

5 http://www.cnbc.com/2013/09/26/whats-in-a-name-lots-when-it-comes-to-obamacareaca.html

Examples of public records[1]

- Census records
- Criminal records
- Consumer protection information
- Court dockets
- Government spending reports
- Agendas and minutes of public meetings
- Legislation minutes
- Professional and business licenses
- Real estate appraisal records
- Sex offender registry files
- Voter registration
- Email correspondence of government officials and employees, especially made on government-owned equipment, during work hours, and/or involving the public business.

Finally, margin of error plays a major role in research and should always be reported. For example, a poll that shows a given presidential candidate is ahead 45 percent to 42 percent may initially be taken to mean that one candidate is doing three percentage points better than the other. However, if the margin of error is $+/-3$ percent, then the candidate at 45 percent may in actuality garner anywhere from 42 percent to 48 percent of the vote, while the candidate at 42 percent falls between 39 percent and 45 percent. Therefore, the two candidates are really in a statistical dead heat.

Finally, find out a little about how the study was conducted and whether the results really are reliable. As an example, small sample size can skew a study. In 1998, Dr. Andrew Wakefield published a study in a peer-reviewed journal that suggested a childhood vaccine may be responsible for autism. This study received a large amount of publicity and was the basis for many parents deciding not to vaccinate their children. However, the study was based on a small sample size (n=12). It was also poorly designed and not controlled.[6] In addition, it was discovered that the data had been manipulated, and the researcher had financial conflicts of interest. However, even though the study has since been refuted and the journal has retracted the article, many people continue to believe the results because of how they were reported and the attention that they received.

Public records, FOIA, and sunshine laws

Public records are documents accessible to the public and often help the public understand

---

6   Ts Sathyanarayana Rao and Chittaranjan Andrade. "The MMR Vaccine and Autism: Sensation, Refutation, Retraction, and Fraud." *Indian Journal of Psychiatry* 53, no. 2 (Spring 2011): 95. doi:10.4103/0019-5545.82529.

1   https://en.wikipedia.org/wiki/Public_records

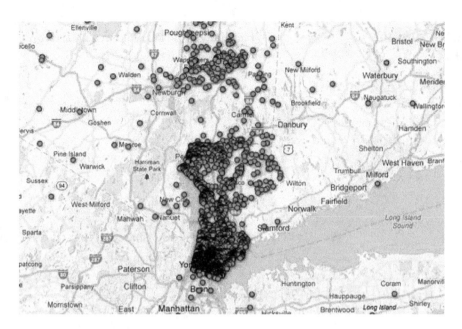

Figure 8.4   Mapping gun owners

how government works. One of the earliest forms of public record keeping pertains to property records. If someone purchased a plot of land, there needed to be a record of its owner.[7] Public records are meant to be free, but reproducing them usually comes at a cost.

As a journalist, you need to consider ethics when considering the use of a dataset. After the Sandy Hook school shooting in Newtown, Connecticut, in December 2012, a local newspaper published a map of all the people who had gun permits in the area.[8] Editors at the news organization received death threats, and many gun owners were afraid their guns would be confiscated.[9] Though this information was public record, mapping and publishing the information constituted a perceived violation of privacy. The newspaper promptly took down the map. (Fig. 8.4)

Many government datasets are readily available in raw form, and you can access them simply by going to the appropriate website and downloading the data. In some cases, even though the data are publicly available, they may not yet have been digitized. If this is the case, then you may need to make a trip to the local office of the appropriate agency to access the information.

---

7   www.publiclibraries.com/records/

8   http://mediashift.org/2013/02/where-the-journal-news-went-wrong-in-mapping-gun-owners053/

9   http://www.nytimes.com/2013/01/07/nyregion/after-pinpointing-gun-owners-journal-news-is-a-target.html

Here is a partial list of government websites where you can download data:

- Internet Public Library (www.ipl.org) details the type of documents available and where to find them.
- The U.S. Government Printing Office (http://www.access.gpo.gov/) will help when trying to track down documents involving laws and legislation.
- For free web-based access to U.S. Census data in the form of table, graphs, charts, etc. (http://factfinder.census.gov)
- Branches of the U.S. Government (http://www.usa.gov)

  - Executive branch of government sites (president, vice president, cabinet)
  - Judicial (Supreme Court, other federal courts)
  - Legislative (Senate, U.S. House of Representatives)

Tips to locating key documents

Data are not always available or accessible. In some cases, the government may not want to release data to the public. However, you may still be able to access the data by filing a Freedom of Information Act (FOIA) request for federal data or a Sunshine Act request for state, regional, or local data.

President Lyndon B. Johnson signed the Freedom of Information Act into federal law in 1966. It allows the public to access government documents from the executive branch. However, even if you gain access, the government does have the authority to redact classified information. The passage of FOIA led to state sunshine laws.

Anyone can file a FOIA request with any government agency that possesses the documents you need, as long as you are a U.S. citizen or foreign national and if the documents already exist. You may not request a special compilation of data. Any corporation, public interest group, organization, or news outlet may also file. Those who *cannot file an FOIA request:*

- Chairs of Congressional Committees
- Federal agencies
- Foreign governments
- Fugitives

Keep in mind that there are limitations to FOIA. The judicial and legislative branches are *not* subject to FOIA. In addition, advisors to presidents are not covered under FOIA, nor are private citizens, corporations, or state governments and municipalities. In addition, presidential resources may not be available until five years after the president leaves office.

Many states have passed Sunshine laws, which act similarly to FOIA. Sunshine laws entitle you to information when covering local boards or other state, regional, or local government entities.

When filing a FOIA request, you do not need to explain why you need the data. You may need to pay a fee, which covers administrative costs involved in compiling the data for you. You may ask for a fee reduction or waiver if the request is in the public interest, and it may be granted. News outlets and non-commercial agencies should have fees waived automatically.

Your request could be expedited given that journalists are primarily engaged in disseminating information to the public or if information is urgently needed to inform the public concerning some actual or alleged government activity.[10] However, just because you are a journalist does not mean the agency or office will give you special treatment.

Sunshine laws

"These laws require agency officials to hold certain meetings in public. These laws do not necessarily ensure that members of the public will be allowed to address the agency, but they do guarantee that the public and the media can attend the meetings. These laws will differ state to state." – Reporters Committee for Freedom of the Press[1]

---

10 http://www.soc.american.edu/journalism/wendell/class_notes/law/foia

1   "Reporters Committee for Freedom of the Press" Reporters Committee for Freedom of the Press. Accessed June 27, 2016, http://www.rcfp.org/.

FOIA timeline

- Agency must respond within 20 working days
- However, no penalty for delays
- Agency can request clarification from you
- Agency must provide an index of existing documents
- Agency must also let you know cost, time frame, unusual circumstances surrounding your information request, and allow you to alter request
- If request is refused, you may appeal
- I appeal is denied, you may file a federal lawsuit
- If request is not granted, you can show proof that information is in the public interest

Figure 8.5 Soldiers saluting caskets

FOIA and sunshine laws are a critical part of news coverage and open access. Many important stories have been brought to light because of FOIA, including the release of images showing the caskets of soldiers who died in the Iraqi and Afghan conflicts. Under the Bush Administration, reporters were banned from publishing images of military caskets because the Administration did not want those images to sway public opinion. A professor from the University of Delaware filed a FOIA request in 2005, citing a public interest to know the whole story. In 2009, then Secretary of Defense Robert Gates lifted the ban.[11]

Above (Fig. 8.5) is a photo released in response to a FOIA request. It shows U.S. war casualties.[12]

FOIA was also in play in connection to the emails on then Secretary of State Hillary Clinton's private server.[13] In 2013, the Associated Press filed a FOIA request. The State Department then agreed to release the emails[14] but did not complete the request until February 2016.

11 http://www.washingtonpost.com/wp-dyn/content/article/2005/04/28/AR2005042802078.html
12 http://www.nytimes.com/2004/04/23/us/pentagon-ban-on-pictures-of-dead-troops-is-broken.html?_r=0
13 http://www.businessinsider.com/associated-press-suing-state-department-for-access-to-hillary-clinton-emails-2015-3
14 http://www.nytimes.com/2016/03/01/us/politics/last-batch-of-hillary-clintons-emails-is-released.html

FOIA and sunshine laws are important tools, critical to a free press and functioning democracy, but they can be misused, and you must take care that you do not misuse these important tools. One way to misuse FOIA is to treat it like a Denial of Service (DOS) attack of a website. Some people file so many FOIA requests that the agency cannot keep up, essentially clogging up agency functions by taking up scarce resources to deal with the multitude of requests, preventing the agency from conducting day-to-day business.

To the right is a sample FOIA request letter. More examples can be found at

http://www.nfoic.org/.

Once you have the data, interview it

"Interview the data." That's according to award-winning veteran journalist Jeffrey Kummer, who has extensive experience when it comes to analyzing statistics and surveys. He is content coach of the Watchdog section of the *Des Moines Register*. Kummer oversees a staff of talented and hard-working investigative reporters who uncover injustices in their community. Through their reporting, knowledge of data analysis, and expertise in accessing public records, this team has uncovered details in criminal cases that remained elusive to government officials.

By "interviewing the data," Kummer says you ask the data questions. It does help if you have skills in such things as tables, charts, pivot tables, and Excel spreadsheets. You analyze the information in public records and ask why things are the way they are. You look for patterns or data that doesn't seem to make sense.

Kummer and his investigative team of reporters often receive story tips from readers. He remembers being tipped by a custodial parent who was not getting the child support they were supposed to be receiving. They wanted help. "As a reporter you ask

Example: Freedom of Information Act request letter

Date

Agency Head [or Freedom of Information Act Officer]
Name of Agency
Address of Agency
City, State, Zip Code

Re: Freedom of Information Act Request

To Whom It May Concern:

I am making this request as permitted by the Freedom of Information Act.

I would like to have a copy of these documents: (List the documents you need here and be as specific as you can.)

It is important that you know that I am a member of the media. This fact should play a role in the assessment of fees for these documents. (Be sure to include your organization's name in this paragraph and cite that the information you are requesting is not for commercial use.)

Thank you for your consideration of this FOIA request.

Sincerely,

Name
Address
City, State, Zip Code

Two websites you should bookmark concerning FOIA requests

To generate an FOIA Letter
http://www.rcfp.org/foia

How to file an FOIA request
http://www.rcfp.org/federal-open-government-guide/federal-freedom-information-act/filing-request

yourself, if this is happening in one instance, then is it statewide? Is it an epidemic? Should we look closer at city, county, and statewide cases?" Kummer's reporters went to the Department of Human Services, which oversees child support. The Watchdog team asked for a database of the biggest child support debtors in the state, but Kummer says the Department of Human Services refused to do it. "Social workers there thought this information would be embarrassing to the children if their parent was seen as a deadbeat. We argued it would be more embarrassing if the child didn't have a coat to wear or school supplies to buy," Kummer explained. He says this story got the Department of Human Services to think about this issue in a different way.

As part of the negotiation for information, Kummer says they wrote a letter to be delivered to the custodial parent so their story could be told. The Department of Human Services agreed. *The Register* had a very positive turnout. Around 85 percent of those custodial parents responded to the Watchdog request and wanted to cooperate. In many cases, Kummer adds, the custodial parent knew exactly where the former spouse or partner was and had all their contact information. "It showed state officials that they were not doing all they could to track down the debtors." Persistence and dedication by these journalists was key to success. It took just six to eight weeks to track down all of the information and eventually help custodial parents get resolution.

Patience is more than a virtue when waiting for documents and public records; it's a way of life for investigative reporters. Such was the case when the *Des Moines Register* Watchdog teams investigated allegations that airport security stole passenger belongings and were handling passengers inappropriately during pat-downs. A FOIA request was filed. Kummer says nothing happened until three years later when a box of photocopies containing the FOIA information from the Federal Aviation Administration showed up on a reporter's desk.

Most of the time, sunshine laws provide more expedient means for information because reporters are requesting data from the state, and not federal government, and there tends to be less bureaucracy at the state level.

Sunshine laws helped the *St. Paul Pioneer Press* promote and pass tougher legislation intended to keep drunk drivers off the road. Jeffrey Kummer was working for the *St. Paul Pioneer Press* at the time. Through initial research, the paper uncovered documents that showed some drunk drivers were arrested on DUIs as many as 35 times. Kummer tracked down a database from the Department of Public Safety that listed all the drunk drivers and their arrest statistics. "There is no way law enforcement could keep them off the road. At the time, Minnesota didn't have a felony for these cases, but after the story ran, the state implemented one," recalls Kummer.

The idea for this story was organic, according to Kummer. "We'd run short stories of fatal car accidents and noticed that the drunk drivers had prior DUI records. When you see this, you ask yourself how many more drivers like this are out there, and how often does this type of thing occur?"

Kummer's advice to students is to be a critical thinker. "You have to question everything, especially the things that seem too good to be true. If you misinterpret data, you have a high likelihood of making hundreds of mistakes from that initial misreading." Most importantly, always be curious about the world around you and keep digging for answers.

Visualizing data

Once you have found and developed your story using data, you need to communicate it to your audience. An effective way to do this is to visualize the data using infographics, charts, mapping tools, or other graphic techniques.

Mapping

Mapping data does not always need to be about location or geography, though that is an effective tool. You can also create story maps, timelines, subway maps, and social media maps. Mapping helps reveal trends, make connections, highlight patterns, and tell larger themed stories. It can also make complex information clear and allow the audience to interact with the data.

Mapping should help reveal stories. Blogger Ben Wellington, founder of I Quant NY,15 mentions in a TED Talk16 that he tells stories with the goal of having a positive impact on people's lives. One of his data map visualizations (Fig. 8.6a) revealed that a designated parking space was responsible for thousands of dollars in revenue. He then discovered that the space

---

15 http://iquantny.tumblr.com/about
16 https://www.youtube.com/watch?v=6xsvGYlxJok

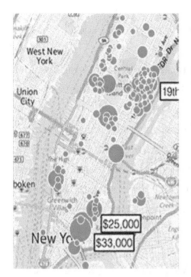

Figure 8.6a

was near a fire hydrant and being treated as illegal by meter maids (Fig. 8b). His story prompted the city of New York to re-paint the space as an illegal parking space (Fig. 8c), saving confusion and frustration for anyone who otherwise may have parked there.

Some simple open-access tools can help you create interesting and informative maps. JS StoryMap,[17] created by the Knight Lab at Northwestern University,[18] allows you to create interactive maps that tell a story. For example, *The Washington Post* used JS StoryMap to visualize the rise of ISIS.[19]

Timeline JS,[20] also created by Northwestern University's Knight Lab, allows you to create interactive timelines. *Time* Magazine used it to map Nelson Mandela's life and work.[21]

The Denver Post used Timeline JS to map a timeline of the Aurora Theater shooting.[22]

Figure 8b

Figure 8c

Infographics

Infographics are charts and visualizations that tell a story, and if done right, they can be highly effective for communicating information and connecting the audience to the story.

17 https://storymap.knightlab.com/
18 https://knightlab.northwestern.edu/
19 http://apps.washingtonpost.com/g/page/world/map-how-isis-is-carving-out-a-new-country/1095/
20 https://timeline.knightlab.com/
21 http://world.time.com/2013/12/05/nelson-mandelas-extraordinary-life-an-interactive-timeline/
22 http://www.denverpost.com/breakingnews/ci_21119904

Strong infographics are not just a collection of numbers, images, and clipart. Your infographic should:[23]

- Have a clear angle or POV. What are you trying to communicate?
- Include accurate data
- Flow well so that the audience may follow the logic and story arc
- Include source information so that people know where it came from

An example of a very effective infographic is "World's Deadliest Animals" (Fig. 8.7).[24] Using data from the World Health Organization (WHO), Gates Notes[25] (Bill Gates' blog) created an impactful infographic showing that the deadliest animals on Earth are not sharks or snakes—rather they are mosquitoes and humans (Fig. 8.7, bottom). Text can only convey the message so far, but this visual has an impact.

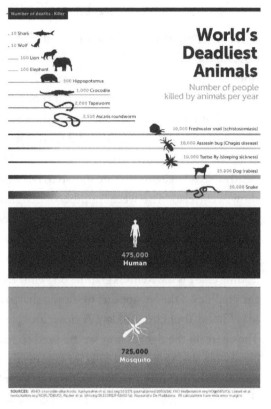

Figure 8.7

There is a science and art to creating strong infographics, which is why it may be smart to enlist the help of a graphic designer. Siege Media studied impactful infographics and came up with its own infographic on "The Science Behind the Most Popular Infographics."[26] It includes recommendations on size, colors, word count, and uses.

Charts and graphs

In addition to fancy mapping and infographics tools, straightforward charts and graphs are also quite effective when it comes to illustrating data. Be sure you are choosing the right chart or graph for the information you are trying to convey. Would it be best to tell your story using a pie chart or a bar graph? Assess your options based on the story you are trying to tell.

23 https://contently.com/strategist/2015/11/25/why-good-infographics-are-more-than-just-pictures-and-numbers/
24 https://s3.amazonaws.com/external_clips/attachments/85507/original/bill_gates_infographic_.jpg?1448481388
25 https://www.gatesnotes.com/Health/Most-Lethal-Animal-Mosquito-Week
26 http://www.siegemedia.com/most-popular-infographics

Data pitfalls and ethics

While data can tell important stories, data can also mislead, confuse, and obscure. If you do not understand what's in front of you, you risk perpetuating misleading and incorrect information. Be sure you understand the data in front of you, including how the data were collected, how to crunch the data, where the data come from, and what may be missing.

One basic level of understanding is the difference between causation and correlation. Just because something seems related does not mean that it is. The website http://www.tylervigen.com/spurious-correlations illustrates this by showing a series of spurious correlations, two clearly unrelated items that are shown to be correlated to each other.[27] One example on the site shows a correlation between "number of people who drowned by falling into a pool" and "films Nicolas Cage appeared in." The point is, just because two things—such as wine drinking and long life/short life—appear to be connected does not mean they are.

Misleading graphs are also a major ethical issue. One of the most egregious examples of a misleading chart is the Reuters graphic on "Gun Deaths in Florida" (Figs. 8.8a–b). At first glance, the graphic on the left appears to show a sharp decline in gun deaths upon the passage of Florida's "Stand Your Ground" law. A closer look, however, reveals that the Y axis has been flipped. The chart on the right is how we are used to reading charts involving X and Y axes. Here, we clearly see that there was a spike in gun deaths immediately after "Stand Your Ground" was passed. Whether the initial graphic was an intent to deceive or simply a creative way to present the information, it was misleading and confusing. Even when trying to be creative, remember that basic conventions, such as the treatment of the X and Y axes, must be followed.

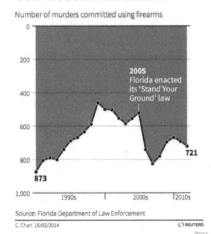 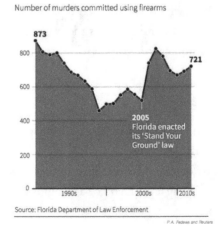

Figure. 8.8a–b

---

27 http://www.tylervigen.com/spurious-correlations

There is also a difference between a data dump and journalism. One of the main differences between WikiLeaks and Edward Snowden was how the data were handled. A data dump is simply providing access. Journalism is curating the information, highlighting the important and impactful information, and providing context to your reader. One way to provide context is to be clear. When you report that attendance to a city council meeting doubled, what does that actually mean? Did it increase from two to four attendees (hardly a news story) or from 200 to 400 (quite a change).

Building relationships with sources

You don't always need to file FOIA requests or take other adversarial actions to get data. If you develop strong sources throughout government, you may be able to get information directly from your sources. Lee Rood, Watchdog columnist for the *Des Moines Register,* says young reporters should "be accurate, treat people fairly and develop sources. People will trust you if they think you are fair and accurate." Rood, a 25-year journalism veteran and award-winning reporter, actually sits down with people and talks to them about the issues that concern them personally. She finds that firsthand information from the source is often the most reliable.

In January 2013, Rood created The Reader's Watchdog to help Iowans find answers and seek accountability from government, businesses, and nonprofits. Before becoming a columnist, she was the *Register's* investigative editor, producing and writing several award-winning projects that spurred new state and national legislation, some leading to criminal investigations, and wide-ranging results for everyday Iowans.

From government offices to city hall to the courthouse to federal courts, there are documents to access and many times layers of data to sort through. Rood says, "The easiest route is always just to ask someone for information or send them an email. It's only when you're looking for a lot of difficult records that it can get tenuous." When sending a request via email, remember to be persistent. Your email could get lost in the shuffle. It's also important to note that, when requesting a court file that involves law enforcement, it might be difficult to retrieve because many states protect this information.

Rood says, "The biggest thing right now deals with police body camera video." This video is government information in the possession of a government employee. Should that be accessible to the public? It's a hot topic for discussion.

Rood adds, "One of the reasons the police officer is wearing this camera is for accountability and transparency. At the same time, these cameras are capturing some very sensitive material in people's lives. Sometimes police are answering domestic dispute calls. There was a case where a police officer was called to a domestic dispute. He walked up to the house, and the couple's German Shepherd attacked him. While the policeman tried to shoot the dog, he shot and killed the wife instead. The family and news reporters attempted to get access to this body camera video but the police department didn't want them to have it."

Public records are not just printed documents. They could be 911 calls. These documents are handled differently according to various jurisdictions around the country. Rood admits there are a lot of problems these days when it comes to requesting public records because of an increasing financial cost to access data.

Investigative stories are everywhere. Rood says you have to be inquisitive. "To do investigative or in-depth work well, a reporter has first to be curious and secondly, cannot be afraid to ask questions. Too many people today accept the pat answer. If something doesn't make sense, you need to investigate. Be persistent and dogged. Where other people would let go, you don't. You keep pursuing as an investigative reporter. That is the only way to get the story. It's the most rewarding kind of journalism."

"Too many people today accept the pat answer. If something doesn't make sense, you need to investigate."

EXERCISES AND ACTIVITIES

1. As a group exercise, find a story in a local news sources or online and ask, "What is the story you want to tell using data"? Does it need telling? What questions are you trying to answer? Brainstorm and discuss what data might be available and where you can find it. How will you visualize the data? Will you use a chart or graph?

2. You want to find out information about your city's budget (in regard to a special area such as education, transportation or social program). Identify where you would go for data. Is the data online freely available? Are there past FOIA requests that someone else has pursued? Create a FOIA request for the data you seek.

3. Go to your city's open data portal (or the portal for the city nearest to you). (EX: https://datasf.org/opendata/ or http://www.city-data.com/city/San-Francisco-California.html). Search for a dataset that interests you. Use the tools in the portal or Tableau Public to create a visual representation of the data.

4. Google Fusion Table: Watch one (or both) of the following tutorials by Kurt Gessler:
   a. https://www.youtube.com/watch?v=ok7gz4nAnFE
   b. https://www.youtube.com/watch?v=oSLyS4-zGeo

Then, find a dataset that interests you and create your own fusion table.

5. Search online for an example of a news outlet seeking a FOIA request. What is notable about the example you found? How long did it take for the journalists to receive the data? Are they still waiting? Discuss the issues surrounding the FOIA process and government transparency.

6. Go to a tool such as Canva or Venngage or Piktochart. Create an infographic that visually tells a story.

Credits

CHAPTER 9

Speeches

" Liberty don't work as well in practice as it does in speech."
—Will Rogers[1]

I n your work, you will most likely be asked to cover some sort of speech. This can include a speech or talk given by a government official, businessperson, pop culture icon, or anyone else making news or discussing a newsworthy topic. It may also include news conferences such as those given by law enforcement, as well as think tank or public affairs forum panels or talks. Basically, the guidelines outlined in this chapter cover any time someone considered to be a newsmaker is speaking in a public place to a group of people, any time thought leaders convene to discuss a newsworthy topic in a public forum, or any time newsworthy information is disseminated to an audience.

For example, during a presidential campaign, a candidate may choose to speak at a fundraising event or in front of a public forum. A group of scientists, thought leaders, and academics may discuss climate change or ocean pollution on a panel convened by a university or think tank. The chief of police in the city where a child was kidnapped convenes a news conference to share updates in the investigation. In all of these examples, there is an audience, and information is being disseminated to a group.

You will in essence be a part of the audience, listening to the speaker(s), noting important information, and potentially having the opportunity to ask a question. Alternatively, you may be asked to cover a ground breaking for a new health center or ribbon cutting for a new youth activity center. In this case, the newsmaker will likely give a photo/video op by cutting a ribbon or pushing a shovel into a pile of loose dirt. That newsmaker may then give brief remarks, giving you another potential opportunity to ask a question of importance to your audience, even if it is unrelated to the event topic. Though a story like this may not provide an obvious news peg, you may want to ask the newsmaker about an entirely different subject. In this case, the speech gives you access, allowing you to ask your question.

---

1   Rogers, Will. *There's Not a Bathing Suit in Russia & Other Bare Facts.* Oklahoma State University Press, 1973.

In some cases, an event may be closed to the public, but journalists may still be allowed in to cover that event. Generally, each news outlet may send someone. However, sometimes the number of journalists allowed in may be limited. In this situation, a **pool reporter** is often assigned. A pool reporter is a reporter from one outlet who agrees to share the information they gather with all other news outlets. Pool reporting is common when space is limited, such as in courtrooms or events with small audiences. For example, when President Barack Obama visited the Bay Area in April 2016, he gave a talk at a private fundraising event and agreed to allow news coverage through a pool reporter. One print pool reporter was chosen to cover that event, and that reporter shared the coverage with other interested outlets. In addition, in the O.J. Simpson murder trial (and several other court cases), a pool reporter was chosen so that the courtroom did not become filled with cameras. If the news media is not allowed to cover the event, you can still try to access the speaker by requesting a meeting before or after the speech or trying to catch the speaker on the way into or out of the venue.

Preparing for the story

If you are assigned to cover a speech of any type, you should first make sure you know who is speaking and on what topic(s), as well as why this might matter to your audience. If you are not up to speed on any of the topic areas or on the significance of the newsmaker, get up to speed. Find out the speaker's history on the topic areas expected to be addressed, as well as whether any controversy surrounds these topics or the speaker. Learn the important points of all sides of the topics. You may also want to do some research on the organization that invited this speaker or convened this panel. Also, reach out to that organization to ask for background information or any other details that may be important.

In addition, assess whether there are other sides to the story. If the speaker is talking about a controversial issue or the speaker themselves is controversial, then chances are that different people or groups may have different perspectives. You may want to also reach out to them to ensure that your story is well rounded and not just a vehicle for allowing a speaker to spread their perspective. For example, if you are assigned to cover a town hall given by the local police department in response to a controversial officer-involved shooting, then you may want to reach out to groups working to reform police responses to incidents involving mentally ill people. This ensures that you are hearing more than one perspective and can craft a well-rounded story.

Setting up

When you arrive to the location where the speech is to be held, you'll need to find a place to sit and assess the technical options. Sitting on an aisle near the center or back of the room may be best if you need to rush out to get back to the newsroom. However, an aisle seat near the front may be the better choice if you plan to try to ask the speaker a question during or after the event. Arriving early is the best way to ensure that you can position yourself as you want.

Figure 9.1

On the technical side, if you plan to record audio, then ideally the organizers will provide a **mult box,** sometimes also called a press box (see Fig. 9.1). The mult box will be plugged into the audio feed. If you plug your audio recorder into the mult box using an XLR cable, you will be able to get broadcast quality audio. If no mult box is available, then you may ask to place your audio recorder on the podium, table, or other area on stage to best capture the voices of the speaker(s). This is less ideal but can still yield usable audio. If there is no mult box and if you are not allowed to position your recorder near the speaker(s), then you must position yourself as close to the stage or speaking area as possible to capture the audio, or you can place your recorder on top of a speaker, but the audio may not be broadcast quality.

If you also plan to capture video, then you will need to find a place for your camera. If the speech or panel is significant enough, the organizers may provide a news media platform at the back of the auditorium where you may set up a camera and tripod. Even if there is no platform, you may still be able to set up your camera and tripod at the back of the room.

You may want to capture still images. If you are unobtrusive enough, you may be able to move about the auditorium or audience space during the event to capture different angles of the speaker(s) and audience. However, the key here is to respect the audience and speaker(s). You are not the story, and you want to do everything you can to avoid disrupting the event with your movements and camera shots. This means remaining in a crouch, turning off your flash, and being judicious. There is no need to snap images during the entire event. Just get what you need.

If you are simply capturing the text of the event, then audio quality will only be an issue in the sense that you will need to understand what was said. Therefore, you can position your recorder at the side of the stage or near an audio speaker. Then, you can sit or stand in the audience and take notes that will help you write your story later. When taking notes during a speech, you will want to note:

- Quotes that you may want to use in your story
- Interesting nonverbal interactions or reactions
- Your own impressions, summaries, or paraphrases
- Audience response or reaction
- Any other relevant information about the event

Tweeting the event

You may be asked to live tweet, Periscope, Snapchat, Instagram or Facebook the speech, talk, or panel. In some ways, this is very similar to note-taking. However, when you push information out to the public in real time, you must take great care that the information is worth sharing with the public—that it is newsworthy, factual, appropriate, and relevant to your audience and not misleading. You may share quotes from the speech, your observations, audience reactions, or any other relevant piece of information. You may also want to share images or videos from the event. Again, consider how the "bite" that you share comes across. Is it a truthful representation of the event or is it misleading? If you share multiple tweets that are connected, be sure to number the tweets so that people know a given tweet is part of a larger string or thread.

Before and after the speech

In addition to covering the speech itself, you may also want to interview the speaker before or after the event, as well as talk with those in attendance and those who organized the event. See Chapter 7 on interviewing for specific interview tips. In this section, we discuss how to navigate the logistics of interviews related to an event.

If there are demonstrators at the event, it behooves you to talk with them, as well, either at the event or before/after the event. If so, be sure to bring your smart phone or an audio or video recorder to capture those quotes. To ensure quality audio, you may also want to use a lavaliere or dynamic microphone. Audience members may also be willing to talk with you.

To set up a separate time with the speaker or organizers, start by requesting an interview from the organization planning the event. If the speaker has a publicist, then reach out to the speaker's publicist, as well. If you know the speaker, then you may reach out to the speaker directly. If you are not granted separate time, then you may try to ask a question of the speaker during or after the event. This is the time to ask about issues that were not covered during the event.

If you are doing a video story, you may also want to capture b-roll of the audience milling about and listening to the speech, as well as b-roll of the speaker, any logos, or other interesting visuals, and cutaways. In addition, you may want b-roll of some of the topics that come up during the event. If so, find out if your outlet has file footage or look online for b-roll or images that will not violate copyright (see Chapter 3).

In addition, take a look around and note your observations. How big is the audience? You can estimate or ask the organizers. However, remember that the organizers may exaggerate the size of the audience. Also, pay attention to the audience as well as the speaker. The audience's reactions can give you clues about what they find important or controversial, giving you potential guideposts for when you craft your story later.

Crafting the story

When it comes time to craft the story, the notes, pictures, video, and sound bites you gathered during the event will help you formulate and focus your story. You may even be able to create multiple stories or sidebars to the main story, which can help add interactivity and interest to your piece.

The key to crafting a speech story is to write about what was significant, whether that is a speaker quote, what wasn't said, or the audience reaction. Do not—repeat, *do not*—just summarize what happened. Your job is to provide context, pull out the relevant information, and help your audience understand how it might impact them. For example, though this is not a speech, it does illustrate this point. When 16-seed UMBC beat top-seeded Virginia in the 2018 NCAA basketball tournament, the story was not that the players ran onto the court before the game to warm up, then went and sat down while the starters jumped for the ball, etc. The story is that UMBC beat a number-one seed. That moment happened at the end of the game. A chronological summary would not work for this story. It does not work for speech stories, either. Find the newsworthy moment and lead with that.

Remember, the topic the speaker chooses to focus on may not be what's newsworthy. Don't just act as a mouthpiece; figure out what the story is, what your audience needs to know, and cover the story from that angle. Find the quotes you think are most relevant and then write around them. For example—again, not a speech, but the lesson applies perfectly—when a U.C. Davis police officer pepper sprayed demonstrating students in November 2011, the chancellor's office spent $175,000 on a PR campaign to improve the university's image online. The chancellor wanted to focus on positive aspects of the university. However, once this expenditure was uncovered, journalists reported on the expenditure itself, catapulting the story and the bad PR back into the public eye and negating the work done under the expenditure.

Your story will sink or swim starting from the very first sentence. A common pitfall many beginning journalists fall into is starting with the event details in what is called a summary lead. DON'T DO THIS. This tells your audience nothing. They can read the event details on Facebook or the organization's website. Your readers want to know what happened and why they should care. It is up to you to tell them.

> **NO–**"Facebook CEO Mark Zuckerberg spoke at the company's F8 developer conference in San Francisco on Tuesday, announcing new functionality on the social media site."

> **YES–**"Facebook users can now use Facebook's save button to bookmark content on any website and save it to their profile. CEO Mark Zuckerberg rolled out the long-awaited added functionality at the F8 developer conference in San Francisco this week."

Note how the second example mentions a specific announcement considered newsworthy to an audience of Facebook users or former users. It goes on to mention some event details but only to add context to the main point.

Also keep in mind that this may not have been the first thing Zuckerberg said. Another sure killer of a speech story is to write about it in chronological order. Instead, talk about the highlights that your audience wants and needs to know. It does not matter when they were mentioned in the speech. Your job is to discuss and contextualize them in order of importance. In fact, what was not said may actually be the most newsworthy part of the speech.

> EX—"The star of this summer's biggest blockbuster avoided mention of an extramarital affair when speaking to a women's safety group."

In this example, the lead was what the speaker did not say, rather than something that was said. After the lead, find a powerful quote that helps advance the story. In the Facebook-save story, the second paragraph might be:

> "I care deeply about connecting the world and bringing people together, so I wanted to put this out there," said Zuckerberg later in a Facebook post. "It's different from any other speech I've given."[2]

The story would then go on to discuss additional details about this and other newsworthy announcements, responses from the crowd or organizers, if relevant, and then details, including audience size, reactions, where and when the event was held, who sponsored the event, etc. See these links for strong examples of speech stories:

- *LA Times* Reporter **Jon Myers** covers Governor Jerry Brown's announcement that a deal has been reached to raise the minimum wage statewide: http://www.latimes.com/politics/la-pol-sac-jerry-brown-minimum-wage-deal-20160328-story.html (03/28/16).
- *SF Chronicle* Reporters **Carla Marinucci** and **Debra J. Saunders** debate preview and live tweeting: http://www.sfgate.com/elections/article/Live-blog-Fact-checking-CNN-s-Republican-debate-6508748.php (09/16/15).

---

2   Ivan Mehta, "Everyone Hates Passwords, So Facebook Now Has An Alternative." The Huffington Post. April 13, 2016. Accessed June 1, 2016, http://www.huffingtonpost.in/2016/04/13/facebook-f8_n_9677306.html.

Conclusion

Speech stories are common, and chances are you will cover many in your career. They are also important. We want to hear from leaders, public figures, celebrities, and other decision makers, as well as hold them to account. Strong speech coverage can reveal important information that audiences need to know to be able to live their lives and understand what is happening in their communities and society. By following the guidelines outlined in this chapter, you can ensure that your coverage will be relevant, interesting, and impactful.

EXERCISES AND ACTIVITIES

1. Choose a speech transcript from the list below or a speech of your choosing. Write a story in less than an hour.
2. Choose three speeches from the list below. What do you think are the most relevant points in each of the speeches? Write a lead for each.
3. Choose three speeches from the list below and select the most impactful quote for your story. Why did you choose this quote?

Transcripts of historical speeches

- **"Women's Right to Vote" - Susan B. Anthony**
  http://www.speeches-usa.com/Transcripts/susan_b_anthony-vote.html

- **"We Ain't Going," Tougaloo, Mississippi, April 11, 1967 - Stokely Carmichael**

  http://www.speeches-usa.com/Transcripts/stokeley_carmichael-weaint.html
- **"Energy Crisis," July 15, 1979—Jimmy Carter**
  http://www.speeches-usa.com/Transcripts/jimmy_carter-energy.html
- **"A Politician and Political Ally," New York, NY, October 24, 1937—Thomas Dewey**
  http://www.speeches-usa.com/Transcripts/thomas_dewey-ally.html
- **"Plea for Free Speech in Boston," June 8, 1880—Frederick Douglas**
  http://www.speeches-usa.com/Transcripts/fredrick_douglas-boston.html
- **"Peace in the Atomic Era," February 19, 1950—Albert Einstein**
  http://www.speeches-usa.com/Transcripts/albert_einstein-peace.html
- **"Farewell to Baseball," Yankee Stadium, New York, NY, July 4, 1939—Lou Gehrig**
  http://www.speeches-usa.com/Transcripts/lou_gehrig-farewell.html

- **"A House Divided," June 16, 1858—Abraham Lincoln**

  http://www.speeches-usa.com/Transcripts/abraham_lincoln-divided.html
- **"Nobel Lecture," Oslo, Norway, December 11, 1971—Mother Teresa**

  http://www.speeches-usa.com/Transcripts/mother_teresa-nobel.html
- **"The Importance of Libraries," Washington, DC, April 1, 1936—Eleanor Roosevelt**

  http://www.speeches-usa.com/Transcripts/eleanor_roosevelt-libraries.html
- **"2000 RNC Speech," Philadelphia PA, August 1, 2000—Colin Powell**

  http://www.speeches-usa.com/Transcripts/colin_powell-2000rnc.html

Resources

How Not to Cover a Speech

http://www.cjr.org/campaign_desk/how_not_to_cover_a_speech.php

Speech sites

- http://www.speeches-usa.com/
- http://www.americanrhetoric.com/speechbank.htm
- Commonwealth Club (audio) https://www.commonwealthclub.org/media/podcast

Credits

- Fig. 9.1: Copyright © by Bob Butler. Reprinted with permission.

CHAPTER 10

City hall, government, and meetings

"If we had failed to pursue the facts as far as they led, we would have denied the public any knowledge of an unprecedented scheme of political surveillance and sabotage."

—Katharine Graham[1]

Introduction

Pick up a newspaper, check an online news source, and tune in to radio or TV news. Chances are at least one story in a newscast will connect the audience to something government-related, such as new tax laws or a mayoral decision concerning transportation fees. Maybe the governor is proposing to cut or extend the state's education budget. There could be a high-profile court story. The state legislature or Congress might be deliberating controversial legislation about abortion or gun control. All of these stories impact people. It is up to you, the reporter, to extract the key points that affect your audience most. It's referred to as "humanizing the story." Make the story relevant to your audience, so they learn whatever it is you are trying to tell them. Show them why this news matters to them and why stories that originate in government matter.

Finding your story and interview research

The key to being successful and knowing everything about your assigned meeting, city hall or other government story is to do a lot of reading about your beat, according to Katherine Perkins, executive producer at Iowa Public Radio. Ask yourself, "What are the burning issues of the constituents?"

---

1   Brian J. O'Connor, *Everything You Always Wanted to Know About Watergate But Were Afraid to Ask.* (Riverdale Avenue Books, July 2017), Accessed March 30, 2018, https://goo.gl/GRcxxc,.

Go to meetings and meet people face-to-face. It establishes who you are and it creates a reputation for you as someone who is working to understand the issues and the government process. It helps with credibility. Perkins advises, "Schedule a meeting to talk with someone. Let the mayor and people on staff know you will be covering city hall and that you want to get to know them and how they stand on the issues." She also says to make sure you do your necessary research to find out if there is a particular issue or project that is especially of interest to the politician you'll be interviewing. "Even if you don't get a story out of this, it's still an opportunity to get the most out of a one-on-one meeting with a newsmaker."

"There is nothing better than to make a human connection with someone, especially if you're a reporter trying to develop sources," according to *San Diego Union-Tribune* reporter Rob Nikolewski.

From experience, Nikolewski says, "You end up wasting a lot of time if you don't know whom to call about a given story, but the best way is to meet people first-hand and to make a connection. To do this you actually have to go the city council or state legislative meetings. If the sources you're trying to connect with see you on a daily basis, covering these meetings, sitting through three-hour meetings, they're able to develop a sense that you're not just parachuting in and out."

It may sound like a cliché, but Nikolewski suggests you "follow the money" when it comes to getting to the heart of most government-related stories. "It's always a good idea to ask your interviewee how much something is going to cost and how it affects the taxpayer." He recommends this be your go-to question every time you do a story about city or state government. "How much is this going to cost?"

Also, research what the legislation means by talking to press aides and staffers. Break down the information and extract the key elements. Keep asking yourself, "How does this affect people or communities?"

Digging deeper for meaning to the bureaucracy

It's not always easy to keep your audience's attention once people realize it's a government story, often because of the complicated nature of these highly political meetings and issues. Even a live shot following a school board meeting can make a viewer's eyes glaze over if it's all about procedure and not relevant to the viewer and his or her life. This is the main reason to always find ways to humanize the story.

Veteran reporters have one important tip for those new to the beat. The tip is to remember that a lot of government stories, city council decisions, for example, will originate in a sub-committee, so it's crucial to be where the basic decisions are made. This way, you are prepared to write about the rationale and history behind the law or new policy affecting the community at large.

According to Perkins of Iowa Public Radio (IPR), it's pretty easy to get caught up in covering the legislature and the maneuvering at the State Capitol between the two parties and the governor. It's harder to keep in mind what is being decided and how it's going to impact people outside the statehouse. "Anytime you are going to explain policy, what you need is someone who relates to that. Whether it's a small business owner, finding a parent whose child has epilepsy, anyone affected by the bill in the legislature. Discover the reason they are concerned about this issue or how this certain piece of policy is going to impact them directly. This gives readers, viewers, or listeners a chance to empathize with others even if the issue or controversy does not impact them." Again, humanize the story.

Veteran political TV reporter Mike Luery of Sacramento's KCRA says, it's "always challenging to make political stories interesting. It's like watching history being made on a daily basis. There are always things happening inside the state Capitol building that people don't understand. In other words, you need to take it outside the building. We did a story about 'willful discipline' where students can be suspended from school for defying a teacher. It's a California law, so if a student does it repeatedly, he or she can be kicked out of school. We interviewed the author and some of the students from around the state who are largely students of color or LGBT students. They claim they are suspended more than others under this law." To get "outside the building," Luery went around Sacramento talking to parents and teachers to get their point of view on the story. He waited until school recessed in the afternoon to ask them what they thought about the proposed legislation. The reaction, he said, was "wide and varied," but still crucial to get their feedback on the measure.

Locating sources

Under the best of circumstances, it can be tough to cold call someone or walk into a business without calling first. It's all about talking to people. That's what reporters do.

It's important to realize there is no typical day when covering meetings or politics. Sometimes news breaks. You might hear something in the hallway while hanging out waiting for a meeting and decide to pursue that story. Experienced reporters in this field say you just never know from day to day what will unfold. Keep ears and eyes open.

"When covering state politics, you have to start with the basics. Know how many legislators there are and how state government works; know the role of state constitutional officers and how their roles differ from the federal or local government officials. Pay attention to high school civics lessons; know about political parties. Having that basic understanding is an integral part of being a good reporter," according to Luery.

If you walk into a small business, find out if the owners are around to talk to. If you are covering a story about a tax increase for small business owners, you'll want to ask small business owners what they think. Will they pass along the cost to their customers? How will they do this?

Chances are those affected will, at some point, show up to talk to a lawmaker. Ask a city council member if he or she has a constituent who might be willing to talk to the media and then contact that person.

Perkins recommends stepping outside your beat to get a perspective from someone who is impacted, whether it's for a breaking story or to add information that has not yet been reported. For example, if a new dog leash proposal is on the table, a reporter might go out to try and find people walking their dogs to find out what they think about this. Perkins says, "Do they like it or not and why? Get the perspective of people who might be impacted by the proposed leash law. It's a way of writing the story. This approach may take a little extra legwork, but try talking to someone at the local animal shelter, too."

How to interview government officials

Above all, be fair. "We all have our biases," says Nikolewski. "People got elected, and you have to respect that. Show courtesy and fairness in your reporting, even if it's a negative story about the politician. Give them a fair shot."

Get to know all of the people behind the counters at city hall. If you have a records request, if you want to know when the meeting has ended or anything else, at least when you walk in the door, they will be familiar with you and your story. They might even know you on a first-name basis because of the friendly terms you cultivated. When covering a government-related story, they're the people you're going to have to talk to on a regular basis.

In a political campaign, politicians and their staff tend to seek out journalists to get their story out to the people. When you are digging for information that may not always benefit the popularity of the politician, these key interviews may very well be difficult to arrange. Unless you've scored a one-on-one interview, keep your questions brief. You may have to wait outside the voting floor of the State House or outside someone's office until they have a moment to talk before you get your sound bite or quote. Always do your homework prior to an interview, so if the politician tries to avoid answering questions, you can quickly find a way to phrase or re-phrase a question so a useable quote will likely follow. Be persistent.

Think in terms of "sequencing" your questions. Have a priority list of questions you absolutely need a response to and others that are subsequent or secondary questions. Nikolewski adds that if there is a highly controversial issue you need to ask, "hit them with the zapper last, for the most part. They might otherwise shut down."

Luery has found that politicians "love to talk about their agenda. Many of them want your attention because they might be running for re-election or have a bill to promote. It's important not to get caught up in the spin. For example, the governor may call a news conference to talk about water conservation. Although that might be Plan A for the day initially in the newsroom, there might be something about prisons or transportation that you've wanted to ask. This is your opportunity to do it. The unscripted moments are your best chance for candor from the politician. Reporters need to hold politicians accountable for their actions."

Using social media for feedback, not quotes

Don't rely on email for obtaining quotes from sources. This is especially easy and common with nearly everyone communicating electronically several times a day. It is convenient, but not reliable nor appropriate for reporters trying to retrieve first-hand attribution and information from any source. Also, a lot of government stories may include highly technical, complicated ideas. You need someone to break down this information for you directly. In case the explanation isn't clear, you can ask immediately for clarification and perhaps examples. This is very difficult, if not impossible, to achieve through email correspondence.

Try to talk to people in person or by phone, so you can receive instant feedback and question follow-up. Lots of nuances get lost if you're communicating by email only. You can't tell their inflection, and answers are likely to be stilted. Never use statements and information from social media, like Twitter or Facebook, without cross-referencing and confirming the information from reliable sources.

Journalists do find social media sites helpful when trying to find out how people feel about a particular issue or community problem. Perkins says talk shows tackle current issues and often rely on Facebook, Twitter or Tumblr to get a "reading" from listeners to find out what they think and feel about particular stories in the news. Input from an audience can also help journalists discover new story ideas.

When it comes to writing online stories, Nikolewski recommends using hyperlinks. He says it can actually help protect the reporter by reinforcing their facts. He's found that hyperlinks help the reader find out more about story background. It also confirms information for the reader and helps him or her better understand the story.

When writing about a legislator, "you can create a link to them, so you know you have the name spelled right, (and the) title right," he adds. "It also helps me fact check."

Keep in mind "bonus" and follow-up stories

When out in the field reporting, always stay open to stories that can be an extension of what you're currently researching. If you meet someone interesting, a politician, staffer or a person you happen to run into in the building, think about doing a profile piece on them. In some way, these individuals might have a personal story that can better define your government story. For instance, if you're pursuing a report about aid for the homeless, the person lobbying for

Activities and Exercises

1. Select at least one of the questions in the discussion section and pursue a story based on the information you gleaned from the answer. For example, if you choose question #2, decide which community issue affects or interests you most. Write a story based on the information you've gathered. Be sure to incorporate basic writing skills such as the inverted pyramid.
    -   If it's a topic such as renewable energy, decide which local politicians and activist groups can best inform you on the subject.
    -   Be sure to find at least two sources that can present different opinions, so you can best inform your audience on the subject.

2. Is there a cultural fair planned for your community? Which country is the focus?
    -   Write a story about the fair and locate background information on the culture or food at this fair.
    -   Find the closest consulate and find out contact information for the cultural attaché. Ask him or her questions via phone call or email about the event and about that country's customs, traditions, and religious norms that will give your story more focus. This will also help your audience better understand the story

3. Run with the information you uncovered from answer #3 in the discussion question box. After researching the meeting minutes, ask yourself these questions and pursue these activities prior to writing the story:
    -   Why is this information important to community members?

the measure or proposing the legislation might have a personal connection with the story. Ask people about themselves. They might provide you with a story that has nothing to do with your current report, possibly a unique angle off the beaten path, but it could make for an excellent profile piece at a later date.

Nikolewski remembers when on a story recently for *The San Diego Tribune* he interviewed an environmentalist. He found out this person used to be an anti-nuclear activist and is now a pro-nuclear activist. How does that happen? You can be assured, there's a story in that transition.

For government stories that take you beyond the United States borders: Social media and diplomacy

These types of stories originate miles away from city hall, but you might find yourself in need of information relating to a government story about another country.

It could be there's an international story where you are required to find a local angle. There are places to search online for background material but be careful where you search. Some sites have a political agenda and will only provide their side to a conflict, whether it's social, economic or cultural. Diplomatic sites are a good place to start.

The Israeli government started years ago implementing social media directors at different consulate sites around the world to develop a diplomatic site. Shaul Hamawi of the Israeli Consulate in San Francisco is one of those social media directors. He says social media is an invaluable tool. "It enables us to reach a global audience of millions who want to know more about their country. Perhaps more importantly, it provides a stream of data and information to journalists around the world."

Hamawi says journalists contact him all the time for information about agriculture, water reclamation and cutting-edge research in the medical field. All of these areas in Israel are quickly growing sectors, so it's crucial that social media keeps reporters up to date. Hamawi admits that most of his time is still spent answering questions and uploading information about the latest in the Israeli-Palestinian conflict.

Social Media coordinator Martin Schwartz of the Swiss Consulate in San Francisco says providing online resources is a huge part of diplomacy. "Not government to government, but government to broad public diplomacy," he says. "If you Tweet or Facebook once a week or once a month, you're not going to build up any reliable following and people won't take you seriously."

Switzerland's financial market status is always in the forefront of people's minds, especially in the U.S. among the business press. Schwartz says a large part of his job is providing the latest answers to questions about Swiss banking. Martin's job emphasis is culture and public diplomacy. He alerts journalists to arts festivals or exhibits not just in the U.S. but anywhere in the world.

Go to embassy or consulate websites when you want to:

- Pursue research on a country's culture and country: Find out why a country is at war or why its government might be failing or why their people are protesting.
- Go directly to the source to confirm information about a country: Call or email the officials in charge of distributing breaking news or facts about an event to the media. Don't assume what you read on social media

- Write down reasons why people in the local community would care about this issue.
- Contact someone on the city or town council who can comment about this issue. Talk in person or call ahead of the interview to make sure you are quoting the most knowledgeable person on the topic.
- Find another person who can provide you with additional quotes from a different perspective or facts that the other source(s) cannot.
- Write a story based on your findings. Start with the most important information first.

Your reference guide[1]

State Government and Offices
Executive Branch
Governor
Lt. Governor
Attorney General
Secretary of State
Commissioners
Auditors

Legislative Branch
Representatives
(49 states have two chambers;
Nebraska has one in its legislature)

Judicial Branch
*State Supreme Court
**Court of Appeals
District

1   https://www.whitehouse.gov/1600/state-and-local-government

Local Government and Offices
***County
****City
Mayor
City Council
City Commissions
School Boards

*May be elected or appointed depending on state constitution

** There are 13 appellate courts in 12 regional districts in the U.S.

***Also known as boroughs in Alaska and parishes in Louisiana

****Sometimes referred to as municipalities. They generally take responsibility for parks and recreation services, police and fire departments, housing services, emergency media services, municipal courts, transportation, and public works for its population.

sites is true. Confirm and vet your sources. You can start with the country's website to find appropriate personal contact information and phone numbers.

- Cross-reference information found in social media: Double-check your facts and source quotes
- Be polite, but persistent

EXERCISES AND ACTIVITIES

1. Who are your government leaders? Governor? Lt. Governor? Congressional representatives? Mayor? Do they belong to a particular political party? Check out old newspaper articles to find out more about a politician's voting history and positions on controversial issues.

2. What are the "hot button" issues in your community? Remember to read local news websites and community-based newspapers to find out what is happening with locally funded programs or issues key to various socio-economic groups.

3. Where can you find minutes from the most recent town or city council? Check the minutes closely. Did anything happen at the meeting that might make a good story? Why would it make a good story? Name at least two people "in the know" who would make key interviews for the story.

4. If you were to write a profile piece about someone in your student body government, who would it be? What are their interests? Why are they in government? What are their goals?

5. Where is your closest Court of Appeals located? How would you retrieve information on a case currently pending? Who would you call?

6. Search the web for a news story about a country confronting serious conflict, whether it's war or toppling of government officials, for example. How would you research more about the history of this conflict?

CHAPTER 11

Crime and courts

"In the criminal justice system, you see the worst people on their best behavior, unlike the civil system, where the best people behave at their worst."

—Edna Buchanan, crime reporter, Pulitzer Prize winner and novelist[1]

Part I: Crime

In an era of decreasing profit margins, lower subscription sales, and shrinking space for news stories, fewer journalists have the luxury of covering specialized beats, such as local politics, technology, or entertainment. It seems that many citizen journalists use smartphones and cameras to take over the watchdog role once occupied by paid professionals.[2]

One beat, however, has stood the test of time, even in lean times. Check out any nightly news program or the front page of almost any newspaper, and you'll find lead stories that include fatal shootings, bank robberies, violent protests, high-speed police chases, terrorist attacks, police officer excessive force—the list goes on. "If it bleeds, it leads" is a common saying among television journalists.

That is why many young people hired by a newsroom will often be assigned to cover crime. The few who stay crime reporters for life will often use their expertise to produce major news features, books, and screenplays. For example, the HBO crime drama *The Wire,* which ran from 2002 to 2008, was created and written by former police reporter David Simon.[3]

---

1 Edna Buchanan, Accessed March 23, 2018, http://www.azquotes.com/quote/1166915.

2 Miranda Spivank, "As Local Coverage Wanes, Residents Become Self-taught Watchdogs," Investigative Reporting Workshop, April 19. 2016. Accessed April 24, 2016, http://investigativereportingworkshop.org/articles/local-coverage-wanes-residents-become-self-taught-/

3 Isaac Chotiner, "David Simon Would Like You to Stop Trying to Understand What's Going on in Baltimore by Quoting His TV Show," Slate.com, Aug. 12, 2015. Accessed April 21, 2016, http://www.slate.com/articles/arts/culturebox/2015/08/david_simon_interview_the_wire_creator_on_his_new_series_freddie_gray_ta.html.

Residents, business owners, politicians and community leaders all want to know if their neighborhoods are safe, and when something bad happens, they want to know how it happened, why it happened, and what can be done to prevent it from happening again. That's why the job of a crime reporter is critical and why so many great crime reporters will go on to get bigger jobs, write novels, or even help create TV shows and movies.

Crime coverage doesn't end when police make an arrest. The community still wants to know if justice will be served. That's why crime reporters may also be tasked to cover the trial of the crime they first reported on. While some newsrooms with a bigger budget might have a specialized court reporter, most newsrooms will turn to the crime reporter to continue informing the public on what happens to the suspects of a crime throughout the court process. That's why a basic understanding of the judicial system is just as important as understanding the basics of covering crime. This chapter will address both.

Covering crime: Preparing for the story

Whether you're assigned to cover a crime beat or simply dispatched to cover a breaking crime story, it's important to know where to go and how to approach law enforcement—before you get to the scene or make any phone calls.

Understanding the basics of law enforcement, so you can speak with confidence, is very useful. Police officers work in paramilitary organizations with a rank structure: police officer, corporal, sergeant, lieutenant, captain, deputy chief, and chief. Police departments exist in cities, while sheriff's departments operate in a county-wide jurisdiction. There are dozens of other law enforcement personnel recognized under the California Government Code, including BART police, University of California police, California Highway Patrol, Harbor Police, and many more. Federal law enforcement officials include U.S. Marshals Service and the Federal Bureau of Investigation. It helps to know the structure so you can navigate who is in charge and who might best be able to provide useful information.

If you're assigned to daily beat coverage in a city/metropolitan area, take time to go the local police precinct and introduce yourself. Hand out your business cards and try to engage in easygoing conversation, so officers know a little bit about you. At a local precinct or headquarters, be sure to ask to see the **police blotter,** which will list recent crimes that occurred in the neighborhood. You can also ask for the **police report** of a particular crime, but these may take days or weeks to obtain, depending on the department's particular policy on releasing reports.

Attend meetings hosted by law enforcement, even if you don't plan to cover the event as a story. Meetings and other events are a great opportunity to get to know key sources that can help you in the future.

Often, reporters asking police for information about a crime will be directed to the **public information officer,** also known as a PIO. The PIO is officially tasked with releasing official statements from police. They are considered the official spokesperson of the department. The spokesperson can give you information about a crime, or even give you the names of the detectives or officers following up on the case.

Once you meet the PIO and other officers who can help answer questions on crime, ask to get on their email list for press releases, newsletters, and community meetings, and follow them on Twitter and other social media platforms. Many times, police agencies will share developments about a particular crime through social media.

Journalists also stay up on police activity by buying a **police scanner** or an app that lets them listen to the police scanner. A **police scanner** is a radio receiver that allows members of the public to listen to two-way radio calls between police, fire officials, and others in law enforcement. The challenge, of course, is making sense of the codes that police officers use to talk about crime. Thankfully, many websites and apps allow journalists to decipher these codes. One site called ScanSF (http://scansf.com/sfpd_radio_codes.txt) offers a long list of codes that can help new folks understand numbers like 187 (homicide) or 207 (kidnapping). It's important to find sites that cover your jurisdiction or municipality because local police codes may vary, but most departments use a very similar radio code structure for describing ongoing activity.

Setting up

When you arrive to the scene of a crime, you may see yellow hazard tape that reads: "Do not enter." Journalists with official press credentials may cross the yellow hazard tape to get inside the scene and ask follow-up questions. Be careful not to get too close to officers as they work to uncover details and do not touch anything. For multimedia packages, start recording as soon as you see images that are relevant to the story, but ask police for permission to set up bulkier equipment that might get in the way of an ongoing investigation. If you plan to record your interviews, be sure to ask permission to record, and try to get full names of the law enforcement officers you interview. If they don't want to give you their names, ask to speak to the officer in charge. If that doesn't work, follow up with the PIO back at the station or police headquarters. Shyness doesn't work in these environments. If you can't get information from one person, keep digging. Call the police chief if you want answers and are getting none.

Other people you'll want to interview include the people actually involved in the crime. Though victims and suspects might be gone by the time you arrive, you can try to follow up with people who have been arrested and jailed by asking where they are being held and trying to obtain a jailhouse interview. If the victim is alive and is recovering at a nearby hospital, you can call the hospital to find out their condition. You'll also need to look for relatives of both the victim and suspects. They might still be at the scene, or you may be able to find out more about them once you obtain the name and other details about the suspects and victims from police. Be respectful of their space, however, and look for an appropriate time to approach them. Identify yourself and ask family members whether they can talk with you now or at a later time. Hand them your business card and let them know they can reach out to you when they're ready.

If the crime occurred near a business, be sure to walk into stores and other shops to ask if owners and others working there saw anything. Also ask them about their reaction to the crime and ask if they have ever witnessed anything like that before.

You can also ask residents the same kind of questions if the crime occurred in a neighborhood.

Crafting the story

To write a breaking crime story, you'll want to use the inverted pyramid. The most important information should come first in a summary lead, letting readers and viewers know who, what, when, where, why, and how it all happened.

Ex: Police are searching for two men who broke into a military surplus store on 14th and Valencia streets last night, taking $5,000 worth of camouflage gear.

In the next paragraph, be sure to offer attribution to back up the lead:

In surveillance video, two men wearing ski masks are seen cutting through a steel bolt on the door of Manny's Surplus Shop, said Public Information Officer Shereal Smethen. The video shows that the break-in happened just after 1:45 a.m., when the store was closed and empty. The men also can be seen in the video smashing glass shelves and tipping over every round of clothing before piling the camouflage into plastic trash bags and running away as the alarm sounds, she added.

Follow up with a strong quote:

"We are asking for the public's help in finding the two men responsible for destroying the owner's shop and taking his valuable merchandise," Smethen said.

Seek comment from those affected:

The owner, Manuel T. Roses, could not be reached for comment. He did, however, tell police that his store has never been burglarized before.

The breaking crime story should also include any comments from witnesses or anyone else in the area. You should search for any information about the store and the neighborhood where the crime occurred. If police on the scene don't talk, be sure to follow up by phone with the PIO or other officers back at the station.

Because the details of a crime can be very disturbing, take care in reporting the facts and consult with your editors and legal team before publishing or airing graphic images and grisly details. In addition, take care when writing about crime that a person accused of a crime is innocent until proven guilty by a judge or jury.

That's why it's important to follow the basic principles of the SPJ Code of Ethics,[4] including:

- Avoid stereotyping. Journalists should examine the ways their values and experiences may shape their reporting.

---

4 "SPJ Code of Ethics." Society of Professional Journalists. Accessed August 25, 2015, http://www.spj.org/eth-icscode.asp.

- Balance the public's need for information against potential harm or discomfort. Pursuit of the news is not a license for arrogance or undue intrusiveness.
- Show compassion for those who may be affected by news coverage. Use heightened sensitivity when dealing with juveniles, victims of sex crimes, and sources or subjects who are inexperienced or unable to give consent. Consider cultural differences in approach and treatment.
- Realize that private people have a greater right to control information about themselves than public figures and others who seek power, influence, or attention. Weigh the consequences of publishing or broadcasting personal information

Summary

Most young reporters hired by a mainstream news outlet are expected to do it all: Write the story, capture the images, record the video, and promote their content via social media. Even so, there is one beat that many newbies will come across, and that is the crime beat.

Part II: Covering courts

It is helpful to know the different stages in court, from the beginning through trial and appeals. This requires knowing the difference between criminal and civil matters. An interview with Oakland, California, attorney Arthur Hartinger, who has offered lessons in covering courts to journalism students at San Francisco State University, helps to round out this section on court coverage.

The **criminal justice system,** according to the National Center for Victims of Crime, is the "set of agencies and processes established by governments to control crime and impose penalties on those who violate laws." State criminal justice systems handle crimes committed within state boundaries, and the federal criminal justice system handles crimes committed in more than one state or on federal property, such as the White House.

A criminal case begins with the State District Attorney or federal U.S. Attorney filing a complaint in court. This is sometimes referred to as an indictment or charges. Most filings are publicly available, and all will be assigned a case number. A District Attorney handles state court criminal violations, and they are empowered under the California Constitution to represent the "people" in prosecuting criminal charges. Every County in California has an elected District Attorney. California state cases begin in a County Courthouse, and the filings are made through the Clerk of the Court. A U.S. Attorney, on the other hand, prosecutes federal crimes, and the cases are filed in the United States District Court. In California, there are four district divisions: Northern, Eastern, Southern and Central.

Similarly, a civil case begins with an individual or entity or the government filing a complaint with the Clerk of the Court. Again, each civil case will be assigned a case number.

The criminal case process

Once a defendant is charged through a case filing, the defendant will appear at an *arraignment*. The arraignment is usually a quick process where the defendant will enter a plea—often "not guilty," but sometimes "no contest" or a request for a continuance to enter a plea pending settlement negotiations. The court will also set the amount for bail—the amount a defendant will deposit as a bond to ensure they will return to court for further proceedings. The arraignment is important for reporters because the defendant will usually have to appear personally in court, and it is the very first time for a court proceeding.

Criminal acts fall into two categories: felonies and misdemeanors.[5] A **misdemeanor** is considered a lesser crime and carries a potential sentence of up to a year in jail and/or a fine. Examples of misdemeanors include petty theft, prostitution, trespassing, and vandalism. A felony is considered much more serious and is punishable by more than a year in prison. Examples include murder, kidnapping, and rape.

In a felony case, if the defendant pleads not guilty, then the court will set the matter for a **preliminary hearing.** The purpose of a preliminary hearing is for the prosecuting attorney to present sufficient evidence to show that there is a good faith possibility of proving the crime at a trial. The presiding judge will rule whether there is enough evidence to hold the defendant over for trial, and, if so, the court will set a trial date. In a misdemeanor case, the court will simply set the case for trial, and there is no requirement to hold a preliminary hearing.

A trial can be a "bench trial," in which the judge hears the evidence and makes a decision with no jury. However, for the most part, every criminal defendant has the Constitutional right to a jury trial. In state court, a jury consists of twelve community residents chosen at random. In federal court, the jury is composed of six residents chosen at random from within the federal district.

The case will end with a verdict, and judgment is then entered. Every case has a "disposition," dismissal, judgment, or plea agreement.

The civil case process

Civil cases involve lawsuits between two people or two parties. For example, a person who wants a divorce will file for "dissolution of marriage," or an employee who is wrongfully discharged can file a complaint for a remedy against the employer.

Once a complaint is filed, the other side is required to file a response—sometimes an "answer" or other response. The parties then engage in discovery, including depositions

---

5   www.justice.gov,https://www.justice.gov/sites/default/files/usao-ri/legacy/2011/04/04/ri_federal_criminal_bro-chure.pdf, accessed on May 7, 2016.

(which are proceedings where sworn testimony is given), sworn interrogatories, and document subpoenas. The discovery process can take months, even years, and it is often conducted in private.

In civil cases, defendants are not usually required to appear in court. The representing attorneys will appear at status conferences, trial setting conferences, and motion hearings, but usually clients will not appear.

If the case does not settle, then the court will set the matter for trial. These dates are often listed on the court's "docket," which is the court's record of all appearances, filings, and court orders. Again, the trial can be a bench trial or jury trial. Trials are usually open to the public.

A useful glossary for legal terms:

Arrest—The act of seizing someone to take into custody.

Arraignment—To call the accused before a criminal court to hear and answer the charge made against them.

Preliminary hearing—A hearing to determine if a person charged with a felony should be tried.

Trial—Allows a judge or jury to examine the evidence and decide the outcome.

Sentencing—The punishment given to a person convicted of a crime. A judge issues the sentence, based on the verdict of the judge or jury.

Lawsuit—A claim brought to court by a person or party to end a dispute.

Motion—A motion is a procedural device for decision. It is a request to the judge (or judges) to make a decision about the case. Motions may be made at any point in administrative, criminal, or civil proceedings, although that right is regulated by court rules, which vary from place to place.

Ruling—An official or authoritative decision, decree, statement, or interpretation (as by a judge on a point of law).

Acquittal—A judgment that a person is not guilty of the crime with which the person has been charged.

Affidavit or Declaration—Written statement of facts voluntarily made under penalty of perjury.

Bail—The surety ordered by the court to allow for the temporary release of an accused person awaiting trial, usually including a condition that a sum of money or property be lodged to guarantee their appearance in court. If there is no bail set, then the defendant will be released on their **"own recognizance."**

Bond—This is an amount of money that, if paid, allows an arrested person to be released from jail.

Venue—The location where the complaint is filed, i.e., in State Court, the County; and in Federal Court, the District. In high profile cases, a party may make a motion for a "change of venue," and if the motion is granted, the trial is moved to another community to obtain jurors who can be more objective in their duties.

Deposition—A proceeding in which a party gives oral testimony out of court but under oath before a licensed court reporter.

Extradition—When a state moves an accused or convicted person to another state or country to face charges or penalties there.

Hung jury—When a jury is unable to reach a verdict of guilty or not guilty. This results in a mistrial. Prosecutors can seek to try the case again.

Indictment—An official statement charging a person with a crime.

Mistrial—A trial that is thrown out because of an error or because the jury can't reach a verdict, or there was some other misconduct during trial.

Plea bargain—A settlement agreement between the prosecution and the defense for the defendant to plead guilty to a lesser offense or to one or some of the offenses.

Probation—A period of time when a person who has committed a crime is out of prison but is being monitored, and can be sent back to prison if they violate any conditions of probation.

Recognizance—A promise a defendant makes with the court to show up as ordered, so they are allowed to leave jail.

Subpoena—A writ commanding a person to appear in court or at a deposition.

Summons—An order to appear in a court of law.

Suspended sentence—A suspended jail or prison sentence that is put on hold if the defendant complies with certain obligations.

Verdict—A decision made by a jury in a trial.

Warrant—A court document that gives police the power to take action against a suspect.

Tackling the story

Often, crime is just the start of a good story. If an arrest has been made, reporters will find out the details of the **booking** in which law enforcement officers will record the arrest and charges against the suspect.[6]

Indeed, many crime stories get much more interesting as they make their way through the court process. Think back to the 2014 fatal police shooting of unarmed 18-year-old Michael Brown in Ferguson, Missouri. Police Officer Darren Wilson, who is white, shot and killed Brown, who was African American. The shooting sparked national outrage, and a **grand jury, a group of citizens** selected to examine the validity of an accusation before trial, was convened.

Officer Wilson, 28, told the grand jury that he was sitting in his patrol car when Brown approached him and punched him.[7] In the following encounter, Wilson fired twelve shots, killing Brown. A few witnesses claimed that Brown had his hands up, but the grand jury

---

6   The Free Dictionary. Accessed May 7, 2016, http://legal-dictionary.thefreedictionary.com/Booking.

7   "Michael Brown Shooting: Ferguson Cop Darren Wilson Not Indicted," NBC News. Accessed May 7, 2016, http://www.nbcnews.com/storyline/michael-brown-shooting/ferguson-cop-darren-wilson-not-indicted-shooting-michael-brown-n255391.

decided not to indict Wilson, citing witness statements that were "completely refuted by the physical evidence."

Announcement of the grand jury's decision led to violent protests, lootings, freeway shutdowns, and marches with protestors carrying signs that read, "Hands Up! Don't Shoot." The fatal shooting of Michael Brown was one in a series of police shootings that called into question police relations with people of color. Thus, while nearly every major news outlet covered the crime, which was a big story in itself, they also reported the case as it made its way through the justice system. That is why coverage of crime and courts go hand in hand.

When you're at the courthouse

Most courtrooms allow members of the public to enter. Remember: Reporters *are* members of the public. There are, however, some exceptions, so be sure to ask your editors or research to find out if the case is closed to the public. For example, a child-protection hearing may not be open to the public to protect the identity of those under 18. When court is in session, you can leave and enter as you like, but try to be respectful and avoid disruption.

A Superior Court will usually have the following personnel: a bailiff, who is often a deputy sheriff assigned to maintain order and security in the Court; a clerk, who logs all proceedings and maintains the case calendar; a court reporter, who formally records all testimony using a stenographer machine; and the judge. It is useful to be polite to the bailiff and the clerk because if you are friendly and respectful, they can provide invaluable information. If you are rude, you will likely be treated in a like manner.

Access to court records

Most court files are open to the public and can be viewed at the courthouse. To view criminal records, you should contact law enforcement. If the court files are being used during a hearing or being reviewed by someone else, a reporter may not be able to access them until later.

Use of cameras and recorders

Rules for cameras, recorders, and other electronic devices vary from state to state, so be sure to check what the laws are in your state before strolling in with a camera. In 1981, the U.S. Supreme Court ruled that states may adopt rules permitting cameras and recording equipment in their courts, according to the Reporters Committee for Freedom of the Press. Some states allow visual and audio coverage; others do not. Cameras in federal courts are limited. The U.S. Supreme Court prohibits cameras at all of its proceedings but does release audio recordings each week.

You can check with the clerk or bailiff to determine the court's rules. Some courts are quite strict, and you could be held in contempt of court if you try to secretly record or photograph anything in the Court. If you ask permission, the court will sometimes permit "cutaway" shots, i.e., photos of the courtroom while the court is not in session, in order to give the story context.

Fourteen courts participated. The pilot program ended in July 2015, but three districts (Northern California, Western Washington and Guam) were continuing the program as of March 2016.[8]

Tweeting in the courtroom

Live tweeting of the news is becoming increasingly popular, as newsrooms try to stay on top of the 24/7 news cycle, but some courts do not allow it, so be sure to check with the courts and your editors to see what the rules are in your state and county. In Seminole County, Florida, a circuit court did allow reporters to tweet while covering the high-profile murder case of 17-year-old Trayvon Martin.[9] Martin, who was an African American high school student, was shot by George Zimmerman, who was then a neighborhood watch captain. A six-woman jury acquitted Zimmerman, setting off huge protests across the country.[10]

How to structure a court story

The first paragraph of a breaking story should include a summary of the latest court development.

Because a trial can last for days, weeks, or even months, a journalist will need to stay on top of each development and decide whether to report on it. For example, the opening arguments in a murder trial could be interesting or newsworthy to the audience, especially if attorneys on either side can shed light on a crime. Motions made by one side, especially if they are to dismiss the case, should also be reported. Get to know the lawyers on both sides so you can stay on top of the story and understand the legal proceeding as they develop. Follow the inverted-pyramid style in most cases, telling readers and viewers what they need to know first. Don't forget to use the full name of the judge presiding in the court.

8   "History of Cameras in Courts," United States Courts. Accessed May 7, 2016, http://www.uscourts.gov/about-federal-courts/cameras-courts/history-cameras-courts.

9   "Be Aware Tweeting Allowed in Some Courtrooms But Not Others," Reporters Committee for the Freedom of the Press, May 28, 2014. Accessed May 7, 2016, http://www.poynter.org/2014/tweeting-allowed-from-some-courtrooms-but-not-others/253548/.

10   "Trayvon Martin Shooting Fast Facts," CNN News, Feb. 7, 2016. Accessed May 7, 2016, http://www.cnn.com/2013/06/05/us/trayvon-martin-shooting-fast-facts/.

Information to include in a court story (for criminal or civil case)

Be sure to note the charges that the defendant faces.

Lead	Start with the latest action first. For example, if you are writing about the verdict, be sure to lead with what the verdict is, not the actual crime or accusation, which may have happened months or years ago.
Elaboration of lead	In the second graph, report the name of the judge, the exact courtroom, and details of the latest action.
Strong quote	Obtain a quote from judge, jurors, defendant, victim, or victim's family and place high up in the story. Often you can get great quotes at the hearing or trial.
Nut graph	Explain to your audience that this was the latest outcome in a trial or case, and let readers know when the case began.
Next step	Has the next step in the trial or case been set? Will there be a sentencing, or will the judge decide damages in a civil case next week? Let your audience know. Don't wait until the end.
Original case or crime details	Tell your audience about the original crime or case. What led to the action today? Be sure to attribute to people you have reached or documents you obtained to review the case.
Background	Were there intriguing details from the original case or crime? Were there moments in previous court sessions worth mentioning again?
Ending	Leave readers thinking about what happens next with a strong quote from a key player in the case. Avoid offering your own insight or opinions about the case.

EXERCISES AND ACTIVITIES

1. Go to the United States Courts website and look for the court locator, http://www. uscourts.gov/courtrecords/find-case-pacer. Type in the zip code of your city and list the locations of the courthouses and the types of cases that are heard at those locations. You may have to choose a category, such as district or bankruptcy, first. Be sure to list the proper name of the courthouse and address.

2. Go to the United States Courts website and click on the "Comparing Federal Courts" link at http://www.uscourts.gov/about-federal-courts. Explain how the selection of judges differs from state to federal courts.

3. Go to the United States Courts website and look up the 2014 Wiretap report at http://www.uscourts.gov/statistics-reports/wiretap-report-2014. What was the most prevalent type of criminal offense investigated using wiretaps? What percentage of arrests was due to federal wiretaps?

4. Jim Bluebird, 68, claims his neighbor cut 20 mature apple trees that were on his side of the fence. He filed a lawsuit in the (your county) courthouse today, seeking $100,000 in damages. Jim, the plaintiff, is suing the defendant, Brownie Stewart, 43, for "wrongful cutting and removal of timber and trespassing." Brownie Stewart, a single mother with three boys who help her care for chickens on her land, told you in an interview that she only cut the trees that were on her property. She does not believe she has done anything wrong but refused to comment further until she had a chance to seek legal representation. Bluebird says he is representing himself in the suit. He says he is "heartbroken" by the loss of his favorite trees. "I rely on those trees to support my fixed income. Why didn't she bother to ask me before cutting my trees?" Bluebird says he runs a small fruit stand on the weekends and was making fresh apple juice to sell to residents. Both Jim and Brownie have three-acre properties in the rural area of your county, and the two have been neighbors for 24 years. Write a 150-word story on the lawsuit. Also, find out what the laws are for cutting down trees on other people's yards and include that information in your story.

5. Find a local crime reporter in your city and interview thenabout a typical day on the crime beat. Be sure to include video and still images in your news package.

6. Visit your local police station and ask to see the police blotter. Look for a crime that you think might be newsworthy and ask for more information about it.

7. Google "police report," and choose one of the categories of crimes to view. Find a recent report in that category and write a 300-word story based on that police report. You may only use facts given in the police report. Do not cite information from other news articles or websites. Avoid police jargon and write in a conversational tone.

CHAPTER 12

Weather and natural disasters

"I think all good reporting is the same thing—the best attainable version of the truth."

–Carl Bernstein[1]

Weather happens everywhere, all the time. Even for those living in the Sun Belt states where there is plenty of sun and people enjoy warm temperatures nearly year-round, dangerous conditions can develop. Weather events can cause conditions to turn deadly fast. For a reporter, covering weather and natural disasters can present the most difficult circumstances from which to gather and deliver news that you will experience. You could be thrown into life-and-death situations.

Top news stories are often weather-related because of story dynamics and the fact that weather affects everyone in a given community, and people turn to news outlets to keep them informed in such situations. The selection of weather as a newscast lead is based on the same decision-making values as any news story: proximity, prominence, and timeliness.

Weather is often unpredictable. The effects of climate change have brought certain weather conditions, such as tornados, hurricanes, fires, and unseasonable snowstorms, to regions that historically have rarely experienced these patterns of wind and precipitation. Reporters need to be prepared to cover any sort of disaster anywhere.

Remember, the focus of any natural disaster or weather-related story is people. Humanize whatever approach you decide to take along the way of reporting the facts. The Who, What, Where, When, Why, and How of the story remain crucial, of course, but how these elements relate to the daily lives of those affected most is paramount. It is your job as a reporter to communicate to your audience the information people will need to survive and keep themselves safe, to the extent possible, throughout the emergency.

Take your writing skills with you. Stay on point. Remember the purpose of your story. It will be easy to get distracted and want to include so much of what you see and hear. For you

---

1   Quote Fancy. Accessed March 30, 2018, https://quotefancy.com/quote/1092064/Carl-Bernstein-I-think-all-good-reporting-is-the-same-thing-the-best-attainable-version.

to communicate as directly as possible to your audience, keep your sentences brief. Stick with the inverted pyramid. You will have several stories to cover for many days. Make each one stand alone with its own purpose.

When reporting a natural disaster from the early warnings of a tornado, tropical storm, hurricane, or the unpredictable earthquake, it can be difficult to not to get personally affected or become part of the story. According to the Society of Professional Journalists, "journalists walk a fine line to balance their professional responsibilities with their humanity when covering disasters. Journalists need to use caution to avoid blurring the lines between a participant and being an objective observer." The SPJ Code of Ethics[2] states the following:

> No one wants to see human suffering, and reporting on these events can certainly take on a personal dimension. But participating in events, even with the intention of dramatizing the humanity of the situation, takes news reporting in a different direction and places journalists in a situation they should not be in, and that is one of forgoing their roles as informants.

Most common natural disasters defined

Tropical depression

An organized storm of clouds and thunderstorms with a defined circulation and maximum winds of 38 miles per hour or less.

Tropical storm

A system of strong thunderstorms with a maximum of 39 to 73 mile-per-hour winds.

Hurricane

An intense tropical weather system with a wind force exceeding 74 miles per hour. Hurricanes are products of the tropical ocean and atmosphere powered by heat from the sea, and they grow with velocity. Moving toward land, hurricanes sweep the ocean inward, pulling water up into their structure. Hurricanes range in strength from Category 1 to Category 5, and Category 5 is the most dangerous.

Hurricanes are becoming more common as climate change progresses. There have been 11 Category 5 hurricanes since 2000 (18 years at the time of this writing), compared to four in

---

2 "SPJ Code of Ethics." Society of Professional Journalists. Accessed August 25, 2015, http://www.spj.org/ethicscode.asp.

the previous 18 years. Hurricanes that reached Category 5 and caused great damage to U.S. communities include Hurricanes Maria and Irma (2017), which caused damage to Puerto Rico that its residents were still recovering from at the time of this writing; Hurricane Matthew (2016); Hurricanes Katrina and Rita (2005), which caused extensive damage to New Orleans and other regions of the U.S. South; and Hurricane Andrew (1992), which pummeled Florida.

According to NOAA (National Oceanic and Atmospheric Administration), there are no other storms like hurricanes on earth. Views of hurricanes from satellites located thousands of miles above the earth show how unique these weather systems are. [3]

Tornado

A tornado is a narrow, violently rotating column of air that extends from the base of a thunderstorm to the ground. Because the tornado itself is invisible, it is hard to see a tornado unless it forms a condensation funnel made up of water droplets and debris. According to NOAA, tornadoes are the most violent of all atmospheric storms.[4]

Preparing and covering the story

Have a plan ready. No one knows when disaster will strike. A hurricane may be brewing off the coast of the Carolinas, but it could downgrade and evaporate by the time it makes landfall. On the flip side, a natural disaster could take people by surprise. For example, Hurricane Katrina in August 2005 was Category 5 when over water, but when Hurricane Katrina struck the Gulf Coast, it had weakened to a Category 3, with sustained wind speeds as high as 174 miles per hour. The hurricane spread destruction for hundreds of miles in and around New Orleans, but it was the aftermath that caused most of the devastation. The unstable levees busted, which led to massive flooding and more deaths.[5]

When preparing for eventual coverage of a natural disaster, create a database containing names of local officials and their cell numbers. Texting these individuals at disaster time may be the most efficient way to contact them and to receive bits of breaking information as it becomes available.

If a disaster forces road closures, how will you get around? Your normal routes about town may change dramatically. If there is no electricity or water for days, how will you manage to report and survive yourself? If you cannot get a live signal from the scene, how will you manage to get the visuals back to the station? Do you find some alternate means of transportation? Could you walk or ride your bike if needed?

---

3   http://www.aomi.noaa,gov

4   http://www.nssl.noaa.gov

5   http://www.history.com/topics/hurricane-katrina

Keep in mind that there will be a lot of misinformation, especially in the immediate aftermath. Reporters can make mistakes and deliver erroneous details during any breaking news story, and coverage of natural disasters is no different. As with all news stories, double-check information and confirm with officials. You can attribute eyewitness reports, but be sure to note if that information is yet to be substantiated by authorities. It's important to relay what neighbors or survivors say they saw or witnessed, but delivering it as fact may need an official sound bite. This is a decision you will need to make as you exercise objectivity on the scene.

Decide what kind of visuals you might need. A "video shot list" is a way of making sure, when the time comes, that you are getting specific shots and not generic "wallpaper" video. Even the most seasoned reporter can get caught up in the panic-driven nature of constant breaking news. Provide yourself with this b-roll reference sheet, so when an emergency situation kicks into high gear, you have a visualization reference point to help illustrate specifics of the story.

Covering a story under dangerous conditions

Two words to remember: Be safe. Don't put yourself or any co-worker at risk.

A big part of being safe is being prepared with a change of clothing complete with durable shoes, rain boots, a breathing mask (preferably N95) for fires, and warm layers. You will also need a stash of non-perishable food. Keep these items in your car always. You may be heading out to cover disastrous conditions with little or no notice. You will need to be self-sufficient, because there is no way to know how long coverage of natural disaster will last. It could be days or weeks of non-stop reporting.

Nancy Dignon, a 20-year TV meteorologist, remembers covering plenty of tropical storms, flooding, and hurricanes during her time at WCTV in Tallahassee, Florida. She says the first thing any news staffer needs to do is plan. Have a strategy for how to cover a weather-related event. "Know where the water is going to surge. You may only have 20 minutes to get a live shot, so you need to know where to get the remote set up, do your live shot, and get out of danger." She notes that when a hurricane gets upgraded to a 3, 4, or 5, it is not advised to send a reporter into those conditions. Dignon says those are "almost always deadly. You prepare for the worst and hope for the best."

Get out the word using social media. Use the most popular means to send out news and emergency information to the community. Facebook, Twitter, Tumblr, and Reddit are good places to start. Let people know to evacuate if that is what local officials are requiring or recommending. Live tweet as often as possible so your audience will know to follow your reports for reliable information.

Remember, you likely will live in the area affected by a natural disaster. In the case of the deadly Joplin tornado of 2011, five reporters in the KOAM-TV newsroom lost their homes.

The tornado destroyed about one-third of Joplin in about 20 minutes. News Director Kristi Spencer said one reporter was injured and went to the emergency room, and the others reported to work. One of those reporters was Lisa Olliges, who says she waited for the tornado to pass while in a relative's basement. After all the noise stopped, she drove to the station to begin her coverage of this historic disaster.

Pursuing interviews during and after a disaster

Always remember that people do not have to talk to you. Many of them will have just experienced a life-altering tragedy. Be aware that people are generally traumatized. If they didn't lose someone close in the disaster or suffer major material losses, it's likely they know someone who did.

Check out local hospitals. That's where the most seriously injured will be taken as soon as possible. You will receive a quick overview of just how serious the situation is, and you might find officials to talk to for an initial overview of casualties. You could also discover where to locate the greatest damage.

"… Don't presume to know how they feel. They may just have seen someone perish."

Be compassionate. KOAM-TV Reporter Lisa Olliges says, "Don't ask someone on the scene, 'Do you feel lucky to have survived?' It's better to be vague in your questioning of people who have just experienced a natural disaster. Don't presume to know how they feel. They may just have seen someone perish." She recommends more open-ended questions that allow the survivors to contribute whatever information they can and are willing to share.

Olliges recalls survivors of that Joplin tornado telling her she needed to interview people holed up inside a local Pizza Hut. She approached it as a good news story until she uncovered all the facts. There was this amazing story, they told her, of an employee who told them to run for safety and stay inside the cooler until the tornado passed. They all survived, but the employee was thrown by the tornado and killed while helping others. It's a good indicator of trying to understand the nuance of the story before asking specific questions.

TIP: You will be inundated with many story ideas once on the scene of a natural disaster. Experienced reporters say write down ideas as you think of them to pursue later.

Many reporters interviewed for this chapter admit everyone is nervous when covering a natural disaster. They agree that one of the best tips to remember when interviewing people during a natural disaster is to record names, phone numbers, and email addresses. In the midst of a chaotic environment, the idea of follow-up opportunities gets lost.

Important disaster story follow-ups

Record names and get phone numbers. You'll want to talk to these sources later to find out how they are doing and see how the situation has evolved and developed. This will enable you to get updates on the injured and anyone affected by the disaster. Being "in the moment" of a breaking news story, you stand the chance of losing an opportunity to write down information for key sound bites in follow-up stories to be used at a later date.

Years after the Joplin tornado and Katrina's devastation in New Orleans, there are still stories to report. These are cities adjusting to their "new normal." Stories of survival are there to be told. Housing is an issue. In Joplin, new businesses are moving in and replacing the ones ruined by the tornado. In the aftermath of the 2017 California wine country fires, reporters discovered that many longtime residents were leaving the area, likely permanently, because they could not find affordable housing. In addition, a second weather event—rain—which would ordinarily have been just part of the normal weather report, became a major story given the concern about mudslides in fire-damaged areas. In Santa Barbara, which also experienced devastating fires, mudslides a few months later claimed lives and caused further damage. Follow-up stories can also investigate the aftermath of how the crisis was handled. Over the years, there have been cases where reporters uncovered corruption in the way in which money, earmarked for rebuilding, was distributed. The promptness and efficiency of first-responders might also be investigated.

In the case of earthquakes, find out if buildings are being retrofitted to protect from future quakes. Are buildings and houses up to code? Is that code safe enough for residents? In the days and months following major flooding, check to see what the city, county, and state are doing to reinforce protection around flood zones. Have new safety measures been put into place? In the days and weeks following a major fire, check on the progress of clean-up, the status of insurance payouts, and the welfare of those in the community.

Tips from the experts when covering a natural disaster

- Stay safe. You are not helping anyone if you place yourself in danger.
- Educate yourself to the current situation; look around and gather details from the scene prior to disseminating your story.
- Be compassionate when interviewing people on the scene.
- Try not to presume you know what happened to people you are interviewing.
- Connect people with the video; make it relevant; write to the visuals.
- Use social media to get your story out quickly; live Tweet.
- Have someone go with you on a natural disaster for safety.
- Make sure you have plenty of phone and camera batteries.

- Dress appropriately. Have waterproof boots, tennis shoes, warm clothing, and rain gear always in the trunk of your car.
- Have emergency food supplies handy, especially water, energy bars, and any non-perishables that you can access quickly when needed.
- Get names and phone numbers for follow up; find out how they're doing.

A day in the life of a newsroom meteorologist

All weather news is as planned as possible. That's the word from experienced meteorologist Tom O'Hare of the 9 and 10 p.m. news and Fox 32 in Cadillac, Michigan.

Tom O'Hare starts his day in the newsroom, usually early in the afternoon, and keeps a close eye on weather maps and graphics until around midnight. The exception happens if there's a storm on the way. "We send emails out to the newsroom or to the entire company to give a heads-up to say it's going to be pretty bad, and then we give updates. This way when the storm happens, there's a plan for team coverage and the impact of it afterwards."

He finds it best to err on the side of caution. "We say it's going to be on the cloudy side and, hopefully, we'll get the sunshine." There could be a couple of things, he says, such as a surprise rain shower or storm where nothing in the forecast indicates it's on the way. He admits no one can have a perfect forecast all the time.

This brings about a constant challenge for meteorologists and weather reporters because weather is sometimes unpredictable. O'Hare has the added responsibility that many local businesses in his Northern Michigan viewing area depend on weather forecast accuracy. Much of the local economy is based on tourism, with summer travelers and wintertime enthusiasts seeking a place for sports like ice fishing, skiing, and snowmobiling. There's also the multi-million-dollar cherry and apple industry to consider.

Figure 12.1 Meteorologist Tom O'Hare on the air

Figure 12.2 In the weather center

Figure 12.3 Checking the latest weather prior to air

In markets such as Cadillac, Michigan, and others with four seasons, there are things you can count on, including snow. "We get at least two to three major snowstorms a year." Eight to 10 inches of snow is considered a big storm. In Northern Michigan 10 to 11 inches is a significant snowstorm."

When waiting for the snow to fall, reporters are assigned a variety of stories to cover. One type is the preparation story. What is the Department of Transportation doing to get ready to keep streets clear? How will blowing snow and high winds impact the roads? What are people doing to hunker down prior to the storm? Are local businesses feeling the impact? Are hardware stores running out of road salt and shovels? Are grocery stores crowded with last-minute shoppers stocking up on food?

Covering weather is not unlike other reporting beats, delivering stories about information people need but also stories involving things people want to know. Social media comes into play to help better understand what a community is seeking.

When O'Hare gets to work, he posts something weather-related as soon as he gets through the newsroom door. In addition, he'll Tweet and Facebook three to four times a shift, maybe more, depending on how active weather conditions might be that day. The frequency of social media postings will increase as storms are approaching.

According to O'Hare, you can find out what people want to know by just posting something quickly on the web. "Just the other day, I put out a graphic (on social media) about hummingbirds and the fact they're coming back to Northern Michigan. It's a story people relate to weather because things are changing, and spring is arriving. A huge number of people watched it," O'Hare said.

If you're thinking about a career in a newsroom weather center, O'Hare highly recommends studying the technical side of weather, so you can better relay information to your audience. He says more stations and news organizations are hiring meteorologists. "The industry wants you to have the background to be able to explain the weather and what's coming tomorrow and why." Weather is getting more complicated with non-traditional weather patterns popping up all year.

He also notices that people often tune in to the local television station in times of severe weather. "Mobile phones or tablets are becoming more popular if people are not home to watch, but when things get really bad, you find people going to the TV for their weather information. They want to see the meteorologist talking about the weather on the screen rather than on the phone, which is a little snippet."

In summary, when weather is the big news of the day, it's all hands on deck for reporting information that is crucial to your audience. Everyone in the newsroom will be called on to gather and distribute information essential to those in your coverage area.

Learn as much as you can about weather patterns where you work and live. It is becoming rarer that there are specific times of year for weather events such as a fire, hurricane, or tornado "season," so be ready for anything. Hot weather is lasting longer in some parts of the country, and it's snowing in the "off months" in other parts. Natural disasters can happen anywhere and at any time. Think ahead about what you would do and how to report in these potentially life-altering, and often dangerous, situations.

Meteorologist vs. weather forecaster/reporter

There is a difference in qualifications between these two titles, although the viewer may not notice. The meteorologist is armed with more of a technical background with an expertise in interpreting satellite and radar images of the atmosphere.

The American Meteorology Society (AMS) recommends that a meteorologist should have at least a Bachelor of Science degree in a subject that includes meteorology and geoscience courses.[1] The AMS is the nation's premier scientific and professional organization promoting and disseminating information about the atmospheric, oceanic, hydrologic sciences. It is a non-profit organization, which provides certification programs of excellence to meteorologists.[2]

A weather forecaster, or reporter, collects forecast information from sources like the National Weather Service and then adds some local footage of a flooded road or other visualization to help tell the story.[3]

Both newsroom positions require an ability to communicate information quickly and efficiently. They also need a polished on-air presence.

1   http://work.chron.com/meteorologist-vs-weatherman-3682.html

2   https://www.ametsoc.org/ams/index.cfm/about-ams/

3   http://work.chron.com/education-needed-weather-forecaster-1819.html

EXERCISES AND ACTIVITIES

1. What would you do in this situation?

   A category 5 hurricane is predicted to make landfall in your viewing area.
   Find answers to as many of these questions as possible:
   How do you prepare? What do you do first as a reporter? Do you interview officials first? Others? What kind of visuals do you shoot to help tell stories involving preparations? How does the story change, if at all, if the hurricane is downgraded to a category 2 or 3?

2. When a natural disaster strikes and damage is all around, how do you prioritize stories?

   a. Scenario: There is a major earthquake. The epicenter of the quake was 20 miles away. A few buildings have collapsed in your city. People may be buried in the rubble. Officials have little information at this time. How do you prioritize this information for your audience? Which stories would you cover first? Possible follow-ups?

   b. Scenario: A tornado touches down in your Midwest community. FEMA (Federal Emergency Management Administration) is warning everyone in your area to stay in a shelter. You are a reporter at a local TV station. What do you do? You realize this could be a major story.

   c. Scenario: A late-winter snowstorm catches everyone, including the meteorologists, off guard. A local senior center loses power, but no one can seem to get through by phone. What is the real story here? Who do you talk to and what do you do to get the story?

   d. Scenario: The city in which you live and work is experiencing a three-day heat wave. Temperatures have hovered around 110 degrees Fahrenheit in the middle of the day. The evenings only dip down to 98 degrees. Air conditioning in homes and office buildings is stressed to the breaking point. The first day you reported on the extraordinary heat. The second day, you reported on how people were coping by heading to the beach, pools, etc. Now in its third day, what is your story? Who do you talk to for new perspectives on the heat?

   e. Scenario: A wildfire is spreading in the fields outside of town. Winds are starting to pick up, and your newsroom sends you and a videographer out to cover the story. What do you do first once arriving at the scene? What is your list of priorities in terms of getting information for this story?

3. Which items would you pack in an emergency kit in preparation for a natural disaster? Be specific.

Credits

CHAPTER 13

Budget and financial stories (working with numbers)

> "*Although reporting on budgets might seem less 'sexy' than the usual suspects of war, disaster, and catastrophe, nothing is more fundamentally important: the budget provides the fuel—the money—on which all else runs. It sets out a government's policy priorities in the social, economic, and military sectors. Given this central role, it is clear that it will be the prime target of special interests both within the state bureaucracy and outside.*"
>
> **–Michael Arkus**[1]

Reporting on budgets and financial news will likely be among the most important work you do as a journalist. State, local, and federal government budgets dictate how much money gets allocated to schools, public health, transportation projects, parks, libraries, protective services such as police and fire, and many other important services. The choices made by government officials impact the lives of citizens, sometimes significantly. Special interests will work to influence how lawmakers allocate and spend funds.

Financial stories can be just as important. Reporting on company earnings, nonprofit spending, or how candidates spend public dollars is critical because of the journalist's role as a watchdog. In addition, making sense of Wall Street, financial reports, global markets, and market trends helps the public understand their world and the mechanisms that influence it.

The main issue with budget and financial stories is that they can be dry, complex, and unwieldy, and often remain inaccessible to the lay person. It is your job through your coverage to make these stories accessible by explaining the information in a way that the public can understand, including highlighting and examining elements that are newsworthy or impactful, and relating budget issues to everyday life. It may be difficult for the public to comprehend or make sense of the fact that public school funding has been cut by $1.5 million, but if you

---

1   "Budget Writing Tips for Reporters," Journalism Backgrounders: Publications: Initiative for Policy Dialogue. Accessed June 27, 2016, http://policydialogue.org/publications/backgrounders/budget_writing_tips_for_reporters/en/.

explain by telling the public how many teachers will be laid off, how many music programs may be cut, or how that cut impacts school lunches, then the public has context.

Studies show[2] that cities and countries with a robust news media experience less corruption than those with weaker or non-existent outlets. The media's role as a watchdog of local, regional, and state government is often carried out by reporting on how money is spent, misspent, collected, and allocated. To be an effective journalist in this area, an understanding of how to develop and craft budget and financial stories is critical.

Even if you are not a financial reporter, you may still be called upon to cover a story involving budget, finance, or other numeric data. Many important news stories deal with budgets, financial issues, or other numeric data, and reporters on many different beats must be prepared to handle those stories. For example, a story about why a politician voted a certain way may become a story about campaign contributions from donors seeking influence.

Preparing for the story

Budget and financial stories are often ongoing, so preparing involves more than just beginning to learn about the story a few hours or days before your deadline. You will want to note and keep track of important dates throughout the year, including state and local budget deadlines, dates for corporate quarterly financial releases, notable anniversaries, and other milestones involved in budget and financial processes. You will also want to follow companies, government entities, and nonprofit organizations throughout the year to pay attention to their spending activities.

In addition, it is important to develop and maintain relationships with those involved in the process. For example, if you are reporting on the state budget, you will want to develop relationships with the chief budget officer and other key office personnel as well as legislative leaders, especially those most directly involved in the process of developing and crafting the budget, and those who represent marginalized groups in the community.

Finally, remember that budget and financial stories rarely happen in a vacuum. If you are covering these types of stores, build your knowledge on the industries, organizations, stakeholders, and other players, as well as any previous financial decisions, connections to other entities, and other important information. This will help you provide context, explain meaning, and make connections for your audience when you report on the story. For example, when reporting on the California legislative budget process, John Meyers, Sacramento Bureau Chief for *The Los Angeles Times,* needs to report on the actual events of the day, as well as what they mean. Questions he may ask include:

---

2   Aymo Brunetti and Beatrice Weder, "A Free Press Is Bad News for Corruption." *Journal of Public Economics* 87, no. 7-8 (June 25, 2001): 1801-824. doi:10.1016/s0047-2727(01)00186-4.

- Why are lawmakers proposing cuts to certain areas?
- Does the governor agree or disagree?
- How do the economy and tax revenue impact their decisions?
- How do their decisions impact taxpayers?
- Vulnerable groups?
- How is this similar or different from decisions made during other budget cycles?
- Are lawmakers keeping promises they made during their campaigns?
- How can you help the reader separate politics from collaboration?

Budget stories

For budget stories, you need to understand the sources of revenue. In California, the state raises revenue primarily through various taxes and fees. Taxpayers and interest groups have differing opinions on whether or not they agree with the taxes and fees as currently structured, as well as how much those taxes and fees cost, and who is getting a break versus who is not. It is also important to understand how money is allocated and whether money can be re-allocated. In addition, the Golden State has an initiative process, and voters often vote to pass propositions that specifically allocate funds to one project/service or another, for example, early childhood education or protection of waterways. The more money that gets allocated to a specific place, the less lawmakers have to work with when trying to cover the costs of other governmental activities.

The bottom line is this: Do some work to understand how money is spent and provide voters with context on lawmaker salaries, funding allocations, whether or not lawmakers can move funds from one pot to another, and how this impacts taxpayers.

Financial stories

More and more people have mutual funds, stock portfolios, and 401k accounts tied to the stock market. Therefore, it is important to shed light on the financial dealings of publicly traded companies, fluctuations on Wall Street, activities within the banking industry, government regulatory structure, campaign finance, lobbying, and any other activity that impacts people's savings and the economic landscape.

The 2007 housing crisis and subsequent recession impacted many people across the U.S. and around the world. Countless people lost their homes. Countless others saw their savings disappear, and countless more lost their jobs and livelihoods. Unfortunately, much of the financial reporting leading up to the downturn seemed to be caught up in the euphoria of ever-rising stock prices and strong housing sales. Strong reporting and a watchdog approach to financial journalism may have helped people understand what is going on, make connections, and perhaps even recognize cracks in the system before they became chasms.

Covering the story

If you effectively keep track of budget and financial processes, you should have an easier time covering stories as they come up.

There are many types of financial and budget stories that you may cover, including:

Nuts and bolts

- Who benefits? (For example: Is this good for the shareholder but bad for the citizen?)
- Informational, such as release of corporate financial statements or government reports
- Economic forecasts
- Corporate takeovers, purchases, and bankruptcies
- History/context/foundational info and short-term and long-term trends

Reaction

- Interest groups
- Taxpayers
- Industry experts
- Finance experts
- Lawmakers
- Board members
- Investors

Impact

- Groups or communities
- Taxpayers
- Psychology of investors

Follow-up stories: Is money being used as promised? Diverted?

For daily financial stories, *Bloomberg News*,[3] one of the largest business news organizations in the world, suggests that four questions should be answered:

---

3   "Covering the Financial Markets Intelligently," Journalist's Resource. March 17, 2016. Accessed June 16, 2016, http://journalistsresource.org/tip-sheets/reporting/covering-financial-markets.

- What happened in investments today?
- Why did it happen?
- How does today's move compare with the past?
- Who said what about all of this?

For stories that come out once a year or once a quarter, prepare by asking:

- What are the changes? Why?
- How will they affect people? Which people?
- What are the priorities? Whose priorities are they?
- What are the impacts? (Money moved or cut? New taxes, fees, fines?)

Of course, you'll want to contact the main players involved in the story. However, consider the sidebars that are also important. If you are covering a story about Wall Street gains after a large company announces that it will take jobs overseas, consider also talking to an expert on how this type of move can impact communities who rely on that industry or what that might do to the cost and quality of the product. If you are covering a local budget negotiation, in addition to talking with the mayor and city council members, be sure to talk to stakeholders who rely on budget dollars to provide services, conduct business, and keep community infrastructure sound.

Also find out the source of the data and how it was gathered and assess whether the source or data collection methods are biased. It is a good idea to have a working knowledge of spreadsheets and data-crunching software to ensure that you know what the numbers are saying.

Crafting the story[4]

When compiling your story to share information with your audience, remember, even though these stories involve numbers and data, they are really about communities, politics, society, and our priorities. In short, they are about us. It's your job to put a human face on the story. Read the data and extrapolate the newsworthy topics and issues within that data to help people connect to the story, understand it, and speak up when they disagree with decisions being made. This section focuses primarily on some important do's and don'ts to help strengthen your coverage.

Numbers can make the mind go numb. Even though budget and financial stories are, in essence. numbers stories, limit mention of numbers to important numerical data, and utilize visuals to help make the information clear. Also, offer your audience comparisons to get a sense of scale, or else the concepts may be difficult for people to comprehend. For example, if the

4 Sarah Marshall, "How To Start Out in Financial Journalism." Journalism Jobs (media, Editorial), News for Journalists. February 10, 2012. Accessed June 16, 2016, https://www.journalism.co.uk/skills/how-to-start-out-in-financial-journalism/s7/a547800/.

parks-and-rec budget is being cut by $750,000, let the public know that this is the same as 12 jobs, or that this is the amount it takes to run the youth sports program for one year.

Avoid simply saying that something happened. Instead, explain it and highlight the important points—the information that the public needs.

> **NO**–"The city council spent five hours discussing the budget last night. They will take up the issue again tonight after failing to pass a budget."

> **YES**–"The city council still cannot agree on a budget after spending five hours debating. Sticking points include whether to allocate money to maintaining roads, sewers, and parks or focusing spending on police and fire services. Social service agencies also attended the meeting to ask that more money be directed at services such as early childhood education, housing for the homeless, and job training, which they say have suffered because of budget cuts in previous years."

In addition, use your own words rather than those of someone who may have a vested interest in spinning the story in a certain way. If there is bureaucratic language, cut through it and tell your audience plainly what is going on. Bureaucratic language, news releases, and summaries can often be used to obscure and spin. Your job is to help shine a light and bring transparency to the process.

> **NO**–(fictitious news release from oil company involved in environmentally impactful oil spill)

> "Our company is committed to the environment. To prove this commitment to communities impacted by the spill, we have dedicated $500 million to habitat restoration and clean up."

> **YES**–(example of using multiple sources to ensure the actual facts are reported)

> "X Oil company lost its appeal in court today and was ordered to allocate $500,000 to habitat restoration and environmental cleanup. The company says it will accept the judgment."

Avoid hyperbolic language. Given the pressure for page clicks and views, social media interaction, and simply recognition and attention in the crowded digital landscape, it is tempting to resort to language such as the "plummeting" stock market or "soaring" revenues, when the reality is much more measured. A one-day drop in the stock market does not constitute a trend. When Apple's stock dipped in 2016 for the first time in several years, anyone consuming news may have thought that Armageddon was upon us. News coverage focused on potential problems at the popular tech giant, and some investors dumped their stock. In reality, nothing goes up forever, and Apple stock is no different. In fact, investor Warren Buffet, not one to pay attention to hyperbolic headlines and absolutely one to seek out bargains on the market, bought Apple shares in the wake of the price dip.

Journalist's Resource, part of the Shorenstein Center at Harvard's Kennedy University,[5] provides some guidelines for how to cover financial activity "intelligently."

- One percent drop or less: Use "fell" or "dropped," as well as "declined." Even "moved downward" is acceptable.
- Two to four percent decline: Any of the above, as well as "dipped" and "slumped," which are slightly more serious grades of a fall.
- Rise of up to one percent: "Gained," "increased" or "advanced" are fine here, as are "rose" and "grew."
- Two to four percent increase: Again, "gained," "increased" or "advanced" are fine here, as are "rose" and "grew."
- Be careful not to give too much weight to one theory or another about the market's movement.
- Markets open 24 hours a day around the world.

In addition, remember that some words have a defined meaning. Words such as "recession" or "depression" mean very specific things, but they are often used in news stories to describe downward trends that have not met the definition. Words carry emotion, and it is your job to tell the story, not play on people's fears and euphoria.

Be sure you are actually comparing apples to apples. Sometimes, data reported one way during one year may be reported differently in another year. For example, student debt default data were reported for several years as within two years of students leaving college. However, between 2009 and 2014, the reporting of student loan default data transitioned from two years to three years. The way the data was being reported changed, so data from 2008 and from 2015 would be conveying different information (two-year vs. three-year loan default rates) and could not be compared.[6] Value jumps from moment to moment may have no meaning at all. If the stock market swings 500 points in one day, it is noteworthy, but it is *not* a trend.

5   Chris Roush. "Covering the Financial Markets Intelligently," Journalist's Resource. March 17, 2016. Accessed June 16, 2016, http://journalistsresource.org/tip-sheets/reporting/covering-financial-markets#sthash.8uqgGhKW.dpuf.
6   "What We Do," The Institute for College Access and Success. Accessed June 16, 2016, http://ticas.org/.

Look at the big picture to see how the market behaves over time, and continue to monitor the stock market for potential upward or downward trends.

Of course, as with any story, avoid errors, bias, or misleading the audience. This could be as simple as correctly reporting whether the number is millions, billions, or trillions, or it may mean larger research. Talk to as many sources as possible to ensure you have the full story. If you receive a financial report, move beyond the summary. Often, summaries are written to favor the organization releasing the information. The actual report will give you the information you need. If the story seems too good to be true, *be skeptical.* Explore, research, investigate, ask questions, and know before you publish. As we know, social media will be unforgiving of mistakes. Above all, use your common sense and journalistic skills, as well as your colleagues to discuss ideas.

Examples of strong storytelling

Because numbers can be so dry and inaccessible, many news and information outlets have come up with innovative ways to tell stories involving numbers. Here are a few examples:

"The price of gas" (Center for Investigative Reporting)[7]

Often, stories about oil or gas focus primarily on the day-to-day price of oil, the actions of OPEC, or gas prices around holiday time, but the larger issue of how the oil trade impacts the globe and the environment remain poorly covered. The Center for Investigative Reporting (CIR) (now called Reveal) tackled this unwieldy story by using animation and a simple script. In "The Price of Gas," CIR reporters, producers, and graphic designers teamed up to tell the story of oil's journey from the ground to our cars, and the impacts that journey has along the way.[8]

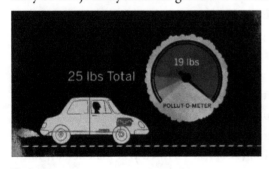

Figure 13.1

Debt buyers (Last Week Tonight with John Oliver on HBO)[7]

Though John Oliver is a comedian and not a journalist, he and his team at *Last Week Tonight* create effective explanatory journalism each week, focusing primarily on one story for much of the 30-minute show. On

---

7   Carrie Ching, Sarah Terry-Cobo, and Arthur Jones. "The Price of Gas" The Center for Investigative Reporting. June 13, 2011. Accessed June 16, 2016, http://cironline.org/reports/price-gas-2447.

8   http://cironline.org/reports/price-gas-2447

June 5, 2016, *Last Week Tonight* helped viewers understand the issues with "debt buying," taking an extremely dry, unsexy, and boring financial story that has a major impact and making it accessible through comedy, stunts, and accessible language and visuals.[9]

Figure 13.2

"#BudgetBeard" & "#NoBudgetNoShave" (Chris Kaergard, Peoria Journal Star)[10]

In 2015, when it became clear that the Illinois state budget would not be passed on time, reporter Chris Kaergard with *The Peoria Journal Star* decided to refrain from shaving until the Republican governor and Democrat-controlled legislature agreed on a budget plan. He thought it would "bring a little color" to the coverage and help focus the audience's attention on this stalemate, which impacted people across the state. Kaergard expected the stalemate to last one or two months. Instead, it lasted until June 30, 2016, and the budget signed on that date was only a six-month stopgap measure. Given the stopgap agreement, Kaergard said on

Twitter that he would shave his beard in a charity event because "the process of negotiation deserves encouragement."[11] Following the progress of the #BudgetBeard was a way to follow the progress of the budget process. A look at Kaergard's Twitter page will show an older picture of a well-groomed and only slightly bearded Kaergard.

As *The Columbia Journalism Review*[12] reports, the paper and other regional news outlets used the beard to help make the story accessible to the audience. They even created an interactive timeline matching the growth

Figure 13.3   Budget Beard: Chris Kaergard

---

9   https://www.youtube.com/watch?v=hxUAntt1z2c

10   Jackie Spinner, "How One Reporter's Beard Gimmick Became a Useful Tool for Covering Illinois' Budget Stalemate." Columbia Journalism Review. April 12, 2016. Accessed June 16, 2016, http://www.cjr.org/united_states_project/chris_kaergard_budget_beard.php.

11   Chris Kaergard, @ChrisKaergard on Twitter. June 30, 2016. Accessed June 30, 2016, https://twitter.com/ChrisKaergard..

12   Jackie Spinner, "How One Reporter's Beard Gimmick Became a Useful Tool for Covering Illinois' Budget Stalemate." Columbia Journalism Review. April 12, 2016. Accessed June 16, 2016, http://www.cjr.org/united_states_project/chris_kaergard_budget_beard.php.

of the beard to story developments. The #BudgetBeard has also been used on social media to help cover the story. "The numbers they are talking about statewide are so staggering, people have a hard time comprehending them," according to Kaergard. "The shtick of the beard gets you in the door, and then you talk about the issues, and you hope you are compelling enough."

In covering the same story, WBEZ put together an effective explainer[13] to help walk the audience through the process. It addressed questions from the audience about how the budget gets passed, how money is allocated, where money comes from, and what is and is not accounted for.

These are examples of well-crafted stories involving numbers, data, and other information perceived as inaccessible. Each story makes the information accessible to the audience by simplifying, breaking information down into manageable chunks, using visuals, and providing examples. The journalists who worked on these stories provide valuable guidance on how to cover a budget or financial story well.

Conclusion

Your job when covering a budget or financial story is to give people information that they can use to understand the story and how it impacts their lives.
To do this:

- Help make sense of complicated budget or financial data
- Pull out and highlight important information and points
- Point out where finances and budget priorities align or fail to align with public expectations and official promises
- Use multimedia and interactive elements, if they will help tell the story
- Use visuals; *be sure they are accurate and tell a story*
- Contextualize to larger societal or community issues

Coverage of financial and budget stories will be among the most important work you do as a journalist. Money makes the world go around, and those in control of the money may not always be taking into consideration more vulnerable populations or even be thinking about the long-term implications of their decisions. A watchdog journalist can help make the process transparent, allowing everyday citizens and taxpayers to understand and, if they choose, participate in the process.

---

13 Dan Weissmann, "Illinois Has No Budget, So Where Do State Tax Dollars Go, Anyway?" WBEZ. April 11, 2016. Accessed June 16, 2016, https://www.wbez.org/shows/curious-city/illinois-has-no-budget-do-where-do-state-tax-dollars-go-anyway/3197f0ba-ce77-44c6-9180-04088ccc8f76.

EXERCISES AND ACTIVITIES

1. Research the status of the budget of your state, county, or city.
    b. Craft a story about the current process
    c. Be sure to choose an audience and write about what that audience may care most about.
    d. Provide historical context, including:
        i. Past spending priorities
        ii. Any controversies during the previous budget process
        iii. How politics played into negotiations.
4. Assess previous coverage of the budget process in your city, county, or state?
    a. What are the effective elements of the coverage?
    b. What do you think the reporters missed?
    c. Do you pick up on any bias? Explain.
4. Choose a company that is publicly traded.
    a. Find recent news coverage on that company.
    b. Explain how the company is being covered.
    c. What do you extrapolate from the coverage?
    d. Do you think the coverage represents what is actually happening? Explain.
5. Find a story written about the U.S. economy, housing market, or stock market in early-to-mid 2007 (before the financial crisis took hold).
    f. How is the story covering its topic?
    g. Do you get any sense that the reporter knew what was coming?
    h. What do you think the reporter missed?
    i. Why do you think the reporter missed information hinting at problems ahead?

Resources

- **Budget writing tips for reporters**
  http://policydialogue.org/publications/backgrounders/budget_writing_tips_for_reporters/en/

- **Tips for covering the budget story**
  http://ugandaradionetwork.com/s/tips-for-covering-the-budget-story/

- **How to report numbers in the news**
  https://www.journalism.co.uk/skills/how-to-report-numbers-in-the-news/s7/a547659/

- **Tips for writing better business stories**

  http://journalistsresource.org/tip-sheets/writing/writin-better-business-stories

- **Understanding numbers as a journalist**

  https://www.journalism.co.uk/skills/how-to-get-to-grips-with-numbers-as-a-journalist/s7/a534975/

- **Covering financial markets**

  http://journalistsresource.org/tip-sheets/reporting/covering-financial-markets

- **How to start out in financial journalism**

  https://www.journalism.co.uk/skills/how-to-start-out-in-financial-journalism/s7/a547800/

- **Budget checklist**

  http://www.sbcc.edu/journalism/manual/checklist/budget.php

Credits

CHAPTER 14

Op-eds and reviews

"The fact that people will pay you to talk to people and travel to interesting places and write about what intrigues you, I'm just amazed by that."

–Nicholas D. Kristof, political commentator and author[1]

In op-ed writing, it's all about you and your views. Whether you're covering the heated presidential race between Donald Trump and former Secretary of State Hillary Clinton or a shooting at a high school, you'll be expected to tell your audience where you stand on the issue.

Of course, you'll need to back up your opinion with facts, and that's where fair and balanced reporting comes into play. Indeed, everything you've learned in your earlier chapters will help you to write clear and powerful op-ed pieces that could be published or aired at major news outlets or articles that could run on your own blog.

The big thing to remember about op-eds is that your opinion counts. Instead of avoiding the use of "I," or "we," you will embrace it—in most instances. Instead of avoiding subjective language, you will welcome it.

In this chapter, we'll learn how to:

- Recognize the difference between mainstream news stories and op-ed pieces
- Understand what questions to ask yourself before writing the piece
- Understand how to structure an op-ed piece for print or broadcast
- Understand how to pitch top editors or publish on your own

The difference between news and opinion

A news story that reaches thousands or millions of people has the power to change a person's life. Sometimes the coverage is positive, meaning the subject is portrayed as a hero, as in the case of a firefighter who rescues a puppy from a burning house. In other cases, the coverage is negative, meaning the subject is portrayed as a villain, as in the case of a banker who has been

---

1 Nicholas Kristof. Accessed March 23, 2018, http://izquotes.com/quote/105389.

arrested for bilking investors out of millions of dollars. In every case, it's important to air or publish truth, which is the first tenet of the SPJ Code of Ethics: Seek truth and report it. There are many reasons why ethical journalists share only what they know to be truthful, but one major reason is that a journalist who has diligently sought to interview all sides and base allegations on verifiable information will have a better chance of defending himself or herself against libel or defamation. In the 1964 *New York Times v. Sullivan* case, the Supreme Court ruled that "a State cannot, under the First and Fourteenth Amendments, award damages to a public official for defamatory falsehood relating to his official conduct unless he proves "actual malice"—that the statement was made with knowledge of its falsity or with reckless disregard of whether it was true or false."[2]

Simply stated, truth was *The New York Times'* greatest defense. Thus, when writing news, journalists avoid basing their stories on gossip, innuendo, and rumor. In fact, many major news outlets will "hold" or delay airing a story that has not been checked out with officials or verified through public records and other official documentation.

Because reporters depend on sources willing to provide truthful information, it's important for reporters to convince sources that they are fair, honest, and willing to hear all sides. Thus, journalists should withhold judgment until they hear from all sides, and even after the story airs or is published, journalists should remain objective about the story because they will in most cases need to talk to the same sources again. If a source feels that you've "burned" him or her, meaning you have not been fair or broke a promise, he or she will never talk to you again. That's especially problematic if you are covering a beat and need to interact with the same sources to find out what's happening each day.

That's why most major news outlets clearly delineate news from opinion and often separate opinion pages from the news section. Students writing for their campus publication can choose to follow a similar model, separating their news department from the editorial pages. A good reason to do this is to show potential sources and subjects of stories that the news side has not taken a stance on an issue and is open to hearing all ideas and all sides in any particular debate or issue.

Indeed, the SPJ Code of Ethics clearly states in its principles that ethical journalists should clearly "label advocacy and commentary."[3]

Furthermore, the SPJ Code of Ethics states that journalists should avoid conflicts of interest, real or perceived. Imagine this scenario: A news reporter announces on Twitter that he does not like Hillary Clinton's political stance on climate change. This reporter, who had been previously been given one-on-one interviews with former First Lady, calls to ask for another interview. How likely will she or her public relations team say yes? Most likely, the PR team

---

2   Justia website. Accessed Jun 15, 2016, https://supreme.justia.com/cases/federal/us/376/254/case.html.

3   "SPJ Code of Ethics." Society of Professional Journalists. Accessed August 25, 2015, http://www.spj.org/ethicscode.asp.

will turn down the reporter's request, and that's because the reporter has revealed a perceived conflict of interest. Any time a news reporter declares a strong stance on an issue, it becomes harder for sources to see that reporter as fair or objective. Indeed, there have been cases where reporters who take a clear position on an issue have been removed from their beat. In March 2014, *The Advocate* reported:

> "*The San Francisco Chronicle* removed its lead city hall reporter and photographer from covering the city's same-sex marriage controversy after the longtime lesbian partners were wed last week. In a decision he characterized as difficult and painful, executive editor Phil Bronstein told the paper's staff on Monday that reporter Rachel Gordon and photographer Liz Mangelsdorf had been pulled from the story after editors concluded there was a potential for the appearance of a conflict of interest."[4]

Even though a reporter has been fair and objective for many months or years, they can be removed from a particular issue or beat because of an action that appears to be a conflict of interest.

In contrast, a news outlet will take a strong stance when writing editorials, articles written by the outlet's editorial board. In addition, news outlets will feature commentary by their own staff writers, clearly marked as commentary or opinion, and feature opinion from the public. The opinion from the public is known as "op-ed pieces." In this section, we will focus on op-ed pieces, which are generally written by politicians, doctors, professors, activists, entertainers, and other members of the public. Op-ed pieces vary in length, depending on publication, and most news outlets accept unsolicited submissions electronically. Anyone, even those not trained in journalism, can get published in the op-ed section by writing a piece that is compelling, clear, and presents a much-needed perspective on a timely issue.

With that in mind, consider these three questions BEFORE you write and submit your op-ed to a major editor:

A. **Why you?**
B. **Why now?**
C. **Who cares?**

---

4 "Lesbian Reporters Removed From Marriage Beat After Marrying Each Other," The Advocate, March 2004. Accessed June 25, 2016, http://www.advocate.com/news/2004/03/17/lesbian-reporters-removed-marriage-beat-after-marrying-each-other-11701.

First question: Why you?

When pitching an editor, they will want to know what makes you an expert in the subject matter. This doesn't mean you have to be a Ph.D., a lawyer, or politician to write op-eds. It just means that you have to know what you're talking about. For example, the president of a local high school might not be considered the top expert on national politics, but she or he would be the best person to talk about campus politics. Alternatively, a bicyclist who rides to work every day could be the perfect person to write about the dangers of commuting by bike.

In addition to knowing a lot about your subject, mainstream news editors are looking for op-eds written by people who are passionate about those issues. One way to demonstrate this passion is through social media and blogging. Writing about what moves you most on Twitter, Tumblr, and other platforms will help others understand that you really know your stuff. Just remember to be thoughtful and fair when sharing your views. Cite your sources and base your opinion on research and facts.

Second question: Why now?

Opinion editors seek commentary that is timely and relevant.

- How can you engage in current events and still write about what matters to you most?
- What makes your view important now? How does it affect more than your circle of friends or family?

Let's say that you want to write about the high cost of tuition at your school. The key is to find out why an editor would publish or air that story now. Are politicians debating legislation that would lower tuition? Did a university president recently say tuition wasn't so bad? Did a new study reveal some new facts about college tuition? That's when you know it's time to write and pitch your story to editors.

If you're having a hard time pinning your story to a timely issue, here are some techniques that can help:

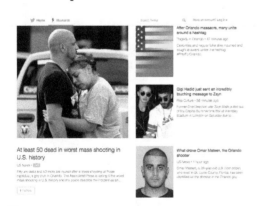

Figure 14.1

Twitter Moments: Twitter now curates tweets, images, and video on hot topics and presents them as collections. By clicking on the tab called "Twitter Moments," you can instantly see what folks are talking about. For example, if you wanted to learn what happened after a gunman rushed into a nightclub and killed dozens of people, Twitter Moments allowed you to see a series of tweets, video, and images that helped you to understand what happened.

Twitter Search: You can also use Twitter's advanced search box to refine a search by keywords, people, dates, and places. You can also search by hash tags. Popular hash tags are a great way to find out what people are talking about. A quick way to find the advanced search tool is by bookmarking this link: https://twitter.com/search-advanced?lang=en.

Instagram Search: On the mobile app, you can search by tying a keyword into the search box, and can narrow a search by top posts, people, tags or places. Instagram will also tell you the number of posts that a particular keyword has generated. This can help you determine what's popular on Instagram, which had more than 400 million users by the summer of 2016.

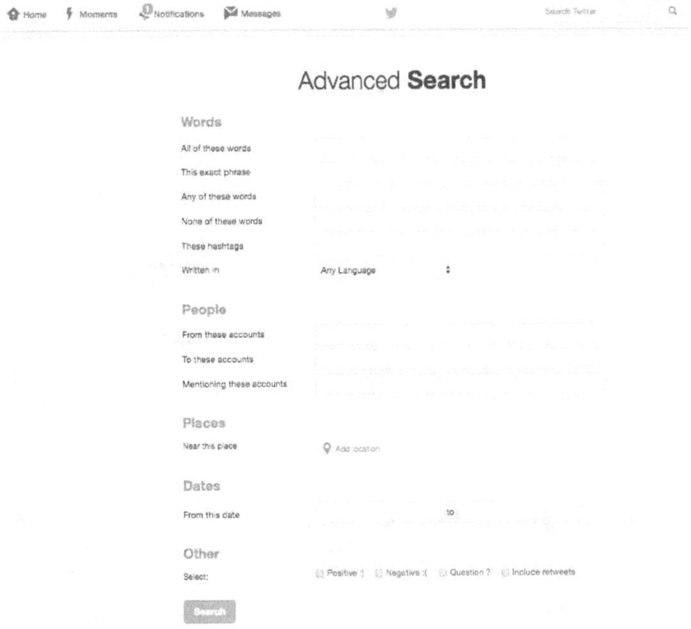

Figure 14.2

Beyond Instagram, a number of apps allow you to search for popular hashtags. One is called Hashtagify, and it's a free app that gives you a great overview of the most popular tags on social media. By using Hashtagify, you can quickly see #love is one of the most popular hashtags of all time. Other popular ones include #tbt, which means Throwback Thursday. This helps to explain why so many people will share an old photo on Thursdays.

Another great tool to find out what news is trending around the world is Google. A search of Google News will yield the biggest stories of the day, stories that you might want to comment on, or use as part of your research in an op-ed. For example, many of the articles and images at the top of the screen appear to be about Donald Trump, indicating that issues relating to Trump are coming up high in search results.

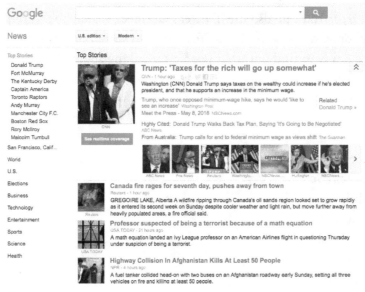

Figure 14.3

Third question: Who cares?

The last question to ask before writing your op-ed: Who is your audience? If you're trying to get your piece in front of powerful politicians in D.C., seek publication at a large newspaper or station, such as *The New York Times* or NPR. They both accept op-ed submissions from the public. If you want to weigh in on a local issue, seek publication at your local news outlet. If you want your commentary to go viral, consider well-crafted messages across social media platforms. In any case, you'll want to study the submission guidelines of each outlet. They all have their own rules. Many sites, such as the Op-Ed Project, http://www.the-opedproject.org/, will give you some idea of where to pitch your piece.

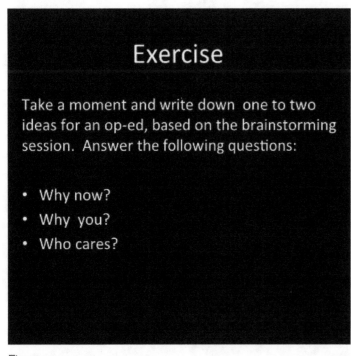

Figure 14.4

Op-ed structure

1. Opening that compels readers to care
2. Nut graph that establishes the focus of the story, why the story is important, and why it's being written now. You must base this nut graph on original reporting (interviews with people and studies that have been verified)
3. Acknowledge opposing views (try to reach an opponent and ask them questions)
4. Two to three points with quotes and/or data (this will usually take anywhere from three to six paragraphs)
5. Solutions or suggestions to the problem
6. Conclusion

Most important, stay focused. When writing about a complex issue such as domestic violence, it is easy to try to cover every aspect of domestic violence, including prevention, the most violent cases, the victims, the perpetrators, and what police or the government is doing to reduce the number of cases. The reality, however, is that your submission has to be pretty short, usually 500 to 1,200 words in print or online and about two minutes for KQED or NPR. Think about what your goal is in writing about domestic violence. Is it to call for more action in Congress? Then tailor the piece around that point, and you'll stay under the word count.

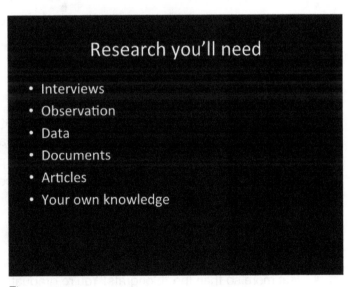

Research you'll need

- Interviews
- Observation
- Data
- Documents
- Articles
- Your own knowledge

Figure 14.5

Radio commentary

- Assert clear point of view/opinion
- Connect personal stories to bigger social themes
- Include opposing points of view
- Keep it short

De-constructing radio commentary

Here is a piece written for an opinion-writing class at San Francisco State. In this piece,[5] which was submitted to *KQED*, Ashley Bowen talks about the experience of graduating from college:

> Groggy eyes at 8 a.m. Ten-hour laborious days spent at school. Eyes bloodshot from staring at a computer's bright radiating screen in the wee hours of the morning.
>
> Wake up, eat, class, eat, class, work, homework. Repeat.
>
> This droning schedule has been my life for the past four years: 1,460 days. 35,040 hours. 2,102,400 minutes. 126,144,000 seconds.

This opening gives a personalized account of what it feels like to study at the college level. The writer also offers statistics to back up what she's saying in her opening.

Nut graph

> This is the hectic and demanding life of a college student aspiring to graduate within four years.

Point one

> Yet at last, this incredible feat I've been climbing towards has been nearly accomplished; it's happening, I'm graduating. Soon I will be striding down the walkway, donning an oversized purple gown with the dangling tassel from the cap swinging in my face, accepting the thin piece of paper I've strenuously worked for.

Point two

> But more so than the "Congrats! You're graduating!" comments I was expecting to hear, different remarks have been consistently chiming in my ears.
>
> "So what are you doing after graduation?
>
> "Any jobs lined up?
>
> "Where will you be working next?"
>
> "What's in store for you?"

---

5   Ashley Bowen, class commentary for radio on life after graduation, April 2016, J750 Opinion Writing Class at San Francisco State University.

Internships, job opportunities, grad school, traveling—these options are the average person's response, and I can even attest to these, as I hope some may come true. I have applied to numerous internships, I have searched for job openings, and I've even considered the possibility of taking a few weeks off to travel.

and the downsides are serious.

Figure 14.6

Yet the future is still so uncertain. I am simply stuck playing the waiting game, and you know what, that's OK.

Solution

Every time someone demands an answer, I just want to honestly say, "Chill out—I just made a major accomplishment."

After spending the last four years trying to hastily achieve a degree on time, I, for once, am content with the fact that I may not have a specific plan directly after graduation. I may start working the week after, or it may take a couple months.

Conclusion

I believe you can just be happy with the fact that you did it, you graduated. I have my whole life ahead of me, and the time to take to figure out what's in store.

A great example of a radio piece is done by Cory Isaacson,[6] who uses her personal experience as a lawyer working with young people to talk about why police on campuses don't make a lot of sense. She does not believe it makes a lot of sense, and she states it in her piece. She also offers data to support her argument.

---

6   Cory Isaacson, "Cops on Campus," KQED Perspectives, Sept. 23, 2015. Accessed June 20, 2016, http://ww2.kqed.org/perspectives/2015/09/23/cops-on-campus/.

To listen to her commentary or to read her piece, you can go here: http://ww2.kqed.org/perspectives/2015/09/23/cops-on-campus/

Elements of a successful op-ed/pitch

- Expertise in the subject matter
- Solid social presence and/or track record in publishing
- Timely news hook
- Unique perspective
- One clear focus
- Offer solutions

Submission guidelines vary from publication to publication. Be sure to go to the website and review the rules before submissions. Editors have strict rules on word count and topic areas they publish or air.

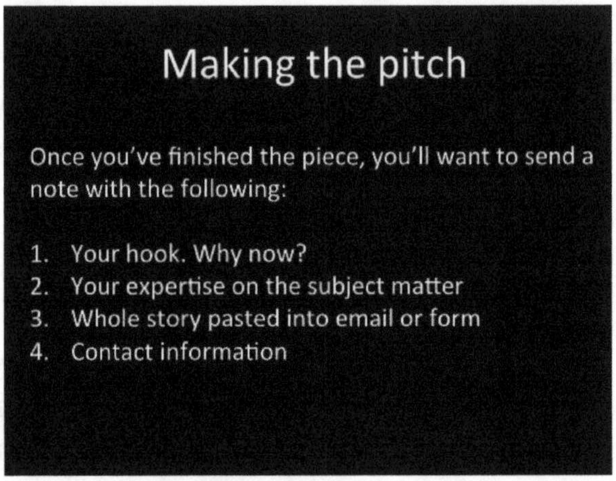

Additional exercises

1. Think about your most recent news articles or papers from other courses. Which of these pieces are you most passionate about? Did one of these news stories get your blood boiling?
2. From your list, choose one that can be turned into an op-ed after answering these three questions:

   a. Why you?
   b. Why now?
   c. Who cares?

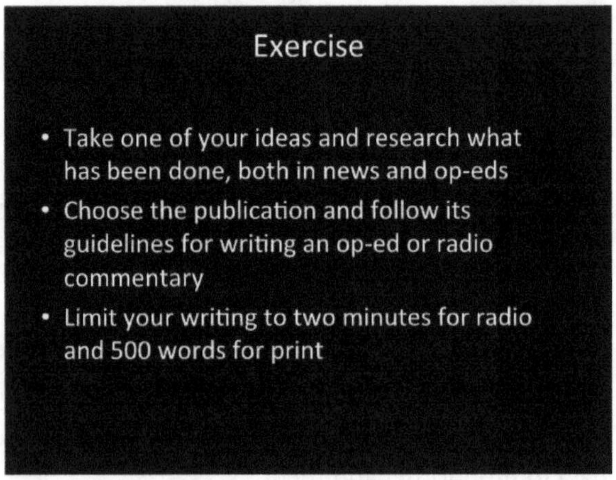

Making the pitch

Once you've finished the piece, you'll want to send a note with the following:

1. Your hook. Why now?
2. Your expertise on the subject matter
3. Whole story pasted into email or form
4. Contact information

Figure 14.7

Exercise

- Take one of your ideas and research what has been done, both in news and op-eds
- Choose the publication and follow its guidelines for writing an op-ed or radio commentary
- Limit your writing to two minutes for radio and 500 words for print

Figure 14.8

Writing reviews

Like commentary, reviews allow journalists and others to express their opinion on a particular topic. In this case, a writer can express their opinion on a restaurant, a movie, a place, a book, just about anything. The difference between a journalistic review and a rant is that the review is fair. Just as you learned in writing op-ed pieces, you want to do your due diligence in seeking truth in reviews. The way to achieve this is simple: Refrain from commenting on a movie, book, or a restaurant until you have watched the entire movie, read all 365 pages of someone's novel, or tasted enough plates at a restaurant to know what's good and bad. You should also attempt to reach the director, the actors, the writer, the owner, and others involved in the event, person, or place you are reviewing.

In many cases, most places will invite the press to a screening, allowing writers to see a movie or show before it opens to the public. This makes sense because you, the reviewer, will have a chance to share your insight on an upcoming event. Just remember, don't be a spoiler. Write just enough about a movie, show, or book that others can discover the ending on their own. In rare instances, when you decide you just have to address the ending in your review, give your audience a spoiler alert. This allows the audience to choose whether or not to read, watch, or listen to your review. Questions to ask when reviewing a movie, book, etc. include:

- Is the story believable?
- What type of genre is it?
- What stands out for you and others watching the movie? The performance of the actors? The cinematography? The sound? Costumes?
- What types of emotions did it evoke in you, or others who watched it? (Be sure to ask others who watched or read it, and feel free to interview them.)
- What was the director or writer's intent? Did they achieve it?
- How long is the movie or show? How many pages are in the book?
- Who wrote the screenplay? Who wrote the book? Who is the director?
- What are the names of the actors playing the main and supporting characters?
- What's the plot?
- Are there other movies, shows, and books like the one you're reviewing?

One way to learn about what others consider exceptional in film is to check out the Oscars. The Academy Awards can be a way for a new reviewer to learn how to dissect a movie or show and offer fair but helpful reviews for the audience.

When writing about restaurants, music venues, or shows, don't forget to talk about the atmosphere. Is the place noisy? Too dark? Crowded? Are the chairs uncomfortable? Be sure to describe the venue because this is important when your audience is deciding whether to check out the show or restaurant.

EXERCISES AND ACTIVITIES

1. List your top three favorite movies. For each movie, explain why you liked it. Find out the name of the director, the screenplay writer, and the names of the major actors. Explain the plot in your own words. Don't copy anything from a website or press release or another person's article. Only comment on scenes you've watched, not what others have told you about.

2. Choose your favorite show and write a 250-word blog post about it. In addition, produce a short video clip or podcast on the piece.

3. Go to your favorite restaurant and write a 450-word blog about it. Be sure to include the name of the restaurant and the owner and be sure to describe the atmosphere on your visit. Also, try the most popular dishes and share with others if possible. Ask them what they think about the food or wine or atmosphere. Before publishing or sharing your piece, try to interview the dining staff and ask to speak to the chef or the owner. Most important, let the restaurant know you are doing a review (wait until you try their food), and let them know when you plan to publish or air the piece. This goes back to a journalist's effort to be fair.

Credits

CHAPTER 15

Digital media 101: Blogging, micro-blogging, and promotion

> *"I get a lot of nasty tweets, and sometimes nasty emails, and sometimes nasty phone calls. But, you know, I believe in facts. I'm here for the facts. It is not personal. I'm not political. What are the facts? People like to make up facts, or they like to act as if they somehow don't have to answer questions, and they do. … I think they are offended that I know the facts, that I'll say, 'Well, here's the study. Let me read it to you.' Or, 'here's the quote that you said six months ago, which completely contradicts what you're telling us now.'"*
>
> **–Soledad O'Brien[1]**

You've gathered your news elements, conducted your interviews, and researched your sources. You are ready to compile your story. Or perhaps you're at the beginning of the process and want to set yourself up online and create a portal for your work. In this chapter, we will focus on both the technical and creative sides of digital media as it relates to journalism. First, we will go over how to set yourself up in cyberspace. Then, we will discuss strategies for effectively presenting your story online.

The set up

Though many people get their news through social media posts, and you should have a presence on social media (which we will discuss in a bit), it is important to have a home or portal for your work—basically, a website.

You have many choices for which platform to use. You may also hear them called CMS (Content Management Systems) or website builders. Each will provide you with a multi-page website capable of hosting and embedding text, video, images, and other content, including

---

1 Wendy Williams, "Soledad O'Brien Says It Like She Means It." YouTube, November 09, 2012. Accessed April 01, 2018, https://www.youtube.com/watch?v=ngRHr-uQHcQ.

blog streams. There are too many to properly cover here, and new platforms will emerge, but we provide an overview of those that are the most popular at the moment.

Before we begin, a few definitions you should know:

- **CMS**—stands for content management system. It is where you build and maintain your website. Also called website builder or platform.
- **Hosting**—When you create content, it must live or be hosted somewhere. This is the host. Many CMS platforms offer hosting as part of the package. Users who have more advanced skills or want a more customized experience may choose to host their website through a separate host, such as BlueHost, HostGator, WP Engine, or GoDaddy (among others). This will be an added cost.
- **Plug-In/App**—A piece of software or code that adds functionality to your website. For example, you may add a slider/rotator plug-in to your homepage.
- **SEO**—Stands for search engine optimization. SEO actions, such as adding tags to your website and posts and infusing commonly searched words into titles and content, help make your site more searchable online.
- **Analytics**—Stats on your website traffic telling you how many people have visited your site, read your work, etc.

As of this writing, WordPress has been the most popular choice for a while, but other platforms are gaining ground. Wix, Weebly, and Squarespace provide an easy user interface, which makes setting up your site simpler than ever.

WordPress

By far the most popular CMS is WordPress, which is used by nearly 75 million websites—that's 25 percent of all websites on Earth. WordPress offers both free and paid options for creating a website, and you can make it as simple or complex as you want. In addition, you can choose from a large variety of free and paid theme options, which set the look and feel of your site. From there, you may customize your theme to give it the look, feel, and functionality you desire. Some customizations are free, but many will require you to pay for the "pro" version of the theme. WordPress does not have its own image library, but you are free to upload your own images, videos, GIFs, graphics, PDFs, and any other media you need. Adding pages and posts is relatively easy. Just go to the section you need, click "add new," and then create your content and configure your page or post.

Some notable companies and organizations using WordPress[2] include:

Forbes.com—A business news and financial site, it boasts a clean interface above the fold, though things get a little less well laid out as we scroll down. The clear, bold images; short, strong, easily readable headlines; and simple color scheme make this a news site that is easy to engage with (Fig. 15.1).

---

2   "Notable WordPress Users." WordPress.com. Accessed June 16, 2016, https://wordpress.com/notable-users/.

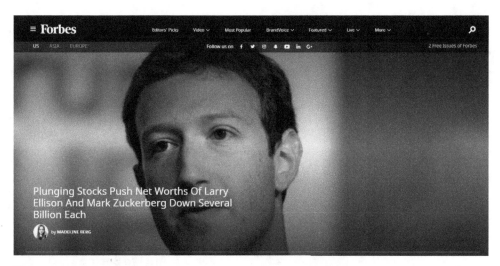

Figure 15.1

TechCrunch.com—A popular technology blog that focuses on startups and new ideas (Fig. 15.2). Though this site is a bit busier above the fold than Forbes, the information is relevant and cleanly presented. TechCrunch also gives users a chance to contribute tips with a prominent link on the top right. A scroll down the page reveals a consistent layout and deep story count. The homepage video plays automatically, which is a plus or minus, depending on taste.

Figure 15.2

FiveThirtyEight.com—A blog written by Nate Silver and dedicated to political polling and other statistical predictions associated with big stories, including sports (Fig. 15.3). The site's theme is clear, and every element supports its mission. Visuals are used thoughtfully and include images, graphs and charts, and interactive elements. The layout is a bit traditional, which works for the content.

Figure 15.3

Sony's PlayStation Blog—A destination for PlayStation fans and gamers, the page offers visuals on top of visuals and can feel too busy and cluttered, but it provides a strong portal for gamers to engage with supplemental content, including video, stories about the industry, interactive elements, social media, and the PlayStation store (Fig. 15.4).

Figure 15.4

Jay-Z's LifeAndTimes.com—A site focused on Jay-Z's hobbies and interests, the layout is a bold visual grid, which offers visitors access to a lot of content. For Jay-Z fans interested in his interests, this site provides an experience that can last as long as the user likes. By clicking on a panel, the user may find music, videos, visuals, and relevant stories (Fig. 15.5).

Figure 15.5

KatyPerry.com—Videos, lyrics, ringtones, and more from the singer/songwriter. This site takes a minimalist approach when it comes to initial content offerings on the homepage but provides rich visuals in keeping with the singer's persona (Fig. 15.6). The scroll-down function feels a bit amateurish. Though the initial presentation is striking, the site may benefit by bringing a few more important elements above the fold.

Figure 15.6

Other sites that use WordPress include General Motors, EBay Inc., UPS Upside, CNN Blogs, Mashable, and BoingBoing.

WordPress.com offers sites hosted by WordPress (more about hosting in a bit). WordPress.org offers sites that you can host using any service you like. For someone just starting out, go with WordPress.com.

WordPress pros

- Large community: If you have issues, the many WordPress users and plug-in creators will chime in to assist you on the WordPress support forum.
- Easy to get started: The step-by-step sign-up and website-creation process for WordPress is simple. However, you may need to consult tutorials for how to add pages and posts, customize your site, or alter the settings. The process is easy but may not be intuitive to everyone.
- Many structured themes: Though themes allow color, font, and widget customizations, the primary design is set. For those with little design savvy, having a structured theme ready to go is a great relief, allowing the user to focus primarily on content.
- Simple platform and plugin updates: Often the user will just need to click a button, and WordPress will do the rest.
- Hosting options: With WordPress, you can choose to host through WordPress (.com) or host somewhere else (.org).
- Offers basic analytics telling you how many people are visiting your site and reading your work.

WordPress cons

- Lack of flexibility / difficult to make large customizations: WordPress themes are fairly structured and standardized, which is great for those who don't want to deal with design but not so great for those who want custom functionality. Any customizations generally become CSS hacks and often look that way.
- Customization options not intuitive: Though a quick online tutorial will guide you in the right direction, it can initially be difficult to figure out how to make the basic customizations or setups offered in the WordPress interface.
- Updates can be a mixed bag: WordPress updates are meant to improve your site and interface, and they often do, but updates may not serve your needs and may even cause problems for your site, especially if you've customized it. Though it is a good idea to accept updates if given the option, you may want to research any concerns or bugs before accepting.
- Not all themes are optimized for mobile, though plenty are; you should check before choosing that theme.
- Cannot switch domain name—this functionality was removed in a recent update.

Wix

Tens of millions of websites now use Wix.[3] The primary draws of Wix are the gorgeous website templates, plug-and-play functionality, freedom to alter the design and elements, and overall ease of use. This platform makes it easy for those with little to no coding or web knowledge to create a nice-looking site. Its drag-and-drop functionality means you can place your elements on the page or canvas and see right away how the page looks. Then you can reposition in real time and publish when you're ready.

Wix's click-and-choose, click-and-change, and drag-and-drop interface is intuitive for many digital users. It is easy to create a simple website with a few basic pages in less than an hour.

Organizations using Wix include:

Hope Care Management—Hope Care, a geriatric-care-management organization, has a site that is clean, easy to navigate, and has an easy-to-use menu. Each page provides basic information in an easily readable format with corresponding visuals (Fig. 15.7).

Figure 15.7

Food Market Chiswick—A farmer's market in a London suburb. This site's job is to entice you to the food market, and it does that with stunning visuals of the food offered at the market (Fig. 15.8). Visitors can get pleasantly lost in the yummy-looking images or scroll or click to find relevant information about how to host, how to visit, or how to engage with the staff.

---

3   "About Us," Wix.com. Accessed June 27, 2016, http://www.wix.com/about/us.

Wix pros

- No coding necessary
- Strong free image library
- Image-editing options included in platform
- Strong free app market
- Modern templates and many customization options
- Apps are not open source, so quality control is better than on WordPress.

WIX cons

- Cannot switch templates
- Design Challenges: The drag-and-drop functionality in Wix can be a nightmare for those with little-to-no design savvy. Without guidance, your website may end up looking cluttered and disjointed.
  - Note: Wix does offer guidelines and snap grids that help line elements up.
- Too many menus: often in Wix, it may feel as if wherever you click, a menu will pop up. This may be disorienting and frustrating at first, but as you learn about the functionality, the disorientation may subside.

Figure 15.8

- It always asks you whether you want to "leave page": This can cause your heart to drop because you may think you made changes that you did not save or accidentally moved something. Just know that Wix will ask this when you close your browser, whether there are changes to be saved or not.
- Analytics function behind a paywall. To see analytics about your site, you must purchase at least the basic package.

Tumblr

Tumblr is both a micro-blog and a social media platform, allowing you to create and share content within a community. The most popular content includes short-form blogs (less than 1,000 words but even shorter in the case of Tumblr), image-focused blogs, and video blogs. Users can choose which genres of content they want to engage with and connect with friends and those who have common interests.

Figure 15.9

Some examples of popular Tumblr blogs[4] include:

Newsweek Science—Focuses on visuals dealing with science and health news (Fig. 15.10). As with many Tumblr sites, content is king, and *Newsweek* takes full advantage, choosing a clean, newsy layout; presenting strong images; and writing clean, simple, newsy copy that compels the visitor to dive more deeply into the site.

Figure 15.10

Comedy Central—Blog filled with GIFs, memes, and moments from the channel's shows (Fig. 15.9). This site is less successful than *Newsweek* in terms of presentation. The background is too sparse, and the theme of the site is not immediately apparent. Only when the visitor takes a look at the stories is a connection made to comedy.

---

4   Megan Rose Dickey, "These Are the 10 Most Popular Tumblr Blogs." Business Insider. May 20, 2013. Accessed June 16, 2016, http://www.businessinsider.com/most-popular-tumblr-blogs-2013-5.

The Daily Show—A blog filled with GIFs from the show, pop-culture moments, behind-the-scenes moments at *The Daily Show*, and other satirical moments (Fig. 15.11). This site is filled with visuals, pop-culture references, and interactivity. The layout is modeled after a straight news site (see *Newsweek*), and similar stories may be covered, but the approach is a bit more irreverent.

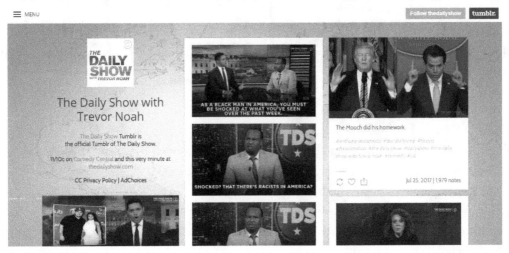

Figure 15.11

American Museum of Natural History—A blog showcasing the specimens on display and in the archives at the museum. Museum site curators do a great job of presenting content of interest to Tumblr users, making it accessible, and bringing its exhibits to life, including such content as a GIF of a dinosaur skeleton, a video featuring animated microbes being interviewed on the streets of New York, and a text conversation between a dinosaur and a blue whale (Fig. 15.12).

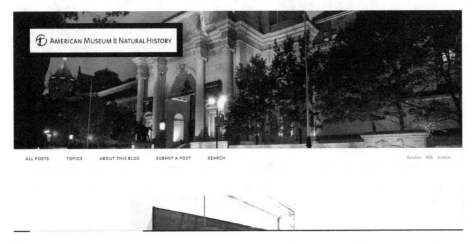

Figure 15.12

RadioLab—Pull quotes, images, and other visuals are connected to the work of this cutting-edge podcast. Though RadioLab uses Tumblr's interface well, there is surprisingly little audio content for a radio podcast. Instead, users must click on links to get to that content. The dark gray, light gray, and blue interface is a bit simple, and there are few other visuals to break it up, but it can be pleasing in its own way.

Figure 15.13

As for more topic-specific Tumblr blogs, check out Nerdology, Reasons My Son Is Crying, and Minecraft News.

TUMBLR pros

- Easy to write and share content
- Strong widget library for customizing your page
- Built-in community and genre-specific tagging
- Great for posting visual elements
- Great opportunities for how-to or topic-specific blog feeds

TUMBLR cons

- Lack of strong SEO options
- Very few themes offer multiple pages, meaning your look may not be as professional as you may want it to be
- More of a personal approach; if you're looking for something more professional, consider another option
- People may not take you seriously

Other strong web platforms you can check out include Weebly, Squarespace, Jimdo, and Blogger. Those with coding experience may be interested in Drupal or Joomla. They all offer varying degrees of cost, design options, and ease of use.

Podcasting

In addition to traditional blogs, you may be interested in podcasting. Podcasts can serve as content for your website and social media, or you may choose to send people to an existing podcasting platform, such as MixCloud, PodBean, Podigree, SoundCloud, Blubrry, or Libsyn. Mixcloud offers lots of free storage, as well as a professional level with additional features. The others offer limited free storage and tiered pricing plans. In addition, the professional or business level in Squarespace hosts podcasts.

To market your podcast, it is a good idea to get it on to iTunes, the TuneIn app, and You-Tube (for video or audio podcasts), as well as any other channels. Also many topic-oriented podcast networks may offer you a good home. Some internet research should point you in a few promising directions.

Hosting

Most CMS platforms offer hosting, so you will not need to worry about this up front. This basically means that the website platform stores your files and content on its servers and ensures that your content and files are efficiently delivered to users who click on your site. However, if you reach a point where you want more power, faster website page loads, greater SEO options, and the ability to have greater control, you may opt to have your website hosted by an external web host.

Many web hosts are available, and this book does not advocate one over the other, but some examples are GoDaddy, HostGator, BlueHost, DreamHost, SiteGator, and InMotion, to name a few. These companies charge a monthly or annual fee to host content for you. They have various plan options, depending on how much space you need, whether you need email storage (and how much), and whether you're willing to share a server with other sites (shared hosting), you want more features (VPS hosting), or you want your own dedicated server (dedicated hosting). Hosting companies can also help you transfer your site from its current location to the new hosted location.

Some things to consider when thinking about whether to go with an external host and how much functionality you will need:

- Are you outgrowing your current setup?
    - Do you have more content than your CMS platform host can handle?

- Are page loads slowing?

- Is this a long-term commitment, or are you simply working on a project?
- Do you need 24/7 customer support? (For most the answer is yes.)
- Does the host have a good record when it comes to site uptime? If your site is offline, then people cannot find you and consume your content.

If you are just starting out, you likely do not need to choose a dedicated host. Stick with the hosting offered by your CMS platform. This section is here for you once you're ready to take it to the next level.

Designing your website portfolio

You've chosen your CMS platform, decided for or against external hosting, and now it's time to create your site. Exactly what elements should a news- and information-oriented website have?

We suggest you consider including the following elements on your website:

Pages

- Homepage
    - Explain the vision and goals of the website.

    - Give visitors some orientation. What are they looking at? Why should they stick around? What are you offering?

    - You may also include access to your work here, especially if you are a journalist. A slider/rotator, feed, or grid of stories may be useful.

    - It is also wise to include social media links on the homepage.

- About
    - This page should include information about you and your company, such as your bio, your company's mission and vision statement, and any other information that helps the visitor get to know you and your work.

    - You may also want to include contact information here or add a separate contact page. This page or section can include an email form, as well as links to your social media.

- Blog
    - This page is where visitors can find your work.

    - Depending on the CMS platform you choose, your blog will be confined to one page (WordPress), or you may be able to add blogs to multiple pages

(Wix). Your choice depends on the work you do. WordPress filters blogs by category, allowing you to set up filters to organize different topic areas. For example, as a local journalist, I may need the following categories: city government, local events, crime and courts, and features. Sites such as Wix will allow you to have multiple blog feeds on either the same page or separate pages.

Beyond these three basic pages, the rest is up to you.

You may want to include a resources page that helps connect visitors to information you find important. For example, keeping with the local reporter theme, I may offer a page with links to city hall, local organizations used as sources in my stories, or embedded videos contributed by my users of newsworthy events in the community.

Beyond pages, be sure to have social media links and feeds and opportunities for the visitor to engage with you, such as through story comments, contact forms, and/or social media.

SEO

A word about SEO or search engine optimization: As a journalist, you not only want to craft incredible, important, and impactful news stories, you want people to read, watch, hear, and share them. To ensure this, you need to spend some time building SEO into your website and each blog post you create.

SEO basically means optimizing your content to ensure that search engines such as Google, Bing, Yahoo, and DuckDuckGo find it and include it in search results, ideally as close to the top as possible.

The primary way to increase SEO is careful use of words. Choose words that reflect your goals and mission and would be used by people searching for the content you provide. If a user types a phrase or word into a search engine, and you happen to have that word in your tags, then there is a greater likelihood that you will appear in that user's search results. If you are unclear which words connected to your topic are most searched, you can do a keyword search to find out.

Here are some ways to increase your SEO:[5,6]

1. *Meta-tags*: If you can access the meta-tags on your CMS platform, fill them out. When choosing which tags (words or phrases) to include, think about your goals, your mission, and your story content, as well as how people might search for that content.

---

5 "Five Ways to Improve Your Site's Ranking (SEO)." Michigan Technological University. Accessed June 16, 2016, http://www.mtu.edu/umc/services/web/seo/.

6 Jayson DeMers, "7 Advanced Ways to Improve Your Site's SEO." Entrepreneur. September 29, 2014. Accessed June 16, 2016, http://www.entrepreneur.com/article/237819.

2. *Post tags*: Each post or page should have an area where you can include tags. Here you want to include names of people mentioned in the story, story concepts or focus areas, and other relevant search terms.

3. *Story Titles, Summaries, and Main Content*: Though you want to write your stories in the most organic fashion possible, it does help to sprinkle searchable terms throughout your titles and story content. This is a slippery slope—while judicious use of this tactic may be helpful, too much of it can make your writing sound stilted, pandering, and disjointed.

4. *Update Your Content Regularly*: If you regularly update content, then the SEO bots are more likely to define your site as relevant and current, and to include your site in search results.

5. *Create Quality Content*: SEO is not all about bots and internet functionality. People have an influence. If you are creating quality content that people share and seek out, search engines will notice and be more likely to include your work in search results.

6. *Avoid "click here"*: Instead, write out relevant content for each of your hyperlinks. Search engines notice this.

7. *Fill Out Alt Text*: Alt Text serves some important purposes. First, it allows visually impaired people to "see" an image, video, or graphic. When a visually impaired person scrolls over a visual, whatever is entered in Alt Text will be read out loud to the user, allowing that user to more fully participate. That is the main reason you should always fill in Alt Text. The other reason is that because it is a text reader, it is read by search engine bots, who will include your work in search results if the Alt Text is relevant.

8. *Consider Your Site Map/Site Navigation*: Search engines will determine the importance of a page based on where it is in a site map. You may also want to customize page name URLs.

A final word about SEO ethics: It is very important that you make ethical SEO choices. The words you use must relate to what you are doing. For example, if I am writing a news blog on city hall and local crime, then it would be unethical for me to include words such as Beyoncé, Justin Bieber, or kittens in my SEO. Even though these words or phrases may be popular search terms, they have nothing to do with my blog. It is unethical to mislead people to drive traffic.

Social media

Many people now find their news on social media. That means you need to be on social media. You have many options: Instagram, Twitter, Facebook, Pinterest, Tumblr (also a blog), Snapchat, Periscope, etc. You do not need to be on all of them. In fact, when you are starting out, choose just one (two at the most), and develop yourself there before branching out, for example, Instagram and Snapchat. If you try to be everywhere, then you will not be able to keep up, and you will doom yourself to failure. Do one (or two) well, and then expand later if necessary.

The most critical factor in choosing a platform is: Where does your audience spend its time? To answer this, you need to figure out your audience. The answer to this question is never "everywhere." It would be great if everyone read our work, but the more specific you can be about who your audience is, the more likely you are to capture that audience and build your audience even further.

For example, when Facebook started, its audience was not "everyone." Its audience was college students at specific colleges. Then, after the platform gained some traction, it was opened up to all college students. Only after it grew in popularity among this audience did it expand beyond college students to the general population. Now, Facebook is not even the platform of choice for college students, primarily because their parents have taken over as the primary audience. Thus, not only can audiences grow, they can also change.

When you are working to determine your target audience, define that audience as specifically as possible, including age range, income level, ethnicity and gender, interests, values, and how you see your audience spending its time. Ideally, have a specific person in mind. Then, you can make choices for this target audience member. This does not mean your work will be relevant to only this audience. Chances are it will be relevant to many audiences, but your target audience helps you define your presence and make content and presentation choices to help you achieve success.

In addition, each social media platform serves a different purpose. Instagram focuses on visuals and is often a one-to-many relationship. However, Snapchat develops a one-to-one relationship, giving a more personal experience for the audience. Live video streaming, such as Instagram, Periscope, and Facebook Live, offer you the opportunity to give moment-to-moment video updates, as well as connect in real time with your audience on in-depth issues. As you develop your social media strategy, weigh the pros and cons of each app and platform to determine what will work best for the stories you are trying to tell and your journalistic goals.

Blog best practices

Once you've built your website, created your website content, and established your social media platform(s), it is time to begin creating content. Best practices for content creation are covered more in depth elsewhere in this book. In this section, we will focus on content choices.

You have many choices in how to present your story. You may write an article that is primarily text with some images and hyperlinks. You may include a slideshow or gallery of images. You may tell your story with video, animation, or audio. You may use an infographic or series of charts and graphs. You may include an interactive element allowing the user to engage with data or information. The two drivers that dictate your choice of media are 1) how best to tell the story and 2) how best to communicate with your audience.

Telling the Story. Some stories are told better through video, some through animation, some through text, etc. Some stories are told best using infographics, photos, and text summaries. You will need to determine this with each story you cover.

Communicating With Your Audience. Even if you think an animation would be the best way to tell a story, will your audience understand how to play the animation? Even if it seems that an interactive infographic would be the best way to simplify complex information, will your audience be able to navigate it? A 20-something audience member may dive right into an interactive infographic, while an audience member in their 50s may prefer a video or text article with separate charts and graphs.

Your ultimate goal is to communicate with your audience. Any media that may be unintuitive to that audience should either be made as accessible as possible or scrapped in favor of media that will better connect with the audience in question.

It is also easy to get carried away. We have access to so many apps and tools that make flashy graphics, interactive elements, and other cool toys, and more are being developed every day. If the new, flashy app or tool does the job of communicating with your audience, then by all means, use it. If not, then take a pass in favor of something that communicates more effectively.

Drawing people in

In the age of digital media, a journalist is not just a journalist. In addition to gathering and reporting news, you must promote yourself and your stories. This can be a challenging task, given how many people are doing the same thing online.

To make the situation even more challenging, the rules of engagement are constantly evolving. People click on posts with visuals at a far greater rate than text-only posts. Beyond that, social media platforms such as Facebook change their algorithms regularly to improve member experience, which means they may prioritize some content over others. For example, in late 2017, Facebook changed its algorithm to prioritize content from friends and family, greatly reducing engagement for organizations and companies on the platform who had built their social media strategies around rules that then shifted. These changes are not always advertised.

As for user engagement with social media content, most people read only the headline without engaging with the rest of the content. It is up to you to write a headline compelling enough to get the user to click into the post and engage with the rest of the content and, even better, to share that content. Keep in mind that different users will click on different types of headlines. Consider your audience as you write to ensure that you are speaking to those people in their language. Also *avoid clickbait.*

In addition to thoughtful and compelling headline and post writing, striking photos, interesting videos, and compelling graphics, you want to directly engage with your audience. This includes suggesting calls to action, responding to inquiries, engaging on social media threads, and following up on story leads from audience members. Currently, Snapchat is a great way to engage using video, graphics, and personalized messages. It also provides a personalized experience in which users can engage directly with you.

Calls to Action: A call to action is a suggestion or request for the user to take some sort of action. You may want the user to share the story on social media, contact a local government representative, share pictures from an event, or contribute information to an ongoing story. The great thing is, if you ask, your audience will often respond positively, so don't be afraid to make the request.

Responding to Inquiries and Engaging on Social Media: Journalism is no longer a one-way street. In the interactive age, the audience can reach out to you easily through social media, on story comment threads, or via email. Taking the time to respond to posts on social media can be a great investment. It shows users that you care about their opinions, builds trust, and could lead to story ideas when users share information with you.

The bottom line is that promoting yourself involves compelling content, strong word crafting, and interaction and engagement with the audience.

Examples of successful bloggers

What does success mean for a blogger? It could mean money/revenue, clicks, and/or respect. Here are some bloggers and blogging websites that have managed to find success in all three areas.[7] Many earn revenue via ad banners or native advertising (posting ads in the form of news stories). Some earn revenue via page clicks, and others sell prime real estate "above

Figure 15.14

---

7   Brock Hamilton, "Bloggers Who Make Amazing Money From Their Blogs," Income.com, October 27, 2015. Accessed June 16, 2016, https://income.com/4100/27-bloggers-who-make-amazing-money-from-their-blogs/.

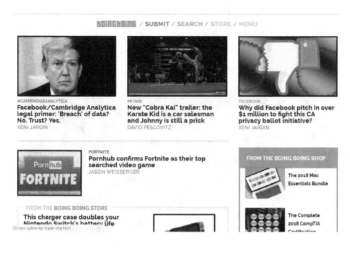

Figure 15.15

the fold" to content providers. These examples have also earned respect among their audience, and audiences for these blogs have grown quite large.

Mashable.com—A blog focused on digital media, its strong header images and clean headlines, as well as its easy homepage navigation make it an easy blog to navigate and peruse (Fig. 15.14). In addition, the content is fun, current, and connects pop culture and entertainment to technology. Its approach to news and information make it popular with Millennials and others.

BoingBoing.net—A group blog on various topics. it bills itself as an "award-winning zine, blog and directory of wonderful things." The interface is a bit old-school and not that flashy, but the content keeps people coming back. NOTE: Very few sites can live by content alone. Presentation is an important way to entice people to check out your content.

Huffington Post—A blog focused on progressive politics, entertainment, and lifestyle. HuffPo is now a monolith in the news blogging realm. Many people find this content in their social media feeds, which speaks to HuffPo's solid social media promotional efforts, as well as the shareability of its content. The site itself features large simple headlines and massive images to draw people into the content.

Figure 15.16

TMZ—Focused on celebrity gossip. The clean interface and tasteful color palette belie the often sensationalistic content. People are drawn to TMZ to try to get insider information, and the site does a good job of walking the line between serious and salacious.

Figure 15.17

PerezHilton—This celebrity gossip blog blog offers a light, fresh color palette and uses its menu structure to showcase big pop-culture icons or stories, rather than topics. PerezHilton.com was one of the first blog sites to blow up, and it has stayed relevant by staying on top of the pop-culture pulse and providing image, GIF, text, video, and linked content on the major pop-culture figures of the day. http://perezhilton.com/http://perezhilton.com/

Figure 15.18

LifeHacker—This DIY blog earns $110,000 per month through banner ads. A true blog site, it has a clean feed right on the homepage offering DIY content of interest to users. Life-Hacker is capitalizing on the trend of life hacks. Another reason the site remains relevant is that it provides news content on things like the most popular passwords—items that tie into its DIY theme.

Figure 15.19

WorldStarHipHop—Entertainment and news media site. This slick content-rich site stays relevant by knowing its audience. WorldStarHipHop breaks big news stories from the hip hop and general music world, as well as aggregates the most ridiculous and shocking moments on the web. So far, the mix has been successful with young people.

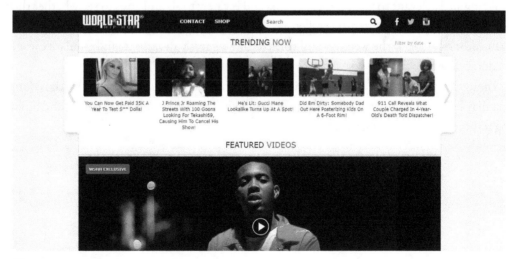

Figure 15.20

BuzzFeed—Social news and entertainment blog. BuzzFeed gained popularity by providing content in a revolutionary way through GIFs and GIF series. The formula has taken off. Now BuzzFeed has moved into more hard news stories, covering them in its own way. This fresh take has drawn loyal followers. The other successful aspect of this website is that it keeps the user on the page by providing related content and clickable options where the user is, keeping the user clicking and perusing for way too long.

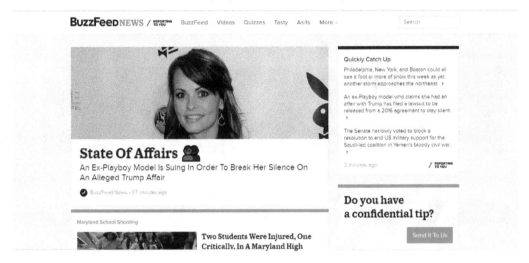

Figure 15.21

Summary

To improve as a blogger/storyteller, it is critical that you pay attention to what other bloggers are doing, including both industry leaders and those new to the scene. Follow bloggers and blogging sites relevant to you on social media and try new tools and apps to see whether they will help you become a better storyteller.

In addition, look at the websites and content of bloggers you respect, and emulate the elements appropriate to your work.

Though many elements are involved in setting yourself up online, once this work is done, you may begin building on it—building your audience, building your story count, and building respect and trust as a journalist.

EXERCISES AND ACTIVITIES

Create your own website

Choose one of the CMS platforms mentioned in this chapter or select a different platform, and create a basic, three-page site.

Before you create your site, answer the following questions:

1. What is your beat?
2. What type of stories will you cover? Ex: Technology, Entertainment, Food, Business, Sports, Fashion, Crime, etc. It is probably best to choose just one area for now, but if you have two related areas, that may be OK.
3. What are other people doing online in this beat area? Social media? Website?
4. Who is your audience? Be specific. Define age range, income level, ethnicity and gender, education level, as well as attitudes and beliefs. What does this person do on a Thursday night?n the weekend?
5. Given the answers to the above questions, which platform best fits your needs? Why?

Then, build your site

6. Choose a platform.
7. Choose your theme.
8. Build your pages: at least home, about, and blog. Add other pages that are appropriate for your site.
9. Add content to your pages.

Once you build your site, write your first post.

Assess social media platforms

Choose an existing social media platform and assess it using the following questions:

1. Why did you choose this social media platform?
2. Who is the target audience for this site?
3. What are the pros of this platform in terms of promotion and content delivery?
4. How could this platform improve for its users?
5. How does this platform influence the choices you're making on social media?

Credits

CHAPTER 16

Future of journalism: Is it bright? You bet.

> "*I became a journalist to come as close as possible to the heart of the world.*"
>
> *–Henry Luce[1]*

You are sharpening your writing and multimedia skills, learning how to shape stories into an inverted pyramid, and figuring out how to meet daily deadlines. You are honing your newsgathering skills and interviewing techniques, so you can talk to politicians, witnesses, and unique personalities for your assigned story. How do you take your talent to the next level and search for your dream job in journalism?

First, you need to figure out how to get hired. Though the journalism landscape has shifted toward consolidation, doing more with less, and part-time and contract jobs over full-time, long-term newsroom jobs, there are still opportunities to make an impact and have a satisfying career. It's important to investigate the field of possibilities. If you peruse job listings, it's clear there are many directions to take your journalism ambitions. More jobs exist than ever before that require knowledge of multiplatform storytelling in a digital world. You could choose to focus on some of the more recent additions to the newsroom, such as social media manager or website curator.

Beyond newsrooms, you'll find many job openings in the corporate and nonprofit worlds. Everyone needs employees proficient in social and digital media and storytelling. You may also find many job openings at tech companies where computer skills are almost as important as storytelling. The key is to stay updated on the latest social media trends and know how best to communicate with your audience. It may be via Twitter, Instagram, Facebook, or another social media outlet. All jobs will require some blending of traditional journalism skills with cutting edge technology. Knowing how to embed information such as graphics, photos, timelines, and hyperlinks into an online story can help communicate important details and add more depth for news consumers.

---

1 The Harvard Gazette website, https://news.harvard.edu/gazette/story/2014/12/ledeing-by-example/, last accessed March 30, 2018.

Some journalism jobs to consider

- News reporter
- News producer
- News anchor
- Social media coordinator
- Multimedia sports journalist
- Beat reporter/writer (politics, business, consumer, health, lifestyle, travel)
- Interactive graphic journalist
- Blogger
- Video journalist
- Video editor

Of course, you can still pursue traditional journalism positions in broadcast newsrooms, such as reporter, producer, writer, or editor. Alerting an audience to your news story via Twitter requires a maximum of 280 characters. That takes practice and skill. Broadcast journalists have more digital duties these days. Reporters often go live on social media for several minutes beyond their live shots for the local newscast. When back at the station, they have online stories and other elements to contribute to the website.

The key to finding a job and success in the business is flexibility. A journalist today needs to be able to file reports across platforms. A print reporter needs to shoot video, obtain audio, and post updates online. Even traditional broadcasters need to file online reports with digital elements, such as photos, graphics, and video clips. Prospective journalists need to be willing to gain experience as unpaid interns or volunteers. Most journalists are likely to begin their career in smaller markets as they hone skills and continue to network with other professionals, so they can move onward and upward.

Knowing how to wear many hats can be considered a bit of job insurance. There is no guarantee, however, that your dream job will come easily or that it will even exist in five or 10 years because of all the consolidation of media companies and staff downsizing. The good news is that having the ability to tell a story and report in a multimedia world does make you more marketable and more prepared for the job interview.

Advice from the experts

Marcy McGinnis is a veteran news executive who ran the London Bureau for CBS News. She says there's no greater way to prepare for an interview than researching the job opening, the company, its history, the people who run the company, and employees, including reporters and anchors. Most of all, know the content they produce. If you're going to an interview at a TV station, you need to watch that station's news broadcasts for at least the previous week and be able to refer to something you saw. According to McGinnis, it's crucial to do your homework. "Pour over their website; know the area they cover. If you are from one city and going to a job in another city, be ready to answer questions about that other city: Who is the mayor? Governor? Senator? Sports teams? Red state? Blue state? Know the basic facts and main players in the U.S. government, as well as the area's city, regional, and state governments. Who is the current Secretary of State? Majority leader and Minority leader in Congress?" In other words, it's difficult to prove that you are the right person for the job if you haven't exhibited some basic investigative skills about the job and company for which you want to work.

If you want to be in the thick of things, try producing. That's a job many news directors say they have the hardest time filling. It's a position that requires organizing, good writing, prioritizing news quickly, and making solid news judgment decisions for morning, afternoon, and evening newscasts. Producers need to know what is going on in the world and at home. Yes, it's a tough job, but it's the one with the most upward mobility to larger markets. For those wanting to report or anchor, News Director Jim Lemon of *KEYT* and *KCOY-TV* has some advice. "Reporters are becoming more self-contained. They work solo shooting, writing, editing, and setting up their own live gear. Those who embrace this style will be successful. Those who do not should move along. There are occasional 'digital only' positions, but fewer of them at television stations because the broadcast product is still by far the bigger revenue generator."

In reality, your success in the industry depends a lot on the choices you make while a student.

In reality, your success in the industry depends a lot on the choices you make while a student.

Greg Esposito, former senior digital manager for the NBA's Phoenix Suns, advises students to get as much experience as possible in the business before graduating from college. Pursue internships or even volunteer to work for free in your field of interest. "The relationships you make and the skills you learn on the job before graduation will be the most valuable to your careers." Esposito also stresses the old adage about networking. "As cliché as it sounds, it's all about the people you know. Those connections will make your job hunt easier, even if it doesn't directly lead to a job."

In addition to tech and digital skills, you need to know about the world around you and beyond. Stacie Chan of Google News underscores the importance of reading a variety of news sources, including magazines, newspapers, websites, and even novels, because "it's good for the brain" and helps journalists to think critically. Chan said the thing to remember is that you are a storyteller. That is at the very core of journalism. Select role models who produce work you admire. She suggests "reaching out to your favorite writers and asking them how they got their job. It can help you better prepare your skill set for the jobs you want."

Journalists, Chan said, need to remain open-minded. They need to be committed to fairness and realize that stories are very complex and can change lives. Blogger and copy editor of FanRag Sports Matt Zemek says you should be a "do-it-yourself" practitioner, someone who doesn't just write and edit, but a journalist who can lay out web pages, take photos, and organize content in a snappy, comprehensive way.

Zemek also says to polish your writing and editing skills. "It surprises me that many writers make errors borne of ignorance. For example, no one in the industry—not an editor, not a publisher, not a colleague, not someone on Twitter—told them that when an athlete pushes through adverse situations to succeed, he was 'unfazed' and not 'unphased.' It seems that seven out of every 10 writers get it wrong. Don't make those mistakes. Check your online dictionary often. I still do. Ask questions to your editors or, before that, your professors."

Students today also have a unique opportunity to shape the future of the industry. "Being able to put forth fresh content and insight matters," says Zemek. "Being an agile, critical, original thinker matters a lot. However, it's more than that. Young journalists should be thinking about what's the next step in the progression of content delivery. Being able to visually and numerically represent new trends in any field of human activity—in addition to painting word-pictures—positions a journalist quite well for the long haul in this industry."

Finding the right job and getting hired

Many employers agree that a creative resume and internship experience play a big role in the hiring process. Employers look at hundreds of applications, so make yours stand out. One absolute MUST is staying current with emerging technology and social media. Have at least one well curated and active social media account. If you want to have multiple social media accounts, then find time to consolidate and organize your newsgathering and dissemination. Applications such as TweetDeck or Hootsuite can help you stay organized.

It's all about personal choice, according to News Director Jim Lemon. "I don't think any one product is the be-all, end-all for reporters, but if I had to point at one, it would be a basic one such as Twitter. Many of the folks that journalists deal with take to Twitter, so some of our folks (and definitely our assignment editors) use TweetDeck, for example. Facebook is still very strong around these parts, too, so some of the 'older' new media would be higher up. Truly, these days it's multiple resources. Sometimes it's through trade channels (the daily media blogs). Other times it's information from corporate or sometimes just from folks who stumble onto something from people they follow on Twitter or through other social media. We are always looking for new ways to stream video or move content, and we're always looking for the easiest and simplest ways to do this."

Esposito says the best way to job hunt, especially in sports, is online. Sources such as TeamWorkOnline.com and "Work In Sports" list the latest jobs with teams and in media. "From there, the key is a strong and unique resume and a quality cover letter." Your best step forward begins with an impressive cover letter, which should briefly highlight your work experiences and educational background.

"The best way to prepare for a job interview is to answer the simple question, 'What can I do to make company x better?'" according to Esposito. "A lot of people want to talk about how the company can help them, but the person who can genuinely answer what value they'll bring to a company is key. Confidence is what convinces us to hire. It's the people who are confident in themselves and their skills that we want. It's the people who are timid or cocky that likely won't get hired."

Matt Zemek highly recommends that a job candidate study the marketplace, be an entrepreneur, and know where opportunities exist. Make inquiries to editors at various publications you're interested in writing for. See what editors and publishers have to say. "Get a sense of how much upward mobility legitimately exists at a publication/outlet. If you can't hit it big at one outlet right away—and that's normal—be prepared to cobble together several side gigs if you're intent on making a living in blogging/journalism. Be tech-savvy and able to convey information through embedded videos, photos, social media, and other platforms beyond the printed or written word."

In general, Zemek says, you have to be your own entrepreneur and know where opportunities exist. Given the rapid changes in the industry, be prepared to recalibrate your expectations every few years. "A typical day for me is comprised of a basket of several activities: writing, loading photos, editing other writers' posts, scheduling posts, laying out our blog homepage (specifically choosing which stories go in our skyboxes at the top of the page), tweeting out our stories on Twitter, re-tweeting colleagues when they tweet out content, interacting with readers, and communicating with staff about the next week's agenda or when a breaking story demands attention from one or two writers on staff."

There's another very important thing to remember when trying to get hired. At the end of the job interview, never say "no" if asked if you have any questions. Marcy McGinnis has hired many network reporters and producers and says, "Don't ask about money or vacation at this point, but rather ask something you really want to know, something about the future of the company, the direction of the news division, plans for covering the political campaign, etc. Near the end, ask about the next steps and when you can hope to hear from someone, and lastly, make one last pitch as to why YOU are the best person to fit their needs."

Types of journalism jobs

Esposito says there are many roles for people interested in sports journalism. Content producers either write or film content for various websites. The photo archivist digitizes photo history. You can also become a social media specialist and post team news onto the organization's social and digital media properties.

If you want a job reporting on sports, Zemek has personal experience to share. "Blogs that cover sports are increasingly trying to differentiate themselves from each other and from traditional forms of sports writing. They know that fans watch the games and don't need to be told what happened. More and more sports blogs want to tell readers why and how things happened and what they mean."

If you are interested in working for an online news aggregator, such as Google News, you'll need to brush up on skills beyond journalism. Chan, at Google, says it's important to remember that tech companies are ultimately tech companies and you need to speak their language with a basic knowledge of coding and engineering. Knowing basic HTML skills is a plus if you want to work at a tech company.

There are non-traditional jobs to consider, as well. For instance, Southwest Airlines has someone who writes and edits a blog about its pilots. That job requires solid storytelling skills, even though it is not a traditional news writing assignment. Art museums, nonprofits, and zoos all need social media writers to contribute content to their websites and blogs.

Once you are working as a professional journalist, continue to hone your skills, learn new skills, and experiment with new apps and tools. This will help you stay on top of your game. Popular journalism sites, such as Poynter.org, have seminars and workshops that cater to sharpening skills for today's marketplace.

Journalist spotlight

JIM LEMON, news director, *KEYT* and *KCOY-TV*, Santa Barbara, CA

Jim Lemon has more than 32 years in the industry. At the beginning of his career, Lemon went to work for a small TV station in Yuma, Arizona, as a reporter and anchor. To rise to the position of news director, he made stops in Boise, Tucson, Topeka, Honolulu, Sacramento, and Milwaukee. Lemon earned his Bachelor's and Master's degrees from the University of Arizona in Tucson. Even before he entered college, Lemon interned with Yuma TV stations.

He has a list of the most important qualities he looks for in a job applicant.

"Intelligence, resilience, fairness, relentless curiosity, thick skin and a great attitude. I want reporters who are always working up stories, not waiting for handouts from the desk. I want them to know how to make stories happen, rather than why they can't. The same is true with producers."

"Intelligence, resilience, fairness, relentless curiosity, thick skin and a great attitude. I want reporters who are always working up stories, not waiting for handouts from the desk. I want them to know how to make stories happen, rather than why they can't. The same is true with producers." Lemon insists, "They must be able to write well! I can't believe how many college graduates I see who clearly have no idea of the best way to write for either broadcast or for digital/online (in the old days, 'print'). I want and desperately need reporters who can pitch stories that are doable. We all have ideas, but not everything will be able to turn for the 5 p.m. news. I want people who can show they are serious about journalism and not just trying to be on TV. I want people who can show me they are constantly finding stories and demonstrating they know their way around the basics: how to look up court documents, police reports, city government records, etc. This is bread and butter for a local journalist, if only they know how to access it,

Key points of review

Learn to write and work on the art of storytelling.

Know how to do everything or as close to everything as possible, including writing, editing, reporting, videography and producing.

Know how to use and manipulate technology; be comfortable with various ways to distribute information and news through social media.

Be your own entrepreneur. See the future of the industry and where it can evolve.

Become familiar with the how and why of things, the industry in which you work, and the industry or industries you cover.

and then translate it into something a viewer/reader will find compelling." Then, of course, there's one quality that could set you apart from other candidates, and that is a good attitude, including a willingness to work long hours.

EXERCISES AND ACTIVITIES:
KNOW WHERE TO FIND JOURNALISM JOBS
AND BEGIN TO BUILD A RESUME

This is intended to be an actual, real-life exercise in finding and applying for work in your field of interest. Look online at the various job openings using some of the links below. Search for an entry-level position, one that requires two years or less experience in the field. This could be the kind of opening that you would apply for at graduation. Write down any relevant work background or courses you have taken to date, and remember any internship will count toward this experience. The objective is to discover which skills you need to achieve and what experience to gain in the time you have between now and graduation. Make it your professional "to-do" list.

News Director Jim Lemon concurs and recommends tailoring your cover letter and resume, plus video clips if you have them, to fit the job opening. He says, "It's easy to create one reel and then upload it to YouTube or Vimeo, etc., but what if the position specifies video journalist and your reel has a bunch of stand ups clearly shot by someone else? Immediately, you're telling the hiring manager that you're not paying attention to the advertisement." If the position is all about politics or digging into complicated or complex stories, you need to put that story up first on your reel.

Former CBS London Bureau Chief Marcy McGinnis wants to remind you that people are not hiring to give you the job of a lifetime. They are hiring because there's work to be done, they have a problem they need to solve by hiring someone to deal with it, and they're looking for the best person for the job. Ask yourself, how can you best fit their needs? How can you convince them or show them that you are the one who is best suited to solve their problem. She says, "If I asked you in a job interview, 'Why should I hire YOU and not one of the other 50 people vying for this job?' the answer should be specific to something I'm looking for and should include an anecdote or two to back up the assertion that it's proof you are the best person for the job. Newsrooms are not hiring you because all your life you wanted to work at CBS News."

Also, remember to keep that to-do list handy as you select classes and make decisions on internships and summer work. These things can help you in achieving your dream journalism job.

Sites and sources for locating jobs and improving skills

- www.poynter.org
- www.journalismjobs.org
- www.journalism.org
- www.pewresearch.org
- www.TeamWorkOnline.com
- http://www.mediabistro.com/joblistings/
- http://www.journalismdegree.com/social-media-careers/
- http://myfootpath.com/careers/media-journalism-careers/
- http://www.indeed.com/q-Social-Media-jobs.html
- http://www.jobsinsocialmedia.com/
- http://www.socialmediajobs.com/
- http://jobs.mashable.com/jobs/social-media-28800948-b
- http://www.simplyhired.com/k-social-media-jobs.html

Epilogue

Doing journalism

"The future does not fit in the
containers of the past."

–Rishad Tobaccowala[1]

We now know that fewer and fewer consumers, especially anyone under 35, are tuning into to the five o'clock news or subscribing to their daily newspaper. Indeed, we now know that most young people are getting their news from their favorite blog or social media platform. We also know that anyone with a decent smartphone can capture news as it happens.

Even so, there are many reasons why the anyone-can-do-it mentality doesn't quite work in journalism. The biggest reason is ethics.

For many years, journalists have been given access to crime scenes, press conferences, and other exclusive events because the public relies on them to provide accurate and fair information. Journalists have also been given interviews with everyone from prisoners on Death Row to prime ministers because the best promise to be fair and transparent with their sources. If this trust is broken, the access that journalists have enjoyed for years will erode. That is why journalists should avoid spreading rumors and gossip unless they can verify it's true. Even then, the journalist should carefully weigh the value of the information to the public to the harm it will cause the individual. As mentioned in an earlier chapter, there is no one code

---

1   Meranda Adams, "15 Quotes to Inspire Journalists," Adweek. com, March 10, 2011. Accessed March 30, 2018, http://www. adweek.com/digital/quotes-inspire-journalists/.

that speaks for all journalists, but many turn to the Society of Professional Journalists Code of Ethics for guidance.

As ethical journalists, we might not be the first to tweet the number of people dead in the Orlando shooting, but we are often right. That is why we introduced journalism ethics at the very beginning of our book and infused ethics into almost every chapter. You'll see what plagiarism is by media standards, and why it's important for students to conduct their own research when producing their work. While it would be easy to copy and paste what *The New York Times* or celebrity blogger Perez Hilton said about pop singer Taylor Swift, our book shows aspiring journalists the importance of verifying rumors and gossip before airing or publishing them.

Above all, remember to attribute every assertion made in your story and base everything on documents, records, and interviews with multiple sources. Always reach out to the person who wrote a press release or the report before you publish. Above all, avoid copying and pasting text from other sites—that's plagiarism, and in the news business, it's a firing offense.

Forging your own path

While it's great to have aspirations of working at *The New York Times* or CNN, most journalists understand that times have changed, and even veteran journalists now know that anyone with a decent smartphone in the right place at the right time has the power to produce a story that has the potential to be seen and shared by thousands or even millions of people. This means that it's important for aspiring journalists to think outside the box when it comes to reporting, distributing, and promoting their stories. While Chapter 16 covered the abundance of freelance to full-time jobs available to those who study and practice journalism, this chapter will focus on how aspiring journalists can carve out a unique niche in a newsroom or fund their own multimedia projects and promote their work through blogging sites and social media.

Journalist spotlight

Interview with **KRYSTAL DAWN PEAK,** journalist

Figure E.1

When Krystal Peak was studying journalism at San Francisco State University, she never thought her experience as editor-in-chief of the campus newspaper would lead to a career in business news and social media, but when the *San Francisco Business Times* offered her an internship, Krystal jumped at the chance. Shortly after graduating in 2010, Krystal took on the role as social engagement manager at the *San Francisco Business Times*.

Q: What does a social engagement editor do?

"You are the voice of all the social media channels coming from *SF Biz Times*: Facebook, LinkedIn, Twitter. A secondary goal is training reporters and editors how to use their social media channels, helping them learn how to create visuals (graphics, GIFs, short videos, etc.)."

Q: How has technology and/or the Internet changed journalism?

"In a couple of different ways. From learning about gathering news to creating news, it's really a great tool. You can follow people and find out what people are talking about. You can use it as a tool to find source. On the other hand, it's a challenge because you have to jump on stories really quickly. [There is a] desire to get as much up as soon as possible, so there's less time to craft stories, and there's a demand for video and visuals [which are] time consuming ... and [you] don't have the time to create all that."

Q: Why did you choose to study journalism?

"I really like the written word. I like the storytelling component. When I was young, I asked myself, 'What allowed for that kind of career?' Really, journalism provided that. Thus far, I've done a lot, and I'm really kind of seeing what I want to do next. I love interviewing people. The hardest part is writing. I love the multimedia experience. You don't have to write everything. Maybe you can tell a story in a short video or blurb. Journalism doesn't just have to be long form. As a Millennial, things have changed since I was in middle school. The only way to tell a story was through an article or book, but now there are these tools that allow us to tell stories in such different ways. This makes way more sense to me. The way I wanted stories delivered ... it's happening. The tools are catching up with the way Millennials learn and consume information."

Q: Are mainstream media outlets doing enough to remain relevant to a younger audience?

"I think they are having a hard time. They are investing in younger reporters and trying new things. They are going outside of their box, but the ones that really stand out are usually the newer players: Vox. They stood out as capturing the Millennial viewer and consumer and creating short explainer videos ... here's everything you should know about Obamacare. When I look how I consume things, I'm more gripped by a lot of these startups that eventually get bought by legacy groups. ... They seem to be handling change by acquiring those with new ideas. They need to look inside themselves and say ... let's start over and change it from the ground up."

Q: What should today's journalists have in their toolkits?

"Obviously, you should have good writing style, technique, and great interviewing skills. You should understand visual media and know what makes a gripping image. You should learn how to make a quick video that tells a little story. You should also know how to edit and create infographics. A journalist who can do it all is hard to find, and I'd love to see more journalists gaining these skills."

Backpack journalism

While some journalists focus on one skill such as writing news, taking pictures or shooting video, an increasing number of people in and outside the newsroom are doing it all—taking the photos, shooting video, and writing the story.

This form of storytelling is commonly known as "backpack journalism," which essentially means that one person is capturing the photos, video, and audio needed to produce a multimedia package. Indeed, many journalism schools have expanded their curriculum to incorporate video journalism, multimedia journalism, visual storytelling and even social media journalism. There are even a number of affordable or even free online courses helping journalists at any age or experience level improve their skills in technology, social media, visual storytelling, and blogging.

In addition, faster and more powerful computers and phones have made it possible for just about anyone to shoot and edit great video, distribute their stories to a large number of people, and even create their own website within minutes.

Students should definitely consider striking out on their own and going the road less traveled as backpack journalists. The challenge, however, is how do you pay for that trip to Nepal or Sudan? How do you pay for the time needed to interview people, travel, conduct research and produce the story?

Crowdfunding

Crowdfunding essentially means asking individuals to help fund a project. Hundreds of websites, such as Indiegogo, GoFundMe, and Kickstarter now make it easy for people to launch a fundraising campaign online and through social media. Even journalists and news outlets are using these sites to raise money for creative work and entrepreneurial projects. In 2015, the owners of the *San Francisco Bay Guardian* shuttered their paper, but within a few days, a group of employees launched an Indiegogo campaign to raise money to help digitize back issues and produce new content for the online edition, now under new ownership.

A January 2016 study by the Pew Research Center found that nearly 660 journalism-related projects on Kickstarter received "full—or more than full—funding, to the tune of nearly $6.3 million."[2] Thus, crowdsourcing is an important step if you are planning to forge your own path.

---

2   Nancy Vogt and Amy Mitchell, "Crowdfunded Journalism: A Small but Growing Addition to Publicly Driven Journalism." Accessed June 15, 2016, http://www.journalism.org/2016/01/20/crowdfunded-journalism/.

Promoting content via social media

Whether you're at a large news outlet or working on your own, you'll want to leverage the power of social media in researching, reporting, and promoting your own story. While our chapter on blogging covered the essential things you need to know, just remember that social media platforms are great places to conduct research, find potential story ideas, and reach out to sources. LinkedIn, the largest professional network at 500+ million members, is a great place to find doctors, lawyers, and other professionals who can help contextualize just about any story.

Twitter is a great place to find out the latest breaking news, and Instagram is becoming a great place for *National Geographic, The Economist,* and other media companies to share their amazing photography. The key for journalists when using these social media platforms is to engage with the audience, so they don't feel like you're giving them a sales pitch. Social media sites are just that: social. No one opens up their Facebook app and gets excited about seeing an ad from a grocery store about what they can do to get their floors nice and shiny. Of course, we all do see those ads pop up or on the sides from time to time, but for the most part, we don't enjoy it. That's why journalists should think about their posts as conversations, inviting potential readers, viewers and listeners to their podcast or program to engage in healthy discourse.

Four basic rules for promoting your news on social media:

1. Take time to build an authentic following or network. Engage with your followers and friends by liking, sharing, and commenting on their content before you ask them to do the same for you. Understand what works well on each platform by searching for popular hash tags and trending topics.
2. Establish a strong, professional identity across social media. If you want to be known as an expert in a certain topic such as sports or entertainment, create a profile that showcases your interest and your experience, and follow it up consistently with posts that reflect your knowledge in those areas.
3. Follow and connect with people and companies that share your common interests, and be sure to engage with their content before you ask them to read your latest article or donate to your crowdsourcing campaign.
4. Vary the way you share an update on each platform. Remember: Most people following you on Instagram might be following you on Facebook, and they rarely want to see the same photo twice.

Credit

Glossary

Accountability—The requirement or expectation that you justify actions or decisions; the act of holding yourself responsible for your work.

Acquittal—A judgment that a person is not guilty of the crime with which the person has been charged.

Affidavit or Declaration—Written statement of facts voluntarily made under penalty of perjury.

Aggregator—A website or program that collects related items of content and displays them or links to them.

Analytics—Stats on your website traffic telling you how many people have visited your site, read your work, etc.

Arrest—The act of seizing someone to take into custody.

Arraignment—To call the accused before a criminal court to hear and answer the charge made against them.

B-roll—Supplemental footage to help visualize your story. Contains content that is descriptive, such as landscape, crime scene, or event wide shots.

Bail—The surety ordered by a court to allow for the temporary release of an accused person awaiting trial, usually including a condition that a sum of money or property be lodged to guarantee their appearance in court. If there is no bail set, then the defendant will be released on their "own recognizance."

Bias — Prejudice against or in favor of one thing, person, or group compared with another, usually in a way considered to be unfair; exhibiting an unjustifiable favoritism in covering the news. When the media transmit biased news reports, those reports present viewers with an inaccurate, unbalanced, and/or unfair view of the world around them.[1]

Blogger—A person who regularly writes material for a blog or online publication.

Body—The main section of an article, which should include backup for the lead and nut graph. It should also include quotes from a variety of sources to make sure that the story is balanced and fair.

Bond—This is an amount of money that, if paid, allows an arrested person to be released from jail.

Checkbook Journalism—Paying for access to news content or a source.

Chilling Effect—Silence on a story that needs to be told.

---

1 David G. Levasseur, "Media Bias," Encyclopedia of Political Communication, (Sage Publications, 2008). Accessed 23 Jan 2017, http://proxy.uscupstate.edu:2048/login?url=http://search.credoreference.com/content/entry/sagepolcom/media_bias/0.

Citizen Journalism—The collection, dissemination, and analysis of news and information by the general public, especially by means of the Internet.

Cleaning Data—The process of detecting and correcting (or removing) corrupt or inaccurate records from a record set, table, or database.[2]

CMS—Stands for content management system. It is where you build and maintain your website. Also called website builder or platform.

Conflict of Interest—A situation in which a person is in a position to derive personal benefit from actions or decisions made in their official capacity.

Context—The circumstances that form the setting for an event, statement, or idea, and in terms of which it can be fully understood and assessed.

Copyright—The exclusive legal right, given to an originator or an assignee, to print, publish, perform, film, or record literary, artistic, or musical material, and to authorize others to do the same.

Creative Commons—Online tool that helps facilitate use of copyrighted material.

Credibility—The level of trust you engender with your audience; the quality of being trusted or believed in.

Data Visualization—A graphic or visual element that helps make the data accessible to the public.

Data Journalism—A specialty focused on using data to tell stories and present information.

Defamation—Publishing a false statement about someone that causes that person to suffer harm to their reputation or mental state.

Deposition—A proceeding where a party gives oral testimony out of court but under oath before a licensed court reporter.

Digital Media Literacy—A set of skills that prepares and empowers people to assess and critique information online, challenge and change messages they hear, and engage more respectfully with others.

Embargo—A request or mandate that a news item not be published until a certain date and time, even if the information is given to journalists early.

Extradition—When a state moves an accused or convicted person to another state or country to face charges or penalties there.

Fair Use—In U.S. copyright law, the doctrine that brief excerpts of copyright material may, under certain circumstances, be quoted verbatim for purposes such as criticism, news reporting, teaching, and research, without the need for permission from or payment to the copyright holder.

---

2   S. Wu, "A Review on Coarse Warranty Data and Analysis," Reliability Engineering and Systems, 114 (2013): 1–11, doi:10.1016/j.ress.2012.12.021.

Fake News—Involves misinformation and the act of delegitimizing quality new outlets. Also called propaganda, misinformation, disinformation, unfounded opinions, or hoaxes.

Fourth Estate—Another name for the news media, highlighting their role as the fourth branch of government, which serves as a check on governmental power.

Freedom of Information Act (FOIA) — Provides the public the right to request access to records from any federal agency. It is often described as the law that keeps citizens in the know about their government. Federal agencies are required to disclose any information requested under the FOIA unless it falls under one of nine exemptions which protect interests such as personal privacy, national security, and law enforcement.[3]

Hard Lead—Hard news leads answer as many of the Five W's and the H as possible. Hard leads should be written in an active voice, meaning starting with the subject followed by a strong, powerful verb.

Hosting—When you create content, it must live—or be hosted—somewhere. This is the host. Many CMS platforms offer hosting as part of the package. Users who have more advanced skills or want a more customized experience may choose to host their website through a separate host, such as BlueHost, HostGator, WP Engine, or GoDaddy (among others). This will be an added cost.

Hung Jury—When a jury is unable to reach a verdict of guilty or not guilty. This results in a mistrial. Prosecutors can seek to try the case again.

Indictment—An official statement charging a person with a crime.

Infographic—A visual image such as a chart or diagram used to represent information or data.

Kicker Ending—End of an article—something that gives readers food for thought. Perhaps it's a quote from one of your sources or thoughts about the future.

Lawsuit—A claim brought to court by a person or party to end a dispute.

Libel—Printed defamation.

Mistrial—A trial that is thrown out because of an error or because the jury can't reach a verdict, or there was some other misconduct during trial.

Motion—A motion is a procedural device for decision. It is a request to the judge (or judges) to make a decision about the case. Motions may be made at any point in administrative, criminal, or civil proceedings, although that right is regulated by court rules, which vary from place to place.

Mult Box—A metal box with multiple outputs of a single audio source (one microphone connected to twenty jacks so that twenty people can record that microphone)." Sometimes called a 'pressbox.'[4]

---

3 "Freedom of Information Act: Learn." Freedom of Information Act. Accessed April 02, 2018, https://www.foia.gov/about.html.

4 Mark Greenhouse,, "Audio Terms of Endearment," NPR. July 7, 2007. Retrieved March 14, 2012. Gary Palamara, "The View From the Back of the Room II: Tips for Reporters and Others Covering Press Events." Radio World. , June 20, 2007. Retrieved May 10, 2012.

Natural Sound or Nat Sound—Sound from the environment. It helps the listener be present and feel as if they are there.

News/Political Interview—Gathering of information to help explain an idea, event, or situation in the news.

Newsgathering—The process of researching news items, conducting interviews, and collecting other elements of a news story for broadcast or publication.

News Peg—An aspect of or angle on a story that ties to currently relevant news and thus makes the story in question newsworthy.

Nut Graph—Once you've enticed your readers, be sure to explain why this story matters to them. How does the story relate to your audience? Why is it news today and not yesterday or last year?

Off the Record—A statement that is not attributable or quotable in a news story. When talking with a journalist, the default is "on the record." Off the record must be explicitly agreed upon.

On the Record—A statement that may be used in publication or broadcast.

Patchwriting—Relying too much on the structure and themes of the original story and writing your own story in a way that mimics that original story too closely.

Plagiarism—Copying of someone else's words, content, or ideas without giving that person credit.

Platform—Websites that provide a social space for the public, such as Facebook or Twitter.

Plea bargain—A settlement agreement between the prosecution and the defense for the defendant to plead guilty to a lesser offense or to one or some of the offenses.

Plug-In/App—A piece of software or code that adds functionality to your website. For example, you may add a slider/rotator plug-in to your homepage.

Probation—A period of time when a person who has committed a crime is out of prison but is being monitored, and can be sent back to prison if they violate any conditions of probation.

Pool Reporter—A reporter from one outlet who agrees to share the information they gather with all other news outlets. Pool reporting is common when space is limited, such as in courtrooms or events with small audiences.

Preliminary Hearing—A hearing to determine if a person charged with a felony should be tried.

Profile Interview—Focuses on an individual. Usually, a news peg is used to justify the profile.

Public Shaming—The collective act of shaming an individual or group in the public sphere, generally carried out by individual members of the public, but the collective nature amplifies the effect.

Recognizance—A promise a defendant makes with the court to show up as ordered, so they are allowed to leave jail.

Ruling—An official or authoritative decision, decree, statement, or interpretation (as by a judge on a point of law).

SEO—Stands for search engine optimization. SEO actions, such as adding tags to your website and posts and infusing commonly searched words into titles and content, help make your site more searchable online.

Slander—Spoken defamation.

Scraping (data)—Extracting data from websites. While web scraping can be done manually by a software user, the term typically refers to automated processes implemented using a bot or web crawler.[5]

Series—Two or more reports that build off each other, yet the stories must stand alone.

Sentencing—The punishment given to a person convicted of a crime. A judge issues the sentence based on the verdict of the judge or jury.

Soft Lead—Used in features. The most important information doesn't come right at the beginning. Indeed, a good feature creates intrigue by starting with a soft lead, which gives readers a hint of what's to come next. The first one-to-four paragraphs should set up the scene with a powerful lead. Remember to tease your readers; don't give it all away.

Sound Bed—A piece of music or ambient sound that is placed "under" your voice track.

Sound Bite—Audio or video cuts from those you have interviewed.

Subpoena—A writ commanding a person to appear in court or at a deposition.

Summary Lead—The most traditional lead in a journalism article. It is to the point and factual. It's meant to give a reader a quick summary of the story in as few words as possible (should be 30 words or less), usually in one sentence.[6]

Summons—An order to appear in a court of law.

Sunshine Laws—State access laws for governmental documents. Each state's sunshine laws are slightly different, and not all states have sunshine laws.

Suspended Sentence—A jail or prison sentence that is put on hold if the defendant complies with certain obligations.

Talking Points—A list of phrases, ideas, and statements designed for framing a message and structuring responses to questions, often used by PR firms, politicians, and others to control, spin, or frame a message.

Target Audience—A specific group that is the focus of messaging campaigns and other communications.

Transparent—Being open to public scrutiny.

Trial—Allows a judge or jury to examine the evidence and decide the outcome.

---

5 G. Boeing, G.and P. Waddell,. "New Insights into Rental Housing Markets across the United States: Web Scraping and Analyzing Craigslist Rental Listings," *Journal of Planning Education and Research* (0739456X16664789). (June 20, 2007). doi:10.1177/0739456X16664789.

6 "How To Write Good Story Leads." Journalism Education. Accessed April 02, 2018, http://cubreporters.org/leads.html.

Venue—The location where a complaint is filed—i.e., in state court, the county; and in federal court, the district. In high profile cases, a party may make a motion for a "change of venue," and if the motion is granted, the trial is moved to another community to obtain jurors who can be more objective in their duties.

Verdict—A decision made by a jury in a trial.

Verify—Checking to make sure that something is truthful or factual. In journalism, you should secure at least two independent verifications before publishing, posting, or broadcasting information.

Visualization—The act of crafting or formulating an image or representation of something.

Warrant—A court document that gives police the power to take action against a suspect.

Watchdog—A person or group whose function is to monitor the practices of companies providing a particular service or utility.

NOTE: Many definitions courtesy Google Dictionary. Google Dictionary relies on Oxford Pocket Dictionary of Current English as its English definitions provider.

CPSIA information can be obtained
at www.ICGtesting.com
Printed in the USA
LVHW061206141220
R16515300001B/R165153PG673954LVX4B/2

9 781516 526789